I0643395

Isaac D. Guyer

History of Chicago

Isaac D. Guyer

History of Chicago

ISBN/EAN: 9783744724777

Printed in Europe, USA, Canada, Australia, Japan

Cover: Foto ©ninafisch / pixelio.de

More available books at **www.hansebooks.com**

HISTORY OF CHICAGO;

ITS

Commercial and Manufacturing

INTERESTS AND INDUSTRY;

TOGETHER WITH

SKETCHES OF MANUFACTURERS AND MEN WHO HAVE MOST CONTRIBUTED TO ITS PROSPERITY AND ADVANCEMENT,

WITH

GLANCES AT SOME OF THE BEST HOTELS;

ALSO THE

PRINCIPAL RAILROADS WHICH CENTER IN CHICAGO.

BY I. D. GUYER.

CHICAGO:
CHURCH, GOODMAN & CUSHING, BOOK AND JOB PRINTERS,
51 & 53 La Salle Street.
1862.

SALUTATION.

THE Title of this Volume defines its subject; and the subject, it is presumed, explains its object. The character of the age is progress—it is practical—and "Commerce is King."

The author of this volume was induced to undertake its publication, after many solicitations by leading commercial and manufacturing firms in Chicago. To our patrons and the public, we submit the result of the invitation.

The necessity that seemed to exist for a more permanent, reliable, and comprehensive guide, for the people throughout the North-West, to the highest class of Commercial Houses and Manufacturing Establishments, forms the basis upon which this work was projected. The public cannot fail to realize improved facilities for the transaction of almost every description of business, by consulting these pages—interesting alike to those who buy, and those who sell; to those who produce, and those who consume.

The various firms, whose business notices appear in this book, are of the highest and most reliable character, and are in all respects entitled to public confidence.

The greatest pains and discrimination have been made in the choice of subjects and the various firms who represent them, as those who are familiar with them will at once see that no attention has been given to anything not fully worthy of the representations offered.

The publisher desires to take advantage of this opportunity to acknowledge his obligations to the patrons of this volume. He would thank especially all who have in any way contributed to its production; for books are the embodiment, not merely of the labor of the author, but of a vast number of persons occupied in seemingly diverse branches of industry. Those who have never carried a book through the press, however humble its pretensions, can form no idea of the amount of toil and trouble involved. There was never a perfect work, so this must bear the general lot of criticism.

We would acknowledge our special thanks, first to the Paper dealers, Messrs. G. H. & L. LAFLIN, for the beautiful quality of paper furnished, and the promptness in supplying — made to our special order — by a New England manufacturing company — in process of making the next day after the order was given for it in this city, — to the Printers, Messrs. CHURCH, GOODMAN & CUSHING, for the general typographical appearance, which is its own best exponent, — to the Pressman, D. A. CASHMAN, whose skill, genius, industry and perseverance, has placed him at the head of his profession, — to the Lithographer, Mr. ED. MENDEL, who has attained a higher degree of perfection in this beautiful art, perhaps, than any other man on this continent, — to the Bookbinder, Mr. CYRUS J. WARD, whose praise will be spoken, when a discriminating public shall have passed their criticism — more effective than anything our pen could add to his fame; whose reputation for an artistic and reliable Bookbinder is an acknowledged fact.

Last, though not least, do we render especial thanks to those who have aided us by their generous contributions in the publication of this handsome Commercial Volume.

PUBLISHER.

CHICAGO, MAY, 1862.

CONTENTS.

HISTORY OF CHICAGO.

NO city or community on this continent, or in the world, shows so remarkable and rapid a growth as CHICAGO. We have men among us to-day, yet in the prime of life, who have witnessed this transformation, as the moving of a panorama—men who have seen all there has been, and all there is, of CHICAGO, and lived out its full history to the present time. Some who trafficked with the Indians, when they were the principal customers of the CHICAGO trader; who afterwards supplied the first permanent white settlement with the necessaries of life; who witnessed all its manifold and wonderful changes, from the insignificant collection of huts, to the magnitude and commerce of our present great city, are here in business now.

While it is pleasant for the early settler, as well as the new-comer, to read a well defined contrast which a few brief years have made, since the Indians built their wigwams where our most thronged and important business streets now run; and since the paddles of the Indian canoes were only heard in our river and lake, which now swarm with vessels having a total tunnage of 400,000 burthen, and which navigate all waters—though a full-drawn sketch of these scenes would be interesting to every reader, we have not the space for a proper and full expose of them. Hence, our "History of Chicago" must necessarily be confined principally to a narration of events, which have to do with our growth in population, trade and commerce.

Although some pretended historians have said "Chicago has no history," there is enough of subject-matter connected therewith, for a good-sized volume. Some of the leading historical facts and incidents we deem of sufficient interest and importance to include in this brief sketch.

ORIGIN AND SIGNIFICANCE OF THE NAME.—We first find upon a map drawn by J. Baptiste Louis Franquelin, dated Quebec, Canada, 1688, (which represents Lake Michigan and the North-West with tolerable correctness,) that "Fort Cheeagou" occupies the precise location of our present city. This map of "New France" is in the Provisional Library of New Canada. Again, in an atlas published by Par le Sr.

Sanson, Geographer to the King, dated 1696, the Mississippi River, from its source to its mouth, is named the "Chacaqua River." In other ancient works it is called the "Chacaqua or Divine River."

The Indians stated that the place had its name from an old and beloved Chief, who was drowned in the river "many — very many moons ago."

Gen. Cass brought from France an old manuscript which purported to be a letter from M. de Ligney, at Green Bay, to M. de Siette, among the Illinois Indians, dated in 1726. In this letter, as well as in the old family letters, and official French correspondence of the earlier days of the present century, this place is alluded to as "Chicagoux."

As to the significance of the word "CHICAGO," it has been contended by some writers, that it was derived from leeks or wild onions which formerly grew profusely in the vicinity at an early day, and was called "Checaque" by the Indians. Others contend that it was derived from the name of the Chief of a powerful tribe of Indians, who formerly held undisputed sway over this region. But the more common acceptance of the term, is that the river was named from the insignificant and unpopular quadruped called "Checague," skunk or pole-cat, and the town named after the river.

The significance of the words "STRONG, POWERFUL, MIGHTY," is the only one that will embrace and harmonize all the different applications of the word. The Indians certainly used it to express this meaning. When they heard loud thunder—"the voice from the Great Spirit," they would reverentially exclaim "*Checaque*,"—meaning powerful, strong, mighty. And it is beyond question that the word was frequently used as an attribute of Divinity—hence the name "*Checaqua, or Divine River*," as applied to the largest and most powerful stream of water known to those tribes who inhabited the Mississippi valley. "Checaqua" the Chief, was a successor of others of the same name, and was the most brave, noble and powerful chief known to the several tribes here at that period. He was chief of the tribe called "Tam-a-roas"—the principal tribe of the Illinois Indians, and the name "Checaqua" was an appellation of dignity, power and superiority, handed down from father to son—from one chief to his worthy successor. The leek or wild onion, called "Checaqua," or "Chi-ka-go," was the strongest and most powerfully scented vegetable known to them—so of the "Checaque" animal or skunk.

From those facts, we conclude that the true significance and meaning of the word "CHICAGO," should be decided upon as being "*Strong, Powerful, Mighty!*"—appellations which the very rapid growth of our city in population, wealth and commercial importance, most richly entitles her to.

EARLY SETTLEMENT OF CHICAGO.—The first white inhabitant of this city was Father Marquette, the Jesuit Missionary, who visited this place in 1673, and the year following erected a dwelling and an edifice for the worship of the Almighty. The French and military afterwards occupied it as a military and trading post.

The author of "Wau-bun, or the Early-days in the Northwest," and some other writers claim that Mr. John Kinzie's residence was the first house built in Chicago—"a part of which was the same rude structure put up by the so-called white man, the negro Jean Baptiste Point-au-Sable, about the year 1796." A Frenchman by the name of Le Mai finally "jumped" the pretended claim of Point-au-Sable, and commenced trading with the Indians. A few years later John Kinzie, then an Indian trader in the St. Joseph country, Michigan, purchased Le Mai's establishment, and in 1804 came with his family to Chicago to reside. Hence, John Kinzie was the first permanent white resident of Chicago—the first to establish permanent improvements—the first to inaugurate a regular trade, and to form a nucleus from which has sprung up to its present marvelous magnitude the city of Chicago. "If any person is entitled to the honor of being styled the Father of Chicago, that person is unquestionably JOHN KINZIE."

In 1804 the United States government established here a Military Post, called "Fort Chicago," and the American Fur Company a trading station. On the 7th day of April, 1812, the massacre of the United States troops occurred, and Fort Chicago was burned by the Indians. In 1817 the Fort was rebuilt at the same location, and its name changed to Fort Dearborn. This Fort was abandoned in the spring of 1837, and thereafter occupied by private families.*

Every city has its "oldest inhabitant"—ours is JOHN H. KINZIE, Esq., who came here with his father in 1804, but subsequently spent several years at other points in the West, and finally settled here, with his family, in 1833. Gurdon S. Hubbard, Esq., a present well-known merchant, first came here in 1818, at which time he says "there were but two families residing here not connected with the military establishment. One of these families was that of Mr. John Kinzie, who resided in the old home he occupied before the war; the other was that of Antoine Ouilmette, a French Canadian, who married an Indian woman, and occupied the same cabin near Mr. Kinzie's, where he resided previous to the massacre. These houses, with the magnificent cabin of Burns, were the only buildings of the settlement of Chicago, which had been spared from destruction.

In the fall of 1828, the Winnebago Indians who then inhabited the country west of this place, became troublesome and threatened the destruction of the Fort. Gurdon S. Hubbard, Esq., went alone on horseback, to the settlements along the Wabash river, and procured reinforcements. He was absent only a week, and returned with a goodly number of hardy pioneers, whose presence acted as a *quietus* upon the Winnebagoes, and rendered them, for the time, very submissive. That one act of Mr. Hubbard's, at such a time, and under such circumstances, endeared him to the settlers here then, and showed him to be brave, valiant and humane. There are a number of "pioneer settlers" still residing in the city, whose relation of incidents would be an honor to them and interesting to readers, but our limits forbid their publication.

*The reader will find a very interesting, and detailed narration of events connected with the Early History of Chicago, in a work entitled "Wau-bun," from the pen of Mrs. J. H. Kinzie, of Chicago.

In 1823 there were but three families in Chicago, all occupying log cabins. Major Long, in his narrative of the Government Exploring Expedition, speaks of his visit to Chicago in 1823, and represents the place as "presenting no cheering prospects, and containing but few huts, inhabited by a miserable race of men, scarcely equal to the Indians from whom they descended" (?)—and their log or bark houses as "low, filthy and disgusting—displaying not the least trace of comfort, and as a place of business affording no inducements to the settler—the whole amount of trade on the Lake not exceeding the cargoes of five or six schooners, even at the time when the garrison received its supplies from the Mackinac." The correctness of his views respecting the inhabitants has been questioned. What he says of the business facilities of the place, and of the amount of business transacted, is probably correct.

The first native of Chicago was born at "Fort Dearborn," in the early part of 1832. This young lady is still one of our citizens—Miss Ellen Hamilton, daughter of Col. R. J. Hamilton.

The Massacre at Chicago.*— In the evening of the 7th of April, 1812, the head of the settlement, Mr. Kinzie, was quietly sitting in the chimney corner, amusing his children by a tune upon his violin, and they were enjoying their accustomed dance before the bright fire light, while the tea-table awaited the return of Mrs. Kinzie, who had gone a short distance up the river some time before, to visit a sick neighbor. Suddenly Mrs. Kinzie rushed through the door, exclaiming, "The Indians are up at Lee's Place, killing and scalping." As before stated, the Fort was situated on the southern bank of the river, directly opposite Mr. Kinzie's mansion. Only a man and boy had escaped from Lee's Place, and were hurrying down to notify Burns' family of their danger. Near the house were moored two old *Pirogues*, into which the family was hurried, and paddled across to take refuge in the Fort. At this time the Fort was officered by Captain Heald, the commanding officer; Lieut. Helm, son-in-law of Mr. Kinzie; Ensign Ronan, and the Surgeon, Dr. Van Voorhees. The Lieutenant and Ensign were both young and inexperienced. The command at this time numbered about seventy-five men, who had little knowledge of military matters, and were quite ineffective.

The recent battle of Tippecanoe, (which had transpired only the preceding November,) had not been erased from the memory of the settlers, which added not a little to their caution and vigilance. Hence the party of a corporal and six men, who had ascended the river on a fishing expedition, when they heard the signal gun from the Fort, extinguished their torches, and dropped down the river as quietly as possible, lying flat upon the bottom of the boat, a distance of two miles. At Lee's Place, how-

* Although "The Massacre at Chicago" is one of the most important events in the early history of the place, we devote less space to its narration, from the fact that it has already been published in several works in detail—first in pamphlet form, in 1836; next in Brown's History of Illinois; then in a widely circulated work, call·d "Western Annals;" and afterwards made the basis of two tales by Major Richardson, "Hardscrabble," and "Wau-nan-gee;" and the same account occupies forty-two pages of Mrs. J. H. Kinzie's "Wau-Bun," published in 1856, which also had a very large sale.

ever, where they stopped to warm, they found the scalped corpse of a Frenchman, in the yard, with his faithful dog beside his master's lifeless remains. Then they knew there was trouble ahead!

The Winnebagoes, who had planned to proceed down the river from Lee's Place, and kill and scalp all the whites outside the Fort, had become frightened at the signal cannon firing at the Fort, and hastily retreated to their homes on Rock River. Strict orders that no soldiers should leave the Fort without special permission, were obeyed. Now and then wandering squads of Indians would be seen in the vicinity after nightfall, and their depredations and boldness increased, until some of the more daring at times entered the houses, and even the Fort, and were looked upon as spies. Thus the little handful of settlers were kept in a state of terror, and hardly dare venture outside their doors after dark. Thus matters continued until the 7th of August following, when Winnemeg, or *Catfish*, a Pottawottomie chief, made his appearance at the post, with dispatches from Gen. Hull, which announced the declaration of war with Great Britain, and that he (Gen. Hull,) at the head of the Northwestern Army, had arrived at Detroit—also that the Island of Mackinac had fallen into the hands of the British. The orders from Gen. Hull to Captain Heald were, "to evacuate the Fort, if practicable, and in the event, to distribute all the United States' property contained in the Fort, and in the United States' factory or agency, among the Indians in the neighborhood." Captain Heald reluctantly yielded to the command, nor did he decide to do so until he had given the subject five days' consideration—five days of dreadful suspense and consternation to all within, as well as outside of the Fort. He argued that "a special order had been issued by the War Department, that no post should be surrendered without battle having been given, and that his force was totally inadequate to an engagement with the Indians."

Finally, on the afternoon of the 12th, the Indians from all the neighboring villages were assembled in council, when Capt. Heald and Mr. Kinzie appeared, to convey to them the information, of which the Indians had heard vague and imperfect rumor, sufficient to enkindle a feeling of impudence and animosity that seemed ready to burst forth at any moment. The other officers, having less confidence in the Indians, remained in the block-houses, opened the port-holes, and directed the cannon so that they commanded the whole assembly, which act alone preserved the lives of Capt. Heald and Mr. Kinzie, as the sequel will show.

Captain Heald informed the Indians, that "it was his intention to distribute among them the next day, not only the goods lodged in the United States' factory, but also the ammunition and provisions, with which the garrison was well supplied." He requested that the Pottawottomies should form an escort for the whites to Fort Wayne, promising to reward them liberally upon their safe arrival there, in addition to what they were to receive of the United States' supplies. The Indians, with their usual shrewdness and deceit, assented to all his propositions, and promised to meet all his requirements. Mr. Kinzie had an interview with Capt. Heald, in which he related his past experience, and his knowledge of the treachery of the Indians, and entreated him not to furnish the Indians, (who must now be looked upon as enemies,) with arms or ammunition. Capt. Heald yielded to Mr. Kinzie's advice, and determined to destroy all the ammunition except what was necessary for his own troops.

On the 13th, the distribution of blankets, calicoes, paints and provision, was made, as previously stipulated. In the evening a part of the ammunition and liquor were thrown into a well, the remainder being secretly transported through the northern gate, the heads knocked in and the contents poured into the river. All the muskets not necessary for the command on their march, were broken and thrown into the well, together with all weapons of defence, and all gun fixtures.

The Indians had heard the knocking in of the barrel-heads, and suspecting what was being done, had stealthily crept, serpent like, as near the scene as possible — near enough to satisfy themselves of the truth of their suspicions. Had other proofs been wanting, the quantity of liquor that had been thrown into the river was so great, that the Indians declared they could taste it as "strong grog."

Having heard, at Fort Wayne, of the order for vacating the Fort at Chicago, and knowing the hostile determination of the Pottowattomies, Capt. Wells, with fifteen friendly Miami Indians, made a rapid march to Chicago, to prevent what he feared would result in a total destruction of his relative Capt. Heald and his troops. He arrived on the 14th—after the ammunition had been destroyed, and the goods and provisions distributed to the Indians. There was no time for a change in the plan, the only alternative being to leave the post next day.

In the afternoon, a second council was held with the Indians, who expressed great indignation at the destruction of the arms, ammunition and liquor—which they prized more highly than all the other presents. Murmurs and threats were unreservedly made by the savages, and it was evident that the first movement of troops from the Fort would expose them to the vengeance of the savages.

On the morning of the 15th, at nine o'clock, all were in readiness for departure. The ammunition had all been destroyed, except twenty-five rounds, and one box of cartridges — which it was then decided were inadequate for the impending conflict, which they saw, too plainly, was before them. Mr. Kinzie and his oldest son had decided to accompany the troops, though warned by a message from To-pee-nee-bee, that the Pottawottomies who had engaged to escort them, were determined to massacre them, and that he should take the boat in which he had placed his family, and thus ensure his safe escape to St. Joseph's.

Mrs. Kinzie, her four younger children, nurse, Kinzie's clerk, two servants, and the boatmen, with two Indians as protectors, had started in the boat, and had scarcely reached the mouth of the river, half a mile from the Fort, when a second message from the chief of St. Joseph's band warned them to remain where they were. With breathless anxiety, the little band watched the movement of the troops with their husbands and friends, as they supposed, to certain destruction. Capt. Wells with his little band of Miamis took the lead. They marched along the lake shore. When they reached the point where a range of sand hills intervened between the prairie and beach, the escort of Pottawomics, numbering some 500, kept the level of the prairie, thus parting from the Americans and Miamis. When they had marched about a mile and a half, Capt. Wells, (who with his little band of Miamis had kept in advance,) rode hastily back, exclaiming, "They are about to attack us — form instantly and charge upon them!"

At this instant a volley of bullets showered among the sand hills, killing a veteran of seventy winters, and wounding Dr. Van .Voorhees, Ensgin Roman, and several others. The firing now became general on both sides. The Miamis fled at the outset — their chief returning, exclaimed in a rage to the Pottawotomies, "You have deceived the Americans and us, the Miamis; you have done a bad action, and I will be the first to join a party of Americans to return and punish your treachery!" Our troops, says Mrs. Helm, who was an eye witness, "behaved most gallantly. They were but a handful, but seemed resolved to sell their lives as dearly as possible." After the first attack by the Indians, the Americans charged upon those who had concealed themselves in a sort of ravine, intervening between the sand banks and the prairie. The savages gathered themselves into a body, and after a severe contest on both sides, in which the number of whites had been reduced to twenty-eight, they succeeded in breaking through the ranks of the enemy, and gaining the rising ground near Oak Woods. There being such a difference in the forces, the contest seemed hopeless, and St. Helm, through a messenger, proposed terms of capitulation, which were, "that the lives of all survivors should be spared, and a ransom permitted as soon as practicable.

"In the meantime a horrible scene had been enacted. A young savage had climbed into the baggage wagon, containing the children of the white families, twelve in number, and tomahawked the entire group. This was during the engagement near the sand-hills. When Capt. Wells, who was fighting near, beheld it, he exclaimed, "Is that their game — butchering the women and children? Then I, too, will kill!"

He rode hastily towards the Indian camp, near the Fort, where he had left their squaws and children. Seeing several Indians in his pursuit, he laid himself flat on the neck of his horse, loading and firing in that position, as he would occasionally turn on his pursuers. At length their balls took effect, severely wounding him, and killing his horse. At this instant he was met by Win-ne-weg and Wau-bon-see, who endeavored to save him from his savage pursuers. As they supported him along, after having disengaged him from his horse, he received his death blow from Pee-so-tum, who stabbed him in the back and scalped him.

Those of Mr. Kinzie's family who had remained in the boat near the mouth of the river, were carefully guarded by Cee-po-tah and another Indian, and after the battle were permitted to return to the mansion of Mr. K., where those who were wounded in battle were cared for. There being no surgeon, Mr. Kinzie extracted the bullets from Mrs. Heath and others with his pen-knife. Here the family remained, closely guarded by their faithful Indian friends, who intended to accompany them to Detroit for security — the rest of the prisoners remaining at the wigwams of their captors.

The following morning the work of plunder being completed, the Indians set fire to the Fort.

On the third day after the battle, the family of Mr. Kinzie, with the clerks of the establishment, were put into a boat, under the care of Francois, a half-breed interpreter, and conveyed to St. Joseph, where they remained until the following November, when they were conducted to Detroit under an escort of Chaudonnai, and their trusty Indian friend Ke-po-tah, and delivered up as prisoneers of war, to Col. McKee, the British Indian agent, and in the month of January following, he was received and paroled by Gen. Proctor.

Capt. Heald and wife was sent across the lake to St. Joseph the day after the battle. He had received two severe wounds and she seven, in the engagement.

Lieut. Helm, who was also wounded, was carried by some friendly Indians to their village on the Au Sable, and thence to Peoria, where he was liberated by the intervention of Mr. Thos. Forsyth, the half-brother of Mr. Kinzie. Mrs. Helm accompanied her friends to St. Joseph. Both Lieut. H. and wife were subsequently liberated, and returned to their friends in Steuben county, New York.

The First Land Trade.—From 1681 to 1795, during the time of the French possession, and after its cession to England, very little is known of Chicago or the surrounding country. After the declaration of peace, between the Colonists and the English, the latter, by intrigue, stirred up the border Indian warfare, which became general in the Western States, and continued till 1795, at which period, having been effectually chastised by Gen. Wayne, the chiefs of the several tribes of Indians, by his invitation, assembled at Greenville, Ohio, and there effected a treaty of peace, which closed the War of the West. Among the numerous small tracts of land where forts and trading posts had been established, then ceded by the Indians to the United States, was one described as follows: "One piece of land, six miles square, at the mouth of the Chikajo River, emptying into the south-west end of Lake Michigan, where a fort formerly stood."

Here we have an account of the *first land trade* of Chicago—the first transaction in that line of business which has at times distinguished Chicago above every other city of the Nation—the first link in the chain of title to thousands upon thousands of transfers that have been made of the soil thus parted with by the Indians.

Illinois and Michigan Canal.—Gov. Bond, the first Governor of this State, in his inaugural, in 1818, called the attention of the General Assembly to the importance of opening a canal to connect Lake Michigan with the Illinois River. In his valedictory, in 1822, he again urged its importance. The session of Congress, 1821-2, passed an act, granting "permission to the State of Illinois to cut a canal through the Public

Lands connecting the Illinois River with Lake Michigan, and granting to it the breadth of the canal, and ninety feet on each side of it," coupled with the condition, "that the State should permit all articles belonging to the United States, or to any person in their employ, to pass *toll free*, forever."

With a hard and protracted struggle by numerous individuals, and especially by Daniel P. Cook, Esq., who was at that time Representative in Congress, and from whom Cook county was named,) an act was passed by Congress, March 2, 1827, granting to the State, for the construction of this work, "each alternate section of land, five miles in width, on each side of the proposed canal." We make mention of these facts, because it was from this act of Congress that the State acquired the title to those lands which have formed the basis for many of the most important financial transactions of the State; from which originated the titles to the valuable Canal Lands, upon which a large portion of the city is built—on which, too, villages, towns and cities have sprung up, all along its line.

In the autumn of 1829, Commissioners authorized the laying out of the "Town of Chicago," on the alternate section which belonged to the Canal Lands—lying upon the main channel of the river, and over the junction of the two branches. The first map of the original town of Chicago, by James Thompson, surveyor, bears date, August 4, 1830. This was the *first beginning of Chicago*, as a legally recognized place among the towns and cities of the world—the first official act of organization, which must accordingly be dated as its birth, or real starting point. Hence this city, with its population of 120,000—the leading mart in the world for grain, pork, and lumber, will have arrived, on the 4th day of August, 1862, at the precocious maturity of thirty-two years!

CHICAGO REAL ESTATE, PAST AND PRESENT.—At one time in her history, Chicago had the reputation of "leading the world," in the way of town-lot speculation. One incident will illustrate to what extent she was entitled to this reputation: An ignorant adventurer had bid off a centrally-located lot, at the Canal Land sales, for $200, which he shortly afterwards had numerous applications for. One day he called at the hotel room of Mr. G., from Kentucky, (who was a large speculator in Canal Lands,) and remarked to him that he had bought a lot for $200, and now there were a dozen speculators chasing him all over town to buy it, and that he hardly dare fix a price, lest he should sell it too low—for less than he could get a short time hence. Mr. G. advised him to ask more for it than he would ever expect to get, and then come down in his price, to suit the purchaser—say $10,000. Soon one of the aforesaid speculators knocked at the door, and asked the owner of the lot if he had fixed upon a price. The owner, who had very little idea of business, and still less of mathematics or money, and had forgotten the amount, with great drops of perspiration upon his face, from excitement, stammered, "Te—te—eighteen thousand dollars!" The applicant asked if that was his lowest figure. Upon being told, hesitatingly, that it was, he replied, "Well, I'll take it—make out the papers." This is but one out of a thousand similar speculations.

Numerous interesting details or contrasts of real estate transactions might be shown, but we insert only the following, which are but a fair sample of the increase in the value of real estate, all over the city:

"Received, Chicago, August 15, 1831, from P. F. W. Peck, Eighty Dollars, in full for Lot No. 4, block 18, in the plan of the 'Town of Chicago,' and in full of all claims to this date.
(Signed) M. F. WALKER."

This lot is situated at the south-east corner of South Water and La Salle streets, fronting eighty feet on the former, and one hundred and fifty on La Salle street—was valued in 1854 at $42,500, and could not be bought to-day, probably, for $60,000!

A lot, eighty feet front, now occupied in part by the store of J. H. Reed & Co., 144 Lake street, was purchased by Jeremiah Price, Esq., in 1833, for precisely the same amount that was paid in New York, in 1844, for one pane of glass, now in Reed's show-window—namely, $100. That eighty feet of ground cannot now be had for $75,000.

Wolcott's Addition, which was bought in 1830 for $130, is now worth fully a million and a half of dollars!

Walter L. Newberry's Addition to Chicago, embracing forty acres, was purchased in 1833 for $1,062, and is now worth fully three quarters of a million of dollars.

From the projection of the Illinois and Michigan Canal, Chicago received her first impulse, and it is to that, more particularly than to any other project or improvement, she owes her present magnitude. It was this that kept her alive when she was, as it were, in her infancy, and she grew with its growth; and this it was that first secured to her the early reputation she possessed as a commercial port. Her rapid growth has created an annually increasing demand for additional outlets and avenues for trade and commerce, until a vast network of railroads have, one after another, been constructed, the early days of many of which have interesting histories of trials and troubles, and of final triumphs.

Since the "march of civilization" is fast obliterating all traces of the ancient landmarks of the pioneers, we will locate a few of them, that they may not be entirely forgotten.

In 1831 the river had a meandering course, sweeping around the promontory upon which the Fort was built, and entered the lake about one-half mile south of its present mouth, so that "these buildings, in fact, stood upon the right bank of the river, the left being formed by a long spit of land, extending from the north shore, of which it formed a part." Directly facing the Fort, on the opposite bank of the river, was the family mansion of J. H. Kinzie, Esq.,—a long low building, with a piazza along its front, having a range of four or five rooms. The Agency House, then known as

"Cobweb Castle," stood at what is now the south-west corner of Wolcott and North Water Streets. This hewed log house, with its several additions, was the early stopping place of many of the new-comers of those days.

The junction of the two rivers was called "Wolf Point." Mark Beaubien, sen., had just completed a white two-story building, with light blue wooden shutters — which from its superior size and appearance, was the admiration of all beholders. A canoe ferry was kept here to accommodate those wishing to cross the south branch. Between the Fort and the Point the land was low, wet prairie, "scarcely affording good walking in the dryest summer weather, while at other seasons it was absolutely impassable." The author of Wau-bun says "a muddy streamlet, or as it is called in the west a slew, or slough, after winding around from about the present site of the Tremont House, entered the river at the foot of what is now State street." A stranger who visited Chicago at that day, (1831) said, "I passed over the ground from the Fort to the Point, on horseback, and was up to my stirrups in water the whole distance; I would not have given six pence an acre for the whole of it." Owing to the wet and marshy condition of the intervening ground, the roads were generally not used, and the usual mode of communication between the Point and the Fort, was by canoes and small flats paddled up and down the river, and this was the usual route of communication by the inhabitants of the Fort to the Agency House.

The family of Clybourne are elsewhere mentioned as among the early settlers. They had previous to this time established themselves upon the north branch, which place they called "New Virginia." Hardscrabble, or Lee's place, was four miles up the south branch, now just outside the city limits. At this time a family named Heacock lived here, and some of the members of that family are among the earliest native born citizens of Chicago.

THE SHIP CANAL.—Notwithstanding five thousand miles of railway have been constructed and put in operation, that are now tributary to Chicago, the old canal (which at one time in the course of its construction came near being abandoned for a single line of railway,) is not only one of the most important feeders to Chicago, but it is now deemed necessary to enlarge its dimensions, to that of a Ship Canal. It was recommended by the President in his message to the 37th Congress, favorably reported upon by the Military Committee, and "the Select Committee on defense of great lakes and rivers." In the able report of the latter, we find this sentence: "The realization of a Ship Canal from Lake Michigan to the Mississippi, for military and commercial purposes, *is the great work of the age.* In effect, commercially, it turns the Mississippi into Lake Michigan, and makes an outlet to the great lakes at New Orleans, and for the Mississippi at New York. It brings together the two great systems of water communication of our country: the great lakes and the St. Lawrence, and the canals connecting the lakes with the ocean, on the east; and the Mississippi and Missouri, with all their tributaries, on the west and south, etc." That this great national work will be accomplished at an early day, there is scarcely a shadow of doubt; and it is probable the present Congress will deem it of sufficient importance to make an appropriation for carrying it forward to an early completion.

HARBOR IMPROVEMENT.—In 1830, the Black Hawk War broke out, with the history of which the general reader is familiar. Gen. Winfield Scott, and others, who were called West to quell the disturbances, passed through Chicago, and upon their return to the East, gave their friends a very flattering and glowing description of Chicago, and the resources of the West. From that date, this section of country was brought into more general notice; and through the representations of Gen. Winfield Scott, Congress made an appropriation for the improvement of the Harbor of Chicago, upon which operations were shortly afterwards commenced.

GROWTH OF CHICAGO.—In 1832, this city was inhabited by but a few families—the total population not exceeding one hundred and seventy-five souls. The principal citizens at that date, were: Archibald Clybourn, George W. Dole, Anson Taylor, Charles Taylor, J. S. C. Hogan, Robert A. Kinzie, Dexter Graves, P. F. W. Peck, John Wright, John S. Wright, Rufus Brown, George W. Snow, Hiram Pearsons, R. J. Hamilton; Robinson, the Indian Chief; J. N. Bailey; Father Walker, a Methodist Minister; J. Lefranbois, J. B. Beaubien, Mark Beaubien, Mr. Reed, Philo Carpenter, H. Compeau, Gholson Kercheval, R. E. Heacock, E. A. Rider, and a few others. Clinging to a lone and solitary military post for protection, and depending upon some chance vessel from Mackinac for subsistence, the mass of our present citizens can form but a very imperfect idea of the trials and privations endured by these "early pioneers of Chicago."

The "City of Chicago" was incorporated March 4, 1837. The following are the names of the Mayors, and the number of population, of the city, at different dates:

Years.	Population.	Mayors.	Years.	Population.	Mayors.
1833,	100		1850,	20,963	James Curtis.
1837,		Wm. B. Ogden.	1851,		Walter L. Gurnee.
1838,		Buckner S. Morris.	1852,	38,733	same.
1839,		Benjamin W. Raymond.	1853,	60,652	Charles M. Gray.
1840,	4,479	Alexander Lloyd.	1854,	65,872	Isaac L. Milliken.
1841,		Francis C. Sherman.	1855,	80,023	Levi D. Boone.
1842,		Benjamin W. Raymond.	1856,		Thomas Dyer.
1843,	7,580	Augustus Garret.	1857,		John Wentworth.
1844,	8,000	Alson S. Sherman.	1858,		John C. Haines.
1845,	12,088	Augustus Garret.	1859,		same.
1846,	14,169	John P. Chapin.	1860,		John Wentworth.
1847,	16,849	James Curtiss.	1861,		Julian Rumsey.
1848,	20,035	James H. Woodworth.	1862,		
1849,	23,048	same.			

OLD DEARBORN STREET (OLD POINT) BRIDGE.

GROWTH OF CHICAGO COMPARED WITH OTHER CITIES.

New York	was	108	years in attaining the same population as	Chicago	in	32	years.
Boston	"	118	"	"	"	"	32	"
Philadelphia	"	137	"	"	"	"	32	"
Baltimore	"	50	"	"	"	"	16	"
Cincinnati	"	50	"	"	"	"	18	"
New Orleans	"	65	"	"	"	"	22	"
St. Louis	"	80	"	"	"	"	26	"

According to the census returns, there were in 1840, ninety cities and towns having a population larger than Chicago, viz: 4,853. In 1850 there were eighteen larger, and by the census of 1860, there were but eight having over 109,263 inhabitants; which is the population of Chicago as shown by the last census. As a result of the War of the Rebellion, however, three of these—New Orleans, Cincinnati and St. Louis have fallen off, and Chicago increased to such an extent that she probably to-day ranks as the sixth city in the Union, and we predict that in 1870 she will rank as second only to New York.

During the brief period that has elapsed, all traces of the former "*Checaque*" have been obliterated—the rude wigwams and log huts have given place to immense warehouses and Railroad depots; the Indian canoes have been superceded by vessels having a total burthen of 400,000 tons, which here find an important port of entry—vessels which navigate all waters; and instead of a mere village, peopled by a few pioneers, who consider themselves secluded from all the rest of the world, we find to-day one of the leading cities of the United States,—a centre for one of the most extensive systems of Railways on this continent—with a population of 120,000 people, transacting a commercial business which in several articles exceed that of any other port or city on the Globe. To those who have been familiar with Chicago from its beginning, the contrast between *what was* and *what is*, must be indescribably great!

THE COMMERCE OF CHICAGO, PAST AND PRESENT.—The commerce of the West is fast becoming the controlling power of the nation. As the geographical and the commercial centre of the Mississippi valley—the most important and productive portion of the North American continent, it is but very recently that Chicago began to attract the attention of her sister cities in the Union. Within the past ten years this city has taken her rank as the greatest primary grain mart, not only in the United States, but in the world; and during the present year, 1862, in her exports and trade in Lumber and Pork she has outstripped every other city on the face of the Globe. Thus, step by step she is wheeling into the ranks, as a first-class commercial city; a position which she must necessarily maintain.

The growth of our commerce will be as well shown by the exports and imports as otherwise:—

	Imports.	Exports.		Imports.	Exports.
1836..............	$325,203 00	$1,000 64	1851..............		
1841..............	164,347 88	348,862 24	1856..............		
1846..............	2,027,150 00	1,813,468 00	1861..............		

TONNAGE OF CHICAGO.—According to the last published volume of "Commerce and Navigation," of the one hundred and thirty-six Shipping Districts of the United States, there are but ten that have a larger tonnage than Chicago. The following is the tonnage of some of the Southern and Western cities:

Chicago,	Total Tonnage,	68,123.30	Louisville,	Total Tonnage,	20,626.72
Detroit,	" "	60,070.45	Cincinnati,	" "	29,514.83
Charleston, S. C.,	" "	61,583.37	Milwaukee,	" "	24,864.30
St. Louis,	" "	90,756.86	Memphis,	" "	7,925.89
Savannah,	" "	37,843.55	Total Tonnage of 136 Districts,		5,145,037.30.

Chicago and Milwaukee compare as follows:

Imported during the year ending June 30, 1859.

	Free of Duty.	Paying Duty.	Total Value.		Free of Duty.	Paying Duty.	Total Value.
Chicago,	$84,006.	$9,402.	$93,588.	Milwaukee,	$7,658.	$21,288.	$28,946.

CHICAGO BOARD OF TRADE.—The first meeting of merchants and business men, was held March 13th, 1848, when a constitution was adopted. An act of incorporation was passed April 15th, 1849, and adopted, and the Board organized May 2nd, 1850. In 1858 the Board consisted of 377 paying members; which had increased to 850 in 1861. Few, if any, similar institutions, number more members, or transact more business on 'change. From the valuable and comprehensive annual statements, prepared by Seth Catlin, Esq., the accomplished Secretary of the Board, we compile the following:

GENERAL SUMMARY OF THE BUSINESS OF CHICAGO.

In some of the leading articles, for the years 1854, 1858, and 1861.

	1854	1858	1861
Barrels Flour shipped	111,627	400,402	1,603,720
Bushels Wheat shipped	2,306,925	8,850,257	15,835,743
" Corn "	6,626,050	7,720,264	21,372,725
" Oats "	3,220,987	1,519,000	1,633,237
" Barley "	147,811	132,020	220,534
" Rye "		7,569	303,813
Pork received, (number of Hogs)	74,870	540,486	675,002
Number of Hogs cut by city Packers	52,840	99,262	271,805
Number of Cattle killed and shipped		140,535	204,579
Number of Cattle packed	23,691	45,504	53,745
Lead shipped, (lbs.)	4,247,128	3,442,870	16,854,706
Tonnage of vessels on the Lake (American)	984,114	404,301	390,611
Capacity of Grain Elevators, (ship bush. per day)		1,340,000	2,095,000
Imports by Lake, Canal, and Railroad		$91,636,000.50	
Exports " " "		83,230,921.20	
Capital employed in Manufacturing	$4,220,000		$6,537,000
Number of Hands employed	5,000		10,613
Value of Manufactured Articles	$7,870,000		$16,948,381
Miles of Railroad completed in Illinois	(1850) 105		2,870

CHICAGO THE GREATEST PRIMARY GRAIN MART IN THE WORLD.—In the "Annual Review of the Commerce of Chicago," for 1854, this announcement was made, and in 1856, the shipments of flour and grain, (reducing flour into wheat,) was shown to be 21,583,221 bushels. As this statement has been called "braggadocia" by some would-be rivals of Chicago, we reproduce a table from the Review, for 1856, showing the exports of the principal grain ports of the world, as compard with Chicago.

	Wheat, bushels.	Indian Corn, bushels.	Oats, Rye & Barley, bu.	Total, bushels.
Odessa	5,600,000		1,440,000	7,040,000
Galatz and Ibrelia	2,400,000	5,600,000	320,000	8,320,000
Dantzic	3,080,000		1,328,000	4,408,000
St. Petersburg		all kinds,		7,200,000
Archangel		"		9,528,000
Riga		"		4,000,000
CHICAGO, (1854)	2,644,060	6,837,899	3,419,551	12,902,310
CHICAGO, (1855)	6,115,250	7,517,625	2,000,938	16,633,813
CHICAGO, (1856)	8,337,420	11,129,668	1,032,188	21,583,241
CHICAGO, (1861)	15,835,953	24,372,725	2,253,384	52,462,062

INCREASE OF THE CHICAGO POST-OFFICE BUSINESS.—In 1828, according to the narrative of events in "Wau-bun," the arrivals of either printed or written matter, were very meagre—few and far between. We quote from that work: "The mails arrived at very rare intervals. They were brought occasionally from Fort Clark, (Peoria) but more frequently from Fort Wayne, or across the peninsala of Michigan, which was still a wilderness, peopled with savages. The hardy adventurer who acted as express, (carrying the mail upon his back,) was, not unfrequently, obliged to imitate the birds of heaven and 'lodge among the branches,' in order to ensure the safety of himself and his charge." During the long and intensely severe winter of 1831-2 the principal population of Chicago occupied quarters in the garrison, and were supplied with the necessaries of life by Geo. W. Dole, Esq., then the only merchant here, except Mr. R. A. Kinzie, who was trading at Wolf's Point (the junction of the North and South branch of the river.) Then there were no mail routes, post roads nor post-office in Chicago, and the only way in which the inhabitants got any knowledge of what was transpiring elsewhere, was by dispatching a half-breed Indian, once a fortnight to Niles, Michigan, or Fort Wayne, Indiana, to procure all the papers he could, old and new. The trip was made on foot, and usually occupied a week. The papers were "handed round" and read in the order in which they were published, so as to keep a correct chronological idea of the events transpiring.

In 1832 a weekly mail was received here from the east, on horseback, J. N. Bailey being Post-Master. Later in 1832 a one-horse wagon was employed to bring the mail. In 1833 a two-horse wagon was required, and in 1834 a four-horse stage line was established semi-weekly — increased to a tri-weekly line in 1835. In 1837 a

POST OFFICE AND CUSTOM HOUSE.

daily eastern mail was first enjoyed — Sidney Abel being Post-Master. There were in 1844, forty-eight mails weekly, and the receipts of the office amounted to $10,000.

To-day, the Chicago distributing Post-Office, in the amount of mail matter it dispatches daily, is second only to the New York office. The 93 clerks and assistants in the different departments, receive and dispatch about one thousand bags of mail matter daily, averaging seventy-five thousand letters per day. The newspaper matter is counted by wagon-loads and tons. One single mail, in March, contained seventy packages of letters in one bill, from Cairo, Illinois,— averaging one hundred to a package, making seven thousand letters to a single mail — these, however, were principally from soldiers who were at points south of Cairo. Packages from St. Louis and New York frequently contain from four thousand to six thousand letters in a single mail. The quarter that closed March 31st, shows the annual receipts to be at the rate of about $150,000.

Mark the contrast! Just thirty years ago the questionable enterprise of establishing a weekly horseback mail was embarked in — now this is, in many respects, the most important Post-Office in the United States, except New York!

Buildings in Chicago, in 1842.— The number and character of buildings in Chicago, in 1842, is as follows:

	South Side.	North Side.	West Side.	Total.
Brick Stores........	37	0	0	37
Frame "	206	10	3	219
Stone "	0	0	0	0
Brick Dwellings....	28	10	3	41
Frame "	444	278	120	842
Stone "	1	0	0	1
	716	298	126	1,140

Number of other buildings, of all kinds, 224. Total, 1364.

In the year 1856 there were built here seven Churches, five Hotels, the City Armory, Hospital and High School edifice; 145 stores, many of them from two to five stories, marble and brick, and several hundred residences — the number erected on the West side alone, estimated at two thousand. The cost of buildings erected in 1856, was — Business blocks, $1,781,900; Residences, $1,104,190; Hotels, $315,000; Churches, Seminaries, Academies, etc., $311,000; other buildings, not included above, $1500 to $1000 each, $1,500,000; city improvements, $427,434, making a total cost of improvements in 1856, $5,708,624. Showing that there was a greater number of buildings erected, at a greater aggregate cost in one year, 1856,) than there were in the city, all told, in 1842.

The Bright Future of Chicago.— Judging of the future by the past, it seems difficult to assign any limit to the advancement of Chicago. Her history presents one of the most remarkable instances of sudden rise to commercial importance to be found in our age. So rapid, indeed, has been her growth — with such gigantic strides has she moved onward in her career, that little space is left to mark and calculate the successive stages of her onward progress.

A few months since, a very able article appeared in Hunt's Merchants' Magazine, (conceded to be one of the most reliable statistical journals of the country,) from which we extract the following sentences, as applicable to this subject:

"Westward Movement of the Centre of Population, Commerce, and of Industrial Power in North America.—In the rapidly developing greatness of North America, it is interesting to look to the future, and speculate on the most probable points of centralization of its commerce and social power. Including with our nation, as forming an important part of its commercial community, the Canadas and contiguous provinces, the centre of population, white and black, is a little west of Pittsburgh. *The movement of this center is north of west, about in the direction of* Chicago. The centre of productive power cannot be ascertained with any degree of precision. We know it must be a considerable distance east and north of the centre of population. That centre, too, is on its grand march westward. Both, in their regular progress, will reach Lake Michigan. Is it not, then, as certain as anything in the future can be, that the central power of the continent will move to, and become permanent on, the border of the great lakes? Around these pure waters will gather the densest population, and on their borders will grow up the best towns and cities. * * * * At the present rate of increase, the United States and Canadas, fifty years from this time, will contain over one hundred and twenty millions of people. If we suppose one hundred and five millions, and that these shall be distributed so that the Pacific States shall have ten millions, and the Atlantic border five millions, there will be left for the great interior plain, seventy millions. These seventy millions will have twenty times as much commercial intercourse with each other as with all the world besides. It is obvious, then, that there must be built up in their midst *the great city of the continent*; and not only so, but that they will sustain several cities greater than those which can be sustained on the ocean border."

After making a comparison between London and New York, in which the writer concludes, (from the past growth of the two cities,) that New York will overtake London in about fifty years; he continues: —

"A similar comparison of New York and the leading interior city — Chicago — will show a like result in favor of Chicago. The census returns show the average duplication to be fifteen years for New York, and less than four years for Chicago. Suppose that of New York, for the future, should be sixteen years, and that of Chicago were only eight years, and that New York now has, with her suburbs, 900,000, and Chicago 100,000 people; in three duplications, New York would contain 6,200,000, and Chicago, in six duplications, occupying the same length of time, would have

6,400,000. It is not asserted as probable, that either city will be swelled to such an extraordinary size in forty-eight years, if ever; but it is more than probable that the leading interior city (Chicago) will be greater than New York, fifty years hence."

If, then, according to these calculations, New York is to outstrip London within fifty years, and Chicago to outstrip New York, the conclusion arrived at is, that *Chicago will, fifty years hence, have become The Largest City in the World!*

INDIA RUBBER AND ITS MANUFACTURES.

NATIVES COLLECTING EAST INDIA RUBBER, OR JINTAWAN.

IT was in the luxuriant vegetation of South America, that the India Rubber tree was first discovered and made known to the world. The botanical history of this gum is peculiar. It is produced only in the intense heats of the equator. It is found, indeed, in the greatest perfection, upon that equatorial ring which modern science has traced around the globe, and which furnishes to the geologist the most convincing proof that, far back in the early dawn of time, before flower, or leaf, or spreading tree adorned the surface of the earth — ages upon ages before his dwelling-place was prepared for man — the solid globe was in a state of fusion.

In South America, under the name of "caoutchouc," this gum is produced from a tree called the *siphonia elastica*, but it is also obtained in the East Indies, and other quarters of the globe. The East India Rubber, as it is called in commerce, is the product oft he *ficus elastica*, one of the most beautiful trees in the world. It is found in Hindoostan, and in the islands of the Indian Archipelago, and among the natives it passes by the name of kasmeer, and the gum is called by the names of juntawan, saikwah, and dallah. It is found also in Africa, but the specimens which have been imported are of inferior quality, and its botanical history is not yet fully ascertained. The native rubber, however, in all its varieties, is comparatively useless. It is only when manufactured into what is now known as "vulcanized," or "metallic" Rubber, that it becomes valuable; and it is of this new substance, and its manufactures, that we propose to give some information to the reader.

India Rubber has been known about one hundred and thirty years; and only in the last twenty-five years has it been found of much practical use. It was brought into Europe, it is supposed, by some French travelers, on their return from South America, in the year 1730, and introduced into America about 1770. From that period to 1791 nothing seems to have been done with the raw material. The grand difficulty seems to have been to find a solvent for it, of such a nature that it might be easily manipulated. In 1791, the first patent for effecting this was taken out by Samuel Peal, who claimed an improved method of making water-proof all kinds of leather, cloth, etc., which he accomplished by dissolving by distillation, or infusion, over a brisk fire, india-rubber in spirits of turpentine, and then spreading it on his cloth, or other material, by means of a brush. Here is the germ of our present water-proof coat.

After hundreds of ingenious mechanics and scientific chemists, in various countries, had occupied years in laborious but fruitless experiments, the all-surpassing genius of an American discovered, and triumphantly perfected, a singular process, by which he is able to combine metals and minerals with this tropical gum, and produce the "metallic," or "vulcanized" Rubber, which has since taken a place in science, and in the mechanic arts, as important as iron or glass.

The late Charles Goodyear, whose name is world-renowned, accomplished this greatest invention of the age, after many years of deep study and wearisome experiments, in the midst of poverty, sickness and ridicule.

India Rubber has already been applied to countless uses, and yet it may be said to be in its infancy. We will attempt to enumerate only a few of the leading articles we saw on a recent visit to the India Rubber establishment of Messrs. John B. Ideson & Co., located at No. 115 Randolph Street, Kingsbury block. This firm is the only representative in the North-West, of the New York Belting and Packing Company, whose extensive manufactory is located at Newtown, Conn., on the Potatook River.

POTATOOK RIVER AT THE MILL-POND.

Mr. Ideson first exhibited some milk of the Rubber tree; ammonia being added to it to preserve it in a liquid state. The milk in the bottle was perfectly white. Then we saw it molded into heavy disks, which form the powerful but elastic and luxurious spring, on which the railroad car, laden with a hundred passengers, rushes along over every iron-belted avenue. It forms the belt which bears the vast power of the steam engine, that mightiest material agent God has given to man, quivering and throbbing through the busy factory.

It is modeled into the delicate billiard cushion, on the smooth green table, where the rolling balls follow the unerring cue. By another process it becomes a substance as hard as ivory, but more brilliant and beautiful in its polish than jet itself, and then it becomes the graceful comb, hidden in a fair girl's tresses, the bracelet on her arm, the ring on her hand or the jewel in her ears. It has already taken the place of ivory, and horn, and shell, in the countless uses to which the ingenuity of man has applied them, for comfort and for luxuries. Among some of the latest appliances of hard, or semi-hard India Rubber we may mention, for machinery, army accoutrements, ornaments and musical instruments, knife, sword, pistol handles and pens. Army accoutrements and ornaments excel those in present use from their lightness, and from the resistance to blows which indent metal, as well as from the facility with which they may be cleaned. As handles to ordinary knives, pistols, or swords, there is a superiority over anything hitherto used, both in touch and wear, the blades not being liable to start when placed in hot water, whilst its application to pens will doubtless, ere long, be as common as steel, combining, as it does, all the qualities of the metal, with the extreme freedom and ease of the quill.

INDIA RUBBER GRINDING MILL.

It has also been applied for the coating of iron pins for insulators, the covering of gun-barrels in place of *browning*, and the coating of harness irons in place of leather, being found far more valuable, not affected by heat or wet, and requiring far less trouble in cleaning.

Since the commencement of the present war, new wants have called forth new applications, and India Rubber promises to be as indispensable for the army and navy, as it has proved in the industrial peaceful arts. Mr. Ideson exhibited to us every variety and style of clothing, and almost every article necessary for army purposes, such as water-proof camp blankets, for officers and privates; some on white and colored flannels, with a slit in the middle, just long enough to slip the head through, thus forming a regular poncho, such as the wild horsemen of the Pampas use. For privates the light blankets are recommended, on account of their cheapness and weight. One of these is rolled in a small package, and carried on the knapsack without inconvenience. Four of these blankets will form a bivouac tent, or a combination knapsack, such as were used by the celebrated regiment of fireman Zouaves.

MACHINE FOR WASHING INDIA RUBBER.

Another very important article we saw, was a Rubber canteen for carrying water. It has an ingenious filterer in the mouth-piece, which always insures pure water. India Rubber hair mattresses and pillows which are water proof, and well adapted for sea and land service, and for invalids, and many other articles which we have not space to enumerate. It is enough to say that every article for the comfort of the soldier, or the luxury and convenience of the civilian, which the art and genius of man can desire, may be found at the representative India Rubber establishment of the valley of the West.

STEAM HEATERS FOR VULCANIZING.

Mr. Ideson came to this city seven years ago; since which time he has perseveringly devoted his time, talent and capital, in developing and bringing to its present position, this important branch of commerce in Chicago. His trade extends over the entire North-West. From the smallest of beginnings in 1855, the business of this establishment has grown into an extent and importance second to few commercial interests in the West. They introduce no article that is not one of decided utility; and make it a point to affirm nothing in their advertisement that is not strictly true.

CUTTING RUBBER INTO SLABS FOR THE WASHROOM.

A leading and very important feature in Messrs. Ideson & Co.'s business, is that of Machine Belting, Steam Packing, and Engine and Conducting Hose, also Solid Emery Vulcanite Wheels, of which they are the sole Western Agents, for the New York Belting and Packing Company.

Before the discovery of the vulcanizing process by Goodyear, Rubber Belting proved almost worthless, but being vulcanized it is not affected by heat or cold. The success of vulcanized belting has been so great that many inventions have been put in the market, made of various materials, and sold for Rubber Belting. These have, in some measure, succeeded for a while, but in every case have proved a failure, and also, a loss to those using them. Any person can test the difference by exposing a piece of each to the action of the heat, when the piece *not vulcanized* will become soft and sticky, while that which *is vulcanized* will remain without any danger whatever. The difference is equally apparent when the belts are exposed to cold weather, as that which is vulcanized will remain perfectly pliable while the imitations and bogus belts will become hard and rigid. From observation and experience we are satisfied that the only reliable Rubber Belting is the "Patent Smooth Vulcanized Belting."

The superiority of this Belting, for most purposes, over the best Leather Belts, has been proved, after a trial of many years. It is manufactured by a process peculiar to this Company, by which unusual firmness and solidity is obtained, thereby obviating some objections heretofore urged against India-Rubber Belting made in the old way. The great improvements in Vulcanized Rubber Hose, combine strength, firmness and flexibility, which render it superior to any other made. Vulcanized Rubber Steam Packing is considered by engineers and mechanics as indispensable wherever steam joints are to be made, as no substance has so much elasticity which stands so high a degree of heat. Since 1840 this packing only, has been used by ocean steamers, and by all the principal steamers and engine-shops in the United States.

The extent, variety and beauty of articles manufactured from HARD GUM is almost incredible; yet opposite as its results are, through all its transformations it preserves its durability, tenacity, impermeability, and the property of retaining the shape into which it is moulded and heated, as well as the most beautiful pol-

PRESSING LEATHER ON THE CLOTH.

ish. This new form of rubber is so far perfected as to form an important staple branch of industry, in which millions of dollars are invested, and the business is steadily increasing in extent and value.

VULCANIZING HOSE.

Solid Emery Vulcanite Wheels, for grinding and polishing metals are of comparatively recent invention. During the past three years, they have been thoroughly tested, and successfully adopted in thousands of the best manufacturing establishments throughout the country. For their great economy, efficiency, and con-

WATERFALL AND MILL-POND FROM BELOW THE DAM, POTATOOK RIVER.

venience, and particularly their perfect adaptation to many kinds of work now commonly done with files by hand labor, they are almost indispensable in every manufacturing establishment. Their durability is such, that even when the wheels are in constant use, the wear of them is hardly perceptible.

This house is also the western agency for the oldest and most extensive Leather Belting manufactories in the East. At all times, there is kept in this establishment, the best and largest stock of Leather Belting to be found in this part of the country. All the belting sold by this firm is sold as low as can be bought at the East, and the quality is warranted. And so we might go on enumerating article after article, of utility, beauty, and ornament, which may be found at this establishment, had we the space. . But we recommend all, whose interest and curiosity would be promoted thereby, to visit the store of Messrs. Ideson & Co., at No. 115 Randolph street, Kingsbury Block, and examine for themselves.

CHICAGO BREWERY.
PREMIUM ALE
PALE ALE
WORKING ROOMS
FERMENTING ROOM
STOCK ALE
PORTER
RACKING CELLER
ICE HOUSE STORAGE FOR 16.000 BRL. STOCK ALE.
ENGINE MACHINE ROOM

THE MANUFACTURE OF ALE, BEER AND PORTER.

ONE of the great things of our Republic is, that it opens to every citizen all the paths that lead to wealth and honor. Here there is freedom for glory, as well as struggle; wealth as well as toil. We shall reckon no Norman conquest in our history; for where we conquer a nation her territory is divided among all our people. We rummage no musty libraries for titles of nobility; but in the United States, every true, brave, daring man is the Rudolph de Hapsburgh of his race. If such institutions, and the universal prevalence of such a spirit, do not make us a great nation, then civilization itself, with all the appliances of political and religious liberty, cannot do it. England has given the world all the grand and bright ideas she had for ages, until the Anglo-Saxons began to develop themselves on this side the Atlantic, in unfettered liberty. The world is astonished at our progress; and we should be ourselves if we could stop long enough to see how rapid it has been. Other countries trace their fortunes to a few men; we do it, comparatively, to many. It is to the concurrent energies, genius, and patriotism of a multitude of men, that we owe what we now are. To illustrate — turn to the frontispiece of this elegant commercial volume, and behold a view of Chicago of 1820 — then to the next page and see Chicago of 1862; a city of only about forty years growth — the admiration of travelers from every part of our own continent — the marvel of those from the other hemisphere. And yet, only a faint conception of the secret of the unexampled progress this city has made in life and power, can be gained by the contemplation of its more imposing palaces, churches, public buildings and hotels. In these we see only surface indications — they are but the saloons and surface decorations of the gorgeous steamer. To understand the power that moves her, we must go below and look at the gigantic machinery which impels her along her way. Behold her manufactories — her men of business: these are the architects whose genius and enterprise have reared this proud structure of commercial greatness on the western shore of Lake Michigan. One of the most interesting spots to visit in this great and growing city of the West, is Messrs. Lill & Diversy's extensive BREWERY, situated in the northern part of the city, on the shore of the lake, whose crystal waters forms so important an item in their article of manufacture.

Ale is a beverage of great antiquity in Great Britain and Ireland. But the Ale of those periods, and until the sixteenth century, contained no hops. Ale is mentioned in the laws of Ina, King of Wessex, who ascended the throne about the year 689. It was one of the articles of a royal banquet, provided for Edward the Confessor, about the middle of the eleventh century.

Some centuries since, ale and wine were as certainly a part of a breakfast, in England, as tea and coffee are at present, and even for ladies. The Earl of Northumberland, in the reign of Henry VIII., lived in the following manner:—"On flesh days through the year, breakfast for my lord and lady was a loaf of bread, two manchets, a quart of beer, a quart of wine, half a chine of mutton, or a chine of beef, boiled. On meagre days, a loaf of bread, two manchets, a quart of beer, a quart of wine, a dish of butter, a piece of salt fish, or a dish of buttered eggs."

Hume relates that the Earl of Leicester gave Queen Elizabeth an entertainment, in Kenilworth Castle, which was extraordinary for expense and magnificence. Among other particulars, we are told that three hundred and sixty-five hogsheads of beer were drank at it. Now in this quantity there are twenty-three thousand gallons; and if there were twenty-three thousand persons present, which is not possible, it would still be an allowance of a gallon to each.

ALE, a fermented liquor, prepared from an infusion of malt and barley. It is called ale or beer; in some places, as in Wilts and Dorset, in England, the terms are used indifferently. In others a distinction is made; Ale being a light colored liquor, prepared from slightly roasted malt, and which gives off more froth or bead. Beer is probably the generic name, hence brewing. Though a German word, its connection with the Latin *bibere* is obvious. Ale is Anglo-Saxon. It is a common beverage in almost all countries in which the climate prohibits the cultivation of the vine; and here it may be observed that the use of some fermented beverage is universal throughout the ancient and modern, civilized and savage world, from Noah to the South-Sea Islanders. Beer or Ale, *cerevisia*, from Ceres the goddess of corn, is said by Tacitus to have been drank in his time by the Germans, the root from which the great beer drinkers of modern times derive their origin. According to Herodotus, the Egyptians prepared it from the barley for which the valley of the Nile is still famous. Diodorus Siculus speaks of two different liquors, one the pure infusion, *Zythos*, the other *Kourmirmi*, prepared with honey. Some, even for the nations which could take their wine, did not despise John Barleycorn; the Spaniards, Gauls and Greeks liked beer; the Gauls in particular had their corma and cerevisea, a barley beer, and a wheat beer, while the Britons imbibed a thin potation, which would hardly pass the lips of their descendants, which they prepared from wheat sweetened with honey. The Chinese, among whom every new-fangled idea has been in use for centuries, have a drink made of barley or wheat, and the Japanese take a rice beer at every hour of the day. Benighted Nubia and Abyssinia claim kindred with Europe, in this one touch of nature — they prepare a drink from various grains. As for the Danes and North-men they placed their hopes of eternal happiness, among other pleasures, in an unlimited supply of beer. The bitter infusion of hops is of less respectable antiquity. Their use does not seem to date earlier than the eleventh century; before that time the Scandinavians are reputed to have used oak bark. What effect the preservative virtues of tannin had on their bodies and health, is not recorded. Root beer, pleasant to Teutons but an abomination to Britons, was invented after the twelfth century; probably first devised as a substitute by some unfortunates during a time of famine; just as sailors who are out of tobacco take to chewing oakum. Hans Kenne, of Nuremberg, (1541) was the father of white Beer, dear to the patriotic Prussian. Ale and Beer was once accounted, beyond dispute, one of the necessities of life, and equally with bread, was subject to an assize of price and quality. Municipal officers, whose duty it was to taste the Ale served out to the public and report defaulters, were appointed by various English statutes. The duty was probably not unpleasant, seeing that the brewers were not likely to submit a bad brew for inspection. The venders of an adulterated tap had to stand in the public dung cart. Beer, though accounted less respectable than wine, perhaps, because the Romans, who served out a ration of parched corn and vinegar to their hungry legions, thought but little of it, has furnished matter to literature and art. Beer riots in Bavaria, malt-tax riots in England, on account of the rise in the price of these beverages, help to teach statesmen that the great food question is at the bottom of all real popular discontent. Hogarth in his Beer Alley and Gin Lane, shows us the infinite superiority of wholesome, sound-bodied Beer, over the detestable alcohol, just beginning to be popular in his day. Every one remembers "John Barleycorn" as a picture of burly strength and substantial solidity. Burns' "happy ale" is the symbol of good fellowship; and to what a depth of contempt does Iago assign "small beer." The government of Bavaria paternally interested in the welfare of of its people, gives considerable attention to the supply of its people with a good and wholesome drink; and although the Bock Beer, so called from the saltatory movements similar to those of a bock (goat), which it induces in its too partial admirers, may bring the beverage into some disrepute with serious people, the excellence of Bavarian Beer cannot be denied.

About the year 1620 some doctors and surgeons, during their attendance on an English gentleman, who was diseased at Paris, discoursed on wines and other beverages; and one physician, who had been in England, said, "the English had a drink which they called Ale, and which he thought the wholesomest liquor that could be drank; for whereas the body of man is supported by natural heat and radical moisture, there is no drink conduceth more to the preservation of the one, and the increase of the other, than Ale; for, while the Englishmen drank only Ale, they were strong, brawny, able men, and could draw an arrow an ell long; but when they fell to wine, they are found to be much impaired in their strength and age."

Wherever a people make Ale a common beverage, spirituous liquors, drunkenness and vice decrease in proportion. A few years ago, in the State of Illinois, the common drink was whisky, or rather a compound of fiery poisons, called whisky. Now Ale is becoming the universal beverage. There are about three hundred and fifty thousand barrels of Ale brewed annually in the State of Illinois, and about two hundred and fifty thousand of Lager. Among the most extensive and popular Breweries in the Mississippi valley is that of Messrs. Lill & Diversy. A visit to this Brewery is full of interest, the gigantic character of business operations, the scrupulous cleanliness which pervades everything is gratifying to the lover of fine Ale. This immense establishment has grown to its present gigantic proportions since 1835, when it was established by W. Haas & Co. The firm was composed of William Haas and Andrew Sulzar, whose combined capital invested amounted to about $3000, giving employment to four men.

These pioneers emigrated to this then far Western Territory, from Watertown, in the State of New York. They brought with them a small brew-apparatus, a lot of malt and about one hundred and fifty barrels of Ale. Soon after their arrival they purchased of Wm. B. Ogden, a lot one hundred by two hundred feet in Kinzie's addition, for two hundred dollars, upon which they erected a frame building, forty by eighty feet, with small additions, where they commenced brewing the finest Ale made in Chicago. Upon that very site now stands the "Chicago Brewery," of Lill & Diversy, whose humble origin dates back twenty-seven years ago, when six hundred barrels of Ale per annum (the amount manufactured by Haas & Co.) supplied the Chicago market, which now requires ninety-three thousand barrels per annum.

About 1836 Mr. Sulzar sold his one-half interest to Wm. B. Ogden, and in 1839, Mr. Haas sold his to Mr. William Lill, the present active partner, through whose indefatigable business capacity, and knowledge of the Brewing interest, the Chicago Brewery has attained its present wide-extended reputation, and extensive sales throughout this great valley, from the frozen regions of the north — the rock-girt shores of Lake Superior — to New Orleans, the Naples of the South — from the Falls of Niagara to the newly discovered gold regions of Pike's Peak. Every where over this wide extended territory, Lill & Diversy's Ale is favorably known and sought for.

The progress of the Americans in brewing of malt and hop liquors, is not less than that made in manufactures and inventions, and we seem to be overtaking John Bull in Ale making, aye, and in Ale drinking. Even temperance men have rejoiced in this, as they look upon the rise of Ale as the downfall of poisonous liquor. But a few years ago, alcoholic liquors were the almost universal drink, and the Ale then made was stigmatized as "swipes." That day has passed, and the most fastidious Britisher and epicurean Teuton quaffs the ripe and sparkling Ale, and the lively, cheering *Lager*, with a gusto equal to what either could in their own country, and the American who used to ridicule the Englishman and the German, now sits down and takes his Lill's Ale with a zest, and protests it is the richest tonic he ever imbibed; while in the homes of American families, we find the barrel and the half-barrel standing ready tapped all the while; and Yankees find that Ale is a cure for dyspepsia, and a capital thing to take and enjoy.

This Brewery occupies two entire blocks, on which there are three large brick buildings, measuring four hundred and thirty by one hundred feet, and four or five stories high, while the rest is devoted to out-buildings, yards, shops, stabling and storage. It was erected at an expense of $125,000, and frequent additions have been made from time to time; the vats, machinery, appurtenances, live stock and wagons, are worth about $80,000; while the value of barley, malt and hops on hand, is always about $110,000. Thus there is a capital of about $300,000 employed in the business, which is far ahead of any similar establishment in the West. They send Ale as far east as Buffalo, north, to Lake Superior and St. Paul, west, to St. Joseph, Mo., and previous to our National troubles, to New Orleans. They also have agents in all the principal cities of the West.

In brewing, the barley is first elevated to the lofts of the main building, each of which measures one hundred by one hundred and forty feet, and is capable of storing one hundred thousand bushels of grain. The barley is raised to the lofts by the elevators, and then passes into a peculiar looking vehicle, called a screening machine, which cleanses it. The first operation is malting. This is the process by which certain of the component parts of barley are converted into a species of saccharine matter, through the agency of an artificial or forced vegetation; and to this are devoted four floors of the entire building, which are as remarkable for their cleanliness and order as for their size, being one hundred by one hundred and forty feet. They have also a Malt House at Janesville, where they malt twenty thousand bushels per annum, also, another, not connected with the Brewery, malting eighteen thousand bushels per annum, and soon they purpose the erection of another building, with facilities for malting one hundred thousand bushels per annum. There are seven immense steeping tubs, capable of holding nine hundred and eighty bushels, and seven drying kilns. Into these tubs the grain is turned, along with water, and remains soaking for many hours — for Ale, it remains twenty-six to forty hours.

There are always four thousand five hundred bushels of grain in process of malting. When sufficiently soaked, the contents of the steeping tubs are emptied upon smooth cemented floors, of which there are two, seventy-eight by two hundred feet in extent. Here the steeped barley remains to grow from seven to ten days; it is then thrown into the drying kilns, and is heated over a coal fire for three days; after this, the barley is again elevated to another floor by the elevators, and falls from thence into the huge mill, where it is completely crushed between ponderous cylindrical iron rollers, which break every corn; then it passes into the malt-bin, and so on to the mash-tun, where the boiling water is added, and is mixed up by a mashing machine capable of mashing one thousand and ten bushels, or more, at a time. This tun is a round wooden vessel, with a movable perforated bottom, and when the barley is thoroughly mixed, it passes through this into a great copper boiler. The hops, at this stage, are added, and the boiling progresses. This is continued until the liquid, or wort, as it is called, is brought to the condition required, and which demands the nicest discrimination on the part of the brewer. The contents of the boilers now pass into the hop-jack, which, having a bottom like the mash-tun, the liquor passes off, leaving the hops at the bottom of the jack. The liquid is then pumped, by steam, into the coolers, which are large shallow vessels, more like boxes, in a separate apartment at the top of the building. As it is essential that the cooling should be rapid, the apartment is almost all windows, overlooking the lake, while over the coolers are fans, which, revolving, keep up a breeze which soon chills the liquor, which passes, subsequently, through pipes to the great fermenting tuns, or tubs, below, (of these there are six for Ale, with a capacity of two hundred and fifty to three hundred and fifty barrels each, and fourteen for Lager, of seventy barrels each,) every tun being furnished with a refrigerator. Fermentation is a process which is the most difficult of all to conduct properly—the most precarious in its results; but, at the same time, of the greatest importance to the operator. For although he has been successful in all the preceding stages, yet should he fail in this, the advantages which he has already obtained will be of little avail, and complete disappointment must ensue, inasmuch as the produce will be wanting in every requisite property—in spirituosity, flavor and transparency. The yeast is added, and the Beer gradually rises in foam, until the tun, which was half full at first, soon brims over. The yeast works out at the top of the Ale, and is skimmed; while it works to the *bottom* of Lager, and the liquor is drawn off, leaving the yeast as a sediment. The process of fermentation takes from three to ten days. From these tuns the Ale or Beer is drawn into puncheons, or hogsheads, of about ten barrels each, situated in the working cellar. When the working has ceased, the liquid passes into the racking vats, where it rests for about six hours, and is then racked into packages for shipment. But it is of course not sold until the article has ripened, which occupies many months, the longer the better; and no brewers but the most extensive can afford their brewing to remain so long on hand. In this respect, Messrs. Lill & Diversy possess facilities beyond that of any other establishment of a similar nature in the North-West—a large capital and extensive capacity for storage, enable them to keep their Ale and Beer longer than the other firms, and this places their productions pre-eminently ahead of their competitors.

In the manufacture of Porter and Brown Stout, the barley, in malting, is roasted, or burned. Stock Ale, which is made in the winter, takes twenty days longer than light Ale in making.

At this Brewery, four thousand seven hundred barrels of Ale are always in process of brewing, and there is always ready stored in the immense ice houses, eleven thousand to twelve thousand barrels of Stock and Bitter Pale Ale, Porter, and Brown Stout, in tuns holding from thirty to two hundred and ten barrels each.

There are two Ice Houses, one of which was recently erected, measuring two hundred and ten by seventy feet. The ice is in the middle of the ice house, in two bodies, one measuring sixty by thirty and twenty-five feet high, and the other sixty by sixty and twenty-five feet high, packed in tanbark, and encased in wood, by which means a temperature of forty degrees is kept up during the year. The absence of cellars has been the greatest drawback to Chicago as a brewing point, but these ice houses overcome all that, and the fame which Milwaukee Lager Beer gained through its cellarage, no longer obtains to the depreciation of Chicago Ale.

Messrs. Lill & Diversy, last year, bought one hundred and twelve thousand bushels of barley, and sold, in the same period, forty-four thousand seven hundred and fifty barrels of Ale, Stout, and Porter, while their facilities will enable them to increase their manufactures at least thirty per cent., when the supply shall fall short of the demand, as soon it must do.

In this Brewery they have a force of seventy-five men, thirty-five horses, a steam engine of twenty-five-horse power, and a boiler of fifty-horse power, which heats the water for boiling and mashing, and warms the entire building. Added to this, there are Malt Vinegar Rectifying Works, which turn out twenty-five barrels per diem. They require two carpenter shops and twelve men to attend to repairs, and making boxes and signs. They have two cooper shops, which employ from five to twenty men, according to the season; while the stables, in neatness and order, are unsurpassed.

Within a few years, Ale of the first quality has been brewed by this establishment, and justly appreciated, until it is now the table drink of nearly every family in easy circumstances — being light, sprightly, and free from the bitterness which distinguishes Porter — no other ingredients entering into the composition than malt, hops, and pure water. The qualities which most distinguish this Ale, are purity, brilliancy of color, richness of flavor, and non-liability to deterioration in warm weather — qualities, the result of the peculiar characteristics of Lake Michigan water, the high intelligence, care, and experience of their brewers, conjoined to the use of apparatus possessing all the modern improvements, of European and American manufacture.

Lager Beer.— The manufacture of Lager Beer was introduced into this country about seventy years ago, from Bavaria. The process of brewing it was kept a secret for a long period. Its reception was not a welcome one; and about twelve years elapsed before its use became at all general. Within the last few years, however, the consumption has increased so enormously, not merely among the German, but among our native population, that its manufacture forms an important item of productive industry. The superior quality of that made by Messrs. Lill & Diversy, has, no doubt, increased the demand, and diminished, to a great extent, the use of spirituous liquors. Lager, signifies "kept," or "on hand;" and Lager Beer is equivalent to "beer in store." It can be made from the same cereals from which other malt liquors are made; but barley is the grain usually used in this country. The process resembles that of brewing Ale and Porter, with some points of difference, and the brewing generally forms a seperate and distinct business.

The Beer used in winter is lighter, and may be drawn five or six weeks after brewing; but the *real* Lager is made in cold weather, has a greater body — that is, more malt and hops are used — and is first drawn about the first of May. It is much improved by age and by keeping in a cool place.

There are about twenty Brewers of Lager Beer in Chicago, employing a capital of about $300,000.

The statistics of the entire Brewing business of Chicago for 1861, are as follows:

PRODUCT.

Ale and Porter, about 93,000 barrels, averaging $6 per barrel	$558,000
Lager Beer, about 50,000 " " 5 " "	250,000
Total Product	$808,000

RAW MATERIAL CONSUMED.

Barley, or Malt, 333,000 bushels, @ 60c	$199,800
Hops, 286,000 pounds, @ 22c	62,920
Total Raw Material consumed	$1,070,720

The Capital invested in Ale, Porter, and Lager Beer Brewing, including *Malting*, is about $1,070,720.

JEWELRY, SILVER WARE, ETC.

PRECIOUS metals are first mentioned in history as a means of facilitating the transfer of property. And Abraham weighed to Ephraim the silver, "four hundred shekels of silver, current money with the merchant." The adoption of gold and silver for personal adornment was subsequent to its use as money, and even to this day the idea of value, in the popular mind, is associated with these metals principally in the form of coin. It will therefore seem surprising to many, that the value of the gold and silver plate in the world has been carefully estimated to be *two thousand millions of dollars*, which is at least *one-fourth more* than all the coin in the world. In the United States, precious metals of the value of at least thirty millions of dollars are annually converted into plate or worked up into ornamental forms. The manufactories for these articles are mostly located in eastern cities, Philadelphia, New York and Newark. In the last-named it partakes of the character of a settled trade. Many of the magnificent services of Gold Plate, Silver Trumpets, Horns, etc., which, at different times, and in different parts of the United States, have been presented by citizens to those whom they delight to honor, were executed in Newark. But beside Gold and Silver Plate, the manufactory of *Jewelry* is largely and successfully carried on, particularly the finer and more costly kinds, as Diamonds and Pearl Jewelry. The taste displayed in setting Diamonds and Pearls, and in Cameo, Enameled, and Filagree work, and the weight and purity of the solid gold work, would astonish those who are familiar only with the work of this description executed in New Jersey.

There are several lapidaries in Newark, constantly occupied in cutting and preparing the various stones — Rubies, Sapphires, Agates, Emeralds — beside the large quantities that are imported from abroad. Although few or none of these articles are manufactured in this city, yet they are on sale here by one of our most enterprising and extensive Jewelry Houses, connected with one of the Newark manufacturing companies. Mr. A. H. MILLER, on the corner of Lake and Clark Streets, represents one of the fairest and most noteworthy houses in this city. His stock presents one of the richest and most beautiful displays of the manufacture of pure silver into objects of taste and utility in Chicago. The burnishing upon their smooth surface, the chasing of scenes and emblems, the various forms into which they have worked these beautiful metals, the originality of many of their designs, the happy adaptation of those which they have borrowed from European artists; have been the theme of remark and commendation from the very highest quarters.

Mr. Miller has spent a life time in this business—he is master of it in all its details. His business relations extend throughout a considerable portion of the North-West; every order is filled with the utmost degree of promptness; his prices are reduced as low as the security of trade and the solidity of a great house can admit. In 1856, he commenced business in Chicago, in the basement of the Marine Bank Building, since which time, his business has steadily increased to its present extent.

Having devoted so many years to the elaboration of the art of working gold, silver, and precious stones into the most exquisite forms, he has contributed in no small degree to the embellishment of our homes, in the North-West.

The building occupied by Mr. Miller, corner of Lake and Clark Streets, has recently been elevated to the grade of Lake Street, and at an expense of about five thousand dollars, it has been made into a first class store — its large, translucent French plate glass windows and doors — the glitter of gems and silver and gold within, reminds the passer-by of the crystal entrance to some Aladdin Palace, where the treasures of earth and sea, refined and polished by cunning workmanship, are all flashing forth their intense splendor. We crossed the threshold of this house of treasures, when the gas light was flashing over these works of genius, and saw them in translucent mirrors, reflected and multiplied — an epic in silver and gems and gold. We saw a coronet of pearls, inwoven with a starry way of brilliants, and lying as though it had just fallen from the brow of a princess — near to it a diamond cross, "which Jews might kiss and Infidels adore," a bracelet, wreathing in a graceful circle flexible links of gorgeous hues and enamelings — a plain chronometer watch, made by the celebrated Jules Jurgensen, of Copenhagen, which follows the sun unfalteringly his three hundred and sixty-five days. This store may well be called a starry way of pearls, diamonds, and opals — brooches, bracelets, and pins of matchless enamelings — vases in lustrous gold and chased silver — objects of rare workmanship; they form a string of sparkling gems of all hues, from the burning ruby to the dreamy, rainbow-hued opal.

But from whence come all these precious stones, and of what are they made? First, as to the diamond, which like the stars, must have cycles to grow — which, though the king and chief of all, may be dismissed in two words — pure carbon. The diamond is the ultimate effort, the idealization, the spiritual evolution of coal, the butterfly escaped from its antennal tomb, the realization of the coal's highest being. Then the ruby, the flaming-red oriental ruby, side by side with the sapphire and the oriental topaz — both rubies of different colors — what are they? Crystals of our commonest argillaceous earth, the earth which makes our potter's clay, our pipe clay, and common roofing slate — mere bits of alumina. Yet these are our best gems, these idealizations of common potter's clay. In every hundred grains of beautiful blue sapphire, ninety-two are pure alumina, with one grain of iron, to make that glorious blue light within. The ruby is colored with chromic acid. The amethyst is only silica or flint. In one hundred grains of amethyst, ninety-eight are simply pure flint — the same substance as that which made the old flint in the tinder-box, and which, when ground up and prepared, makes now the vehicle of artists' colors.

Of this same silica are also cornelian, cat's eye, rock crystal, Egyptian jasper, and opal. In one hundred grains of opal, ninety are pure silica, and ten water. It is the water, then, which gives the gem that peculiarly changeable and irridescent coloring which is so beautiful, and which renders the opal the moon-light queen of the kingly diamond. The garnet, the Brazilian — not the oriental — topaz, the occidental emerald, which is of the same species as the beryl; all these are compounds of silica and alumina.

Many of these precious objects, which in their intensity, beauty and suggestiveness, seem like living things, have in their diverse pilgrimages been gathered into this Jewel House of A. H. Miller, late A. H. Miller & Bros., at 126 Lake, corner of Clark Street. But they will be scattered again, for they were purchased to be distributed again by this enterprising merchant, who has done so much to embellish our homes, and dispense luxuries amid the families of the opulent, who have come here from every quarter of the civilized world.

MUSICAL INSTRUMENT MANUFACTURE.

THERE is nothing more encouraging to our artistic life, than the progress of the Fine Arts in this country. It is encouraging, because we see rapid progress in all directions; and it is affecting, too, because we find that every branch of art has required heroic perseverance and prolonged sacrifices of the early apostles, who have led the way to a period of more refined taste in everything that adorns and embellishes civilized life. Mr. JULIUS BAUER, No. 99 Clark street, opposite the Court House, had long been associated with one of the great musical manufacturing houses at Leipsic, so well known to the musical world. From time to time large orders from America were received in Leipsic, and it was believed that the demand here would warrant the establishment of a manufactory, and Mr. Bauer, after visiting several of the large cities in this country, resolved to locate in Chicago, which he did in 1857, since which time he has prosecuted the manufacture here with great success. The Musical Instruments that are made by this house (which is the only establishment of this kind in Chicago,) comprise Melodeons, Accordeons, Concertinas, Violins, Flutes, Guitars, Drums, Tambourines, Banjos, and German Silver and Brass Band Instruments. All of these articles are of a superior quality, having never been surpassed in tone, finish and construction by European manufactures; for Mr. Bauer supervises every Instrument made at his establishment. He is now furnishing Instruments of his manufacture to music dealers in Cincinnati, St. Louis, and indeed to nearly every dealer in this Western Valley. Composers, performers, and lovers of music throughout this section, have written their unqualified commendation. Mr. Bauer is supplying the Government with nearly all the Instruments for the Army of the West. The Concertina is a new instrument, somewhat similar to the accordeon, though its construction is stronger, and by an echo attachment similar to the pedal of a piano, the tone may be sweet and delicate as that of a flute, or changed to the deep and powerful volume of the organ, or may present the effect of a full band. His Drums are sold in large quantities to New York and Philadelphia dealers. It is said they cannot be *beaten* by any in the world. There are two kinds of these, one of which has a patent contrivance for straining the head of the Drum to a uniform tightness.

The Violins and Guitars manufactured by Mr. Bauer, are of a peculiar construction. The two extremities of the body of the instrument are so connected as to increase its strength beyond the old system, and the sound-board is left perfectly free and elastic in all its vibrations. The strings are so fastened, that a single note, instead of appearing to come from the string, with a vibration from the sound-board, is more like a gush of melody, poured forth from the whole instrument. It gives forth sounds deeper, richer, and prolonged into more voluptuous strains, the first time it is struck, than the old instruments of former years. The Guitar can be traced far into antiquity. The name itself is derived from the Greek. It is one of the most touching and inspiring instruments; and around it is woven a net-work of tender associations, which belong to the history of love and passion in moonlit hours, from grove and river's bank, and castled balcony; from the cold North in its genial summer season; and the purple South, where the arctic winter never comes, and the light of the tropics blushes eternally.

During the few years that Mr. Bauer has been engaged in business in this country, he has received Medals in Gold, in Silver and Bronze, from State, County, and United States Fairs. He is winning a reputation in his business which entitles him to implicit confidence; so that in the purchase, the sale, or the exchange of one Musical Instrument for another, or in procuring any Musical Instrument which can be had in the world, he can be safely confided in; for his connections with houses in Berlin, Leipsic, Dresden, Paris, and other places in Europe, are such as to enable him to produce them in the shortest time, and at the lowest prices. His Music Store is one of the most attractive spots in this city for the lovers of this elegant art, which has thrown its enchantments over the homes of the refined and the cultivated classes of every nation, and which seems destined to command in this country a wide, if not a universal influence.

STAINED GLASS.

THE origin of this beautiful art is lost in the dimness of antiquity. It has been much revived of late years. It loses more than any other branch of pictorial representations, by detracting of color. The public taste has become, of late, much directed towards the chromatic decorations of interiors, both in churches and in private houses. It is, however, the fashion for a certain class of writers, to decry all attempts of modern art to reproduce the stained glass of the middle ages. It is sometimes even asserted, that we no longer possess the secrets of the rich colors, whose unfaded glories still dye the light-beams from the oriel of old churches of the time of the eleventh century. Such assertions can be founded only in ignorance of the resources of modern chemistry, whose list of metallic oxides, capable of producing any tint of the spectrum, was never so complete, nor so fully under the control of the operator, as at the present moment. If we have failed to equal the compositions of the masters of former ages, it is because modern artists of equal talent have thought it is not worth their while to engage in an occupation, which by some strange perversion, has been considered as, in some degree, unworthy the attention of men of genius. It is quite time that artists should abandon the silly notion, now quite too prevalant, that easel pictures in oil, and works in marble, are the only objects worthy of their attention, and that all other forms of art are, in their nature, somewhat menial. BENVENUTO CELLINI was not ashamed of the craft of a goldsmith, although he dared to treat the Pope and his Cardinals with deserving contempt. RAPHAEL and MICHAEL ANGELO, and a hundred other glorious names, had no fear of being mistaken for plasterers, because they lay whole days upon their backs, working up their immortal designs in fresco, upon the very mortar which their own artistic hands had spread. It is not easy to say why an artist is not as worthily employed in decorating a set of porcelain with original designs — in producing his effects in colored glass, or in modelling the forms of beauty for whatever purpose, as when he is starving behind a canvas.

We have in our own age — in our own city, if not a Michael Angelo, yet one, who possesses the genius of the artist, and the skill of the artisan, found in one and the same person; which is congenial with the practical spirit of the present time; and whose useful results are applicable to the wants of our present life. That man is Mr. Robert Carse, whose place of business is at number 164 Clark Street, opposite the Custom House. During a recent visit to his rooms, we were made acquainted with the process employed in modern times of Staining Glass. After the figure to be put upon the plate is drawn upon paper, and painted as desired, it is transferred to receive it. This has to be done with artistic skill, equal to that employed upon an oil painting, and requires much more care in its execution. In transferring fruits and flower pieces, all the delicate tints of the object must be copied with the greatest nicety. The glass is then put into a kiln, and submitted to a heat almost sufficient to fuse it, which not only has the effect to add greatly to the beauty of the painting, but makes it a part of the glass itself, no power being able to remove it. Mr. Carse was the leading artist in this business in New York City for a period of thirty-five years; for the last five years he has been a resident of Chicago, during which time he has executed works of art, in Stained Glass, which will long exist as mementos of his genius, and skill. As some of the more leading ones, we may refer to St. James Church, Trinity, St. Patrick's, Church of the Holy Family, and more recently the Cathedral at Dubuque, Iowa. One of the surest indications of advancing civilization, is the increased taste directed toward the chromatic decorations of interiors, both in churches and in private houses. The place of worship does not demand a profusion of ornament. But so far as the ability of the worshipers goes, if it is accompanied with good taste, it may enrich the house of God with architectural decorations with little danger of carrying the thing too far. "It is one of the affectations of architects," says a late writer, Ruskin — Seven Lamps of Architecture — "to speak of over-charged ornament. Ornament cannot be over-charged if it be good, but it is always over-charged when it is bad." The ancient Temple stands forever as the divine sanction of the adornment of the place of worship; and until the historical account which the Old Testament gives of the wealth of cedar and gold, which went into its construction is proved to be a myth, all the talk, so prevalent, about the abuse and wrong of building costly churches, must be accounted as worthy of notice as the complaint against Mary for breaking her alabaster box of precious ointment on the Savior's head. The ointment might have been sold and given to the poor, undoubtedly, as Judas intimated. And so the gold lavished on the temple might have been used in some other way. But God chose to have them both used as they were, and if any one is disposed to blame the costliness of the temple, or of the churches of our day, let him remember that he blames God more than he does man. The sin, if any, is not in building expensive churches, but in not so building them that the poor, as well as the rich can have the benefit of them. There is abundant room for decoration in the house of God. He who accepted the ancient Temple, delighted in it and most gloriously manifested his presence there, will never forbid our utmost adornment of the humbler structures which we dedicate to his praise, if only it be done aright. The gorgeousness of gold is not too good. The cunning skill in mingling hues is not misplaced. It is quite a mistake, as some suppose, that a great amount of light is needful in a church. Milton did not use the expression, "dim *religious* light," without good reason. Our religous emotions seen to shun the glare of the unsubdued light. Every one must be sensible that the shadows of evening, or the grey dawn of the morning, are far more likely to induce serious thought and devout feeling, than is the garish, full-orbed day. On this account the employment of colored glass, though liable to abuse, is not to be indiscriminately condemned, as it often has been. We are glad to notice the growing taste for this department of church embellishment. All persons who take an interest in this art, should find time to visit the store of Mr. Carse, at 164 Clark Street.

HARDWARE AND CUTLERY.

THE term Hardware, is one of those indefinite, comprehensive nouns of multitude, of which it may be said that it almost includes, as its name imports, every ware that is hard. Popularly, it is understood to embrace all the various manufactures of Iron, Steel and Brass, including all the different appendages of the Mechanic Arts, from a file to a locomotive; many of the details of common life, from a needle to a sewing machine, articles as varied in appearance, size and use, as can well be conceived.

By Cutlery, is understood to mean Steel manufactured into different varieties of Pocket-Knives, Table-knives and Forks, Butcher-Knives, etc., of the various styles of which articles there is an almost infinite variety.

In view of the almost endless number of articles which come under the general head of Hardware, the utmost that we shall be able to accomplish, is to lay before our readers the state of the business in the leading branches, and the character, mercantile reputation, and business facilities of the firm who most fully represents this important branch of commerce in the City of Chicago.

Of the eighteen or twenty Hardware and Cutlery establishments of this city, both Wholesale and Retail, there is none of whom we can speak in higher terms, and with more confidence, than that of MR. EDWIN HUNT, located at No. 84 LAKE STREET, nearly opposite the Tremont House.

Mr. Hunt came from Birmingham, England, in the year 1833, and established himself in the Hardware trade in New York City. From that time, he has always been an extensive Importer of English and German Hardware, and has also dealt largely in Hardware of domestic manufacture.

In 1848, he opened a branch store in Chicago, which was carried on for some years under an agency; but the business becoming larger than was at first anticipated, and finding it would be advantageous to take personal supervision of the same, he removed to this city, and has since then extended his business until it has become second to that of no house of a similar kind in the North-West. He still retains an office in New York City, for the purpose of purchasing his goods on the best terms from the various manufacturers scattered throughout the Eastern States.

Formerly, nearly every article of Hardware used in the United States was imported from Europe, but within the last thirty years, a great revolution has taken place in the trade of this country with Europe. Manufactories of Hardware have sprung up in this country, which, under a heavy protective tariff, have succeeded in a great measure in supplanting the foreign made goods, the American article having attained a very fair character.

In some tools for working in wood, of which branch of Hardware Mr. Hunt keeps the largest and best selected supply of any house in Chicago, the English makers have the preference. Every mechanic knows that Mr. S. Butcher's Chisels, and Spear & Jackson's Saws, are better than those of any other manufacturer.

The Axes, Augers, Hatchets and Hammers that are made here are decidedly better than any that can be imported, and when we contrast them with those that were made and used twenty-five or thirty years ago, we feel highly gratified with the advancement we have made, and are fully convinced that in a few more years, nearly all the tools made in England will be reproduced here, of such superior styles and quality that we shall not be under the necessity of purchasing outside our own country.

One of the leading articles in Mr. Hunt's trade, an article which he imports to a very large amount every year, is Sheffield Cutlery, so famous throughout the world for its superior quality, style and finish. The best makes of Pocket Cutlery come from Sheffield, made by the following celebrated manufacturers: "Geo. Wostenholm & Sons," "Rodgers & Sons," "W. & S. Butcher," "Thomas Turner," and others; a stock of which goods, as varied in styles and prices as can well be imagined, can always be seen on the well-stocked shelves of Mr. Hunt.

Of Table Knives and Forks, the importations are still large, though a very good article is made in this country, by "J. Russell & Co.," and by "Samson, Goodnow & Co.," of Connecticut.

In Files and Rasps, the manufactures of this country have never succeeded in producing any that will compete with those from the celebrated works of Messrs. "W. & S. Butcher," of Sheffield, which have been acknowledged to be the best for the last twenty-five years, during which time Mr. Hunt has imported them regularly, and they have always sold in preference to those of any other manufacture.

In Mr. Hunt's store we find Circular Saws of the celebrated manufacture of "Welch & Griffiths," of all sizes, from a Saw of three inches in diameter, to a monster Saw not less than *five feet* in diameter.

Of the thousands of different articles which Mr. Hunt keeps for sale, we have enumerated above a few only; but to those who want to purchase *any* article of Hardware, we can only say, go to Hunt's, at 84 Lake Street, and you will find it there.

We take pleasure in speaking of this as one of the representative mercantile firms of this proud Metropolis of the West; for during the last thirty years, Mr. Hunt has transacted his business upon such principles of uprightness and integrity, that *none* have had reason to complain, and all that have had any dealings with him have confidence in his word as to the quality of his goods, and know that he sells as low as the lowest.

His place of business is 84 LAKE STREET.

LINE ENGRAVING.

THIS is the general term for the process of engraving on the two metals commonly employed—Copper and Steel. It is the highest style of engraving, of which but few men attain to eminence. The common impression that genius is independent of circumstances and surroundings, and that a first-class artist may spring up any where, and, irrespective of his age and nation, blaze out in glorious beauty, is a great error. There are indeed a few noble souls so richly endowed that they will shoot far ahead of their cotemporaries and will so earnestly cast about for the means of sustenance and growth, that they flourish, rich and vigorous, where others starve. Such a one we name as an illustration of the truthfulness of our position. In referring to Mr. Thomas J. Day, the successor of the late J. J. O'Shannessy, Bank Note Engraver; whose place of business is at No. 40 Dearborn Street, opposite the Tremont House, we only say of him, what a generous public sentiment have long since awarded—he stands in the very front rank of his profession.

Nothing great is ever produced until the popular thought and heart set toward it, and get ready to welcome its advent. Therefore, art appears in fair development, only where popular taste and public appreciation foster art-talent, encourage artistic genius, and reward the artist's toil. Such has become the popular feeling in regard to line engraving, and the peculiar branches of this art which Mr. Day represents, and excels in. So great has become the demand for the elegant and chaste engraved *Marriage, Invitation and Visiting Cards*, that Mr. Day has found it necessary to remove to a location more convenient for his numerous patrons, and extend his facilities to meet all demands. Inscriptions on *Jewelry and Silver-Ware*, also *Silver Plated Door and Number Plates*, and all kinds of *Stencil Brands*, forms a very important branch of his business.

The old method of copper-plate engraving in general use when the demand for impressions was comparatively limited, has nearly fallen into desuetude. Softened steel has set it aside, and its glory is as the glory that has departed. When the copper-plate with careful handling, will yield only a few thousand impressions, without retouching, the number of impressions which the steel plate can multiply is positively illimitable. Mr. Day's patrons are not confined to the limits of Chicago, but extend throughout the North-West. His promptness, integrity and high artistic merit secure for him patrons wherever his name is known.

In a Marriage, Visiting, or Invitation Card, there often is a power, a mysterious influence exerted over the mind, that causes a thousand pleasing and varied associations to rush upon the fancy. We have often gone into this establishment, and when we saw parcel after parcel dispatched by express to distant quarters, and by the post boy through the city; we have thought what fountains of joy or grief will these little white-winged messengers of power open in the hearts of those who read them. Some, with a few words added in pencil, will record the rapturous emotions of reciprocated love; some will carry messages of sadness that will cover life's pilgrimage with gloom; some will announce that a new being has burst joyfully upon creation, to begin its endless career; some that warm and generous hearts are being united in the holy bonds of wedlock; some to summon to the festive scene, and others to the bed of death; each hath its mission to fulfill — the more elegantly engraved, the higher the art-style, the more impressive. Therefore the greater need of employing an Artist who is master of his profession.

AMERICAN LITERATURE.

WHEN Edmund Burke, the wisest statesman and the greatest political philosopher that the world has yet seen, drew in the British House of Commons, his famous word-painting of the future grandeur and prosperity of the American Colonies, his short-sighted and time-serving cotemporaries, aided by superficial buffoons and satirists, caricatured that lyrical prophesy, which time has more than verified! If we could now, as he did then, imprint upon our minds a picture of the wealth, culture, and prosperity of our country, as it shall be seventy-five or a hundred years hence, and could describe it with Burke's matchless eloquence and inspiration, our English haters, doubtless, would ridicule our language, as their wise predecessors, on a former occasion, did the glowing predictions of "that prodigy of nature and acquisition." But, what fates decree man cannot alter; and that our destiny as a Nation is incalculably splendid, the most superficial must perceive. Our physical power, our sources of wealth, luxury, and happy independence (save the temporary cloud that darkens our horizon) are too well developed to need illustration; but there is yet a noble field — the mental one — the National culture of which is but in its infancy. Yet that infancy is expanding, and developing, with a power hitherto unknown. The Americans are a reading people. If intellectual superiority is not a qualification that entitles one to respect, ignorance is surely among the numerous misfortunes regarded with mingled pity and contempt. And it matters not how active may be the business pursuits of an American, he carries with him wherever he wanders, a love for education and enlightenment. In the camp, upon the battle-field, wherever he settles, in the fastnesses of the wilderness, or on the wide prairies, among the first erected objects of his enterprise will be found that peculiar trinity of civilization — the church, the school-house and the press. And it matters not that his residence may be a log cabin, or a modern palace; the Bible will be found in his parlor, and a periodical and newspaper on his breakfast table, and in his pocket. The great and increasing demand for literature, in a cheap form, is daily becoming more obvious. In order to meet the wants of that demand, Depots or Stores are opened, exclusively for the sale of Periodicals, cheap literature, and Newspapers, from far and near; newspapers big and little, newspapers daily and weekly; newspapers comic, and newspapers serious; newspapers political, and newspapers religious; newspapers illustrating every event of interest; newspapers of all characters and opinions; newspapers without number, we had almost said may be found at these Depots. As an illustration of this fact, we would invite the reader of this article to visit WALSH'S NEWSPAPER AND PERIODICAL DEPOT, on the corner of Madison Street and Post-Office Place. From early morning till late at night, it presents a scene of activity, such as is rarely witnessed in any other place of trade in this city. For here may be found every publication which is issued from the press in a cheap form. The scholar, the professional man, the merchant, the soldier of the camp, the citizen, and the man of humble means, may all alike, be seen here in pursuit of the *last publication*, or the *latest news* — news from both hemispheres. Walsh is a *live representative man*, he has been educated in, and for this business. Few men have we ever known, better adapted to its management. His arrangements are such with eastern publication firms, that every popular work, magazine, and newspaper, which is thrown from the press, reaches his store as soon thereafter as steam can convey it. His facilities enable him to supply the trade, to a great extent, as he is doing in almost every interior town in the North-West. Recently, Mr. Walsh has made an addition to his store, by which he is enabled to keep every article of Stationery, and many other articles usually kept by leading Book Stores. He may well be called a representative man in this comparatively new branch of literature, for no other man in the North-West has ever equaled him.

It is about ten years since Edward Furner established the first Periodical Depot in Chicago, the business at that time amounting to about two thousand dollars per annum. So rapid has been the increase, that at the present time there are probably half a million daily papers, and one hundred and fifty thousand weekly papers, besides the magazines sold in this city weekly. The business employs a capital of only about $25,000, as this amount is turned over in the trade nearly every week. There are four principal firms engaged in the business, who make it their speciality to supply New Books, Periodicals, Newspapers, etc., to the country trade, besides nearly one hundred smaller dealers in different parts of the city. Mr. Walsh, who stands pre-eminent in this line of trade, supplies over two hundred and fifty agents. He also deals extensively in Patriotic papers and Envelopes, Prints, Pictorials, Maps, Charts, etc., also every variety of Stationery. He supplies to order, any book, new or old. All new books are received as soon as issued and supplied to the trade at publishers' prices, adding only charges for transportation.

INTERIOR DECORATION.

INTERIOR Decoration has been practiced in different countries from the most remote period, and it has assumed national and marked characteristics, as among the Egyptians, Assyrians, Hindoos, Chinese, Greeks, Romans, and Saracens. From the greater freedom of intercourse in later periods, the peculiarities of the art have been less decidedly pronounced, yet there has always been in each style sufficient to render it national and unique; as the Renaissance, and the Arabesque. The latter, whose suitability to modern times has caused it to be so widely diffused, was commenced and invented by Ludius, a painter of the time of Augustus Cæsar. The exquisite Frescoes of the Bath of Titus, buried for centuries in the devastations of the Roman wars, were resuscitated in the sixteenth century; and the sight of them revived the style of the Arabesque, which was brought out and perfected by the prince of painters, Raffael d'Urbino.

Greece and Italy have been foremost in all the arts of design, and the ornaments of their dwellings and public buildings have remained as examples and authorities of taste, down to our own age. The Greeks carried the arts into Italy, and the paintings at Pompeii and Herculaneum are the works of Greek artists. The Italian houses are still decorated, from the abode of the artisan to the palace of the noble. Germany, in the present day, is following Italy in Interior Decoration, and has produced some of the finest works of modern times, under the patronage and direction of Louis I., ex-King of Bavaria.

In England, where wealth might be expected to minister to taste, the upholsterer, not the artist, is consulted by the nobility; there is therefore abundance of paper and gilding, but little art, or genuine taste, in the disposition of ornament in English mansions. New York and some other large cities in the United States bid fair to surpass London.

Among the cheerful evidences of increasing refinement and taste among our people, is the constantly increasing attention being given to the art-decorations of the better class of our dwellings, churches, educational and other public edifices. Blank, bare, unmeaning walls, or walls covered with crudely designed paper hangings, are beginning to be looked upon as an eye-sore and a deformity, by the more intelligent portion of the community; multitudes of whom, since the rapid transit across the ocean, by means of weekly lines of steamers, is secured beyond peradventure, are taking up, temporarily, their sojourn in the elegant capitals of Europe, catching glimpses of the art-glories that have cost ages of development to produce. These glimpses are rapidly transmitted into the elements of a higher taste, and a desire to see reproduced in our own country and our own homes, similar creations. The result of this shows itself in the great attention very generally paid, especially in our own cities, to the styles and designs that are to adorn the walls of the *Heaven of Home*, where every form must daily meet the eye, turn as it may, and where beauty and harmony of spirit too often become fatally affected by discordant surroundings. Hitherto we have been obliged, in this country, to employ the foreign artists to do all this kind of work. It has grown to be a mania with many men of wealth in the large cities of America, to secure foreign architects and artists, who too often are obstinate second-rate copyists of inferior ideas and designs, to erect our dwellings and our grandest public edifices. We have been led to this expression of a well-considered conviction, from an extended examination of the various specimens of Fresco Paintings which have been executed in this city; among which those of Messrs. JEVNE & ALMINI take a prominent position.

We take pleasure in referring to several buildings, where interior decorations are in Fresco, the work of these two Artists; among which we may mention Trinity Church; First Presbyterian; Wabash Avenue Methodist Church; the palatial residences of T. King, Esq., on Michigan Avenue; B. F. Haddock, Esq.; the Sherman House, and many others.

Messrs. Jevne and Almini have been residents of Chicago for the last nine years, during which time they have inculcated and infused a higher love of Fresco Painting.

We wish we could announce the more rapid progress of Frescoe Painting, the most beautiful of all the arts for interior decorations. But as wealth is flowing in upon us as to no other nation on the globe, it is gratifying to know that our enterprise and successful efforts in arts are acknowledged on all hands. In an incredibly short space of time, we have subdued almost a continent of wilderness, filled the cultivated country with villages and cities, and all the forms of human industry, and obtained reputation by some of the most important practical inventions which any people have produced. It was naturally to be expected, that the Fine Arts would have a slender growth; coming, if at all, after nearly everything else was perfected. Yet in these, as in whatever else is of the physical or intellectual life of man, the American mind has shown its capacity. We believe the time has now come in this country, when *labor* is to be expended on ideal conceptions; that the forms which arise to the gifted in the "stillness of musings," shall find, through intense and long effort, "a local habitation and a name." There is at least genius and desire enough; it only remains for the people of this country to give sufficient encouragement; and we think that this, also, is in a measure being afforded—in a word, that the era of *Art* is beginning on the Western Continent. Yet we are surprised, and it is greatly to be regretted, that cultivated Americans, who enjoy the luxury of art abroad, should be content with whitewashed walls at home.

We regret to say, that there are but few mansions of the opulent in Chicago whose walls are embellished with Frescoe; that *highest style of painting*, in which RAPHAEL achieved much of his reputation; and Michael Angelo himself has been as extensively known, perhaps, as the author of "The Last Judgment," and "The Creation," both of which were in the Sistine Chapel.

There are palatial residences in this city, whose Interior Decorations, we are proud to say, are from the pencil of our own Artists, Messrs. Jevne & Almini; yet we suppose there are very few of the "Lords of these Mansions," who would not regard the application of a stranger to be allowed to see their embellishments, as a piece of impudence—while everybody knows that all over Europe, it is expected that the fortunate possessor of an exquisite work of art, or taste, in Fresco, will at all proper hours allow visitors to see it. There is not a royal palace on the Continent whose doors are not thrown open, whenever convenience will allow, for strangers to inspect the works of art which adorn them. It will be so here as soon as our standard of taste has been far enough elevated for strangers of culture to make such applications. As it is now, a man of taste can have no motive for going through a magnificent house. He sees nothing but gaudy and expensive furniture—rooms lumbered up with mahogany or rosewood, with velvet-cushioned chairs and sofas, blazing carpets, curtains and drapery, with, perhaps, a few contemptible daubs by men who paint such things, either because they dream that they are artists, or because they can make more money by humbugging rich men than by painting signs or barns, or wood-houses. There are a few exceptions, and we might mention them; and it would be with a sentiment of respect we cannot feel except towards those gentlemen who devote a portion, at least, of their income to the purchase of statues and pictures, thereby showing that they prize intellectual and moral refinement higher than expensive furniture, cashmere shawls, fast horses, and *imported wines, warranted pure Chicago vintage.*

HAIR JEWELRY.

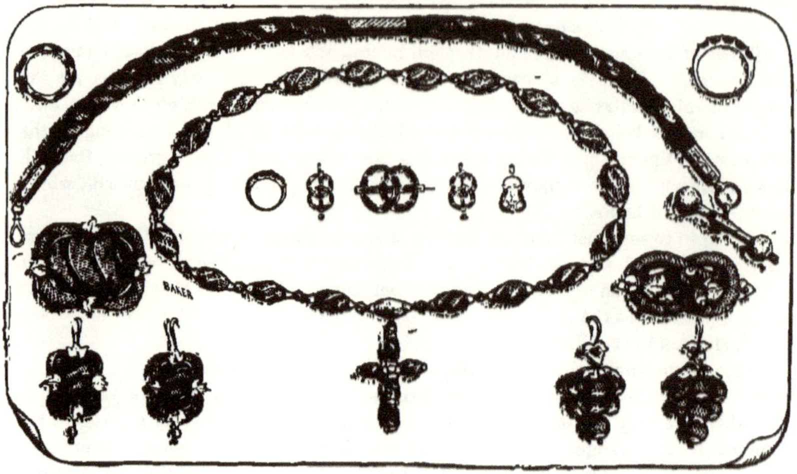

THE most powerful thing, says an Arab proverb, is a *beautiful woman*, and as "a thing of beauty is a joy forever," whether it be on canvas, in the breathing marble, in words, or of fancy undefined in the brain, which betrays something of the re-creative power that is within every soul — whether it be in the human face and form divine, or the gem that decks the brow and bosom of beauty, and sparkles on the lily-white hand, it matters not, if only a thing of beauty, 'tis a joy forever. It is forever thus with CAMPBELL's productions of the beautiful jewels for the hair, jewels for the bosom, and jewels for the hand — they sparkle in the sunbeam, and flash forth their splendor in the gas-light — these gems of *Hair Jewelry*, interwoven with a starry way of brilliants, or the pearl, that gem which is interwoven with the pure image of our little eternity of time — they call into being thoughts and emotions of affection — remembrances of husband or wife, lover or child, parents and children. Who that has gazed upon the hair wrought in many a strange and artistic device —

secured from the wavy ringlets of some beautiful girl, or the brow of the loved or the lost, but will cherish them as *gems of the beautiful* forever?

This Hair Jewelry Store of Campbell's, located on Clark Street, opposite the Court House, has become a place of no inconsiderable attraction, for Campbell's inventive genius and artistic skill in works of Hair Jewelry have inspired a love for personal embellishment, which has made it popular and sought for, far more than the flashy jewelry, which have no souvenirs of affection entwined as remembrances of the loved and the lost.

It is only a few years since the first introduction of Hair Jewelry as an article of commerce. Now it is sought for, and considered indispensable to every lady who dresses fashionably, and with becoming elegance and taste. There are many workers of Hair Jewelry, though but few who excel in artistic merit — in chasteness of style — variety of designs, and cunningly wrought devices. Campbell has made it a life-study; he has brought genius, skill and high intelligence to his aid in fashioning gems of beauty. He is preparing for publication, a work treating on the whole subject of Hair Jewelry; describing minutely, in detail, the whole *modus operandi*, adapted for common instruction in the art.

To those who know the power of Art, to educate and reform the taste — the social life and character of a people — it has always been a cause of regret that the appreciation and enjoyment of it should have been confined to the few whose wealth was equal to the purchase of its costly productions.

We believe that art is capable of accomplishing all that is claimed for it by its most enthusiastic friends, when our life, in all its pursuits, is brought into daily contact with its productions; when its works are no longer a monopoly, but an every-day possession, within the reach of the mechanic and tradesman, as well as the opulent and noble. If the beautiful were daily placed before us, surely our social life could not fail to be ameliorated and exalted by its silent eloquence. All these elegant gems of art manufactured by Campbell come within the reach of any honest, upright and industrious person. There is no establishment of a similar kind in the United States that will excel the variety and beauty of Hair Jewelry, and it must be a dainty taste which cannot be gratified with some object of beauty there.

Who that has lost a dear friend, be it husband, wife, lover or child, would not be made happier by having a lock of their hair, wrought in beauty, encased in cunningly devised objects of gold, to remain "a joy forever," and treasure up as a souvenir in the remembrance of the loved?

There are few Jewelers in this country so well sustained as Campbell, at No. 81 Clark Street.

PICTURE FRAMES AND LOOKING GLASSES.

ON one of those dreamy Indian-Summer afternoons during last autumn, while standing in the elegant *salon* of one of those palatial residences, in Marble Terrace, Michigan Avenue, before a grand French plate mirror, extending from the ceiling to the floor, reflecting the beauties of the lake and sky, and looking more like a sea of glass, surrounded by a golden shore, we involuntarily exclaimed, if this be not the highest ideal of domestic luxury, where shall wealth or fancy go to find it? It breathed an atmosphere of refinement through the appartment it adorned. From the crown to the base it was significant of beauty. Along the gilded border, silver waters were leaping — the white-sail yacht was dancing on the wave, where the sheen lies shimmering like moonlight on dream-land. The frescoed walls hung with rare pictures, in frames of artistic beauty and rich workmanship, they bore unmistakable marks of having been made by a man of taste and genius, and were in harmonious keeping with the graphic and luxurious pencil of the painter. We sought out the maker of these frames; and what promonader on Randolph Street has not lingered in front of the translucent French plate glass windows of HENRY WIGGERS to admire the works of art, in elegant frames. Mr. Wiggers has studied picture frame making as an art of design; he began life as a workman in the trade, and he has thoroughly mastered it; he is familiar with every stage of his business, from the first selection of appropriate woods, and other materials for framing, up to the study and elaboration of pleasing and graceful forms. Once, significance in artistic emblems was hardly thought of, but that time has gone by in this country. Now those who manufacture anything to embellish domestic life, have a far higher taste to administer to — our mechanics are successful just in proportion as they outstrip competition in knowledge and refinement. The road to fortune for the manufacturing world, in many of its great departments, lies through those entrancing regions of the Ideal, over which art breathes the magic of beauty. Mr. Wiggers has been engaged in this business, in this city, eight years. His manufactory located on South Wells Street, is driven by steam, thereby enabling him to produce every article in his line at greatly reduced rates. At his finishing and gilding rooms may be seen the moulder in plaster modeling forms of beauty — then comes the gilder with the leaf of gold, and warms it into life, and then the burnisher, who gives the gleam of beauty. The gold and silver leaf used by this establishment amounts to $3000 annually. Mr. Wiggers not only manufactures frames, but has built up an extensive jobbing business, supplying mouldings in the strip. His Sale Rooms are located at No. 153 Randolph Street. There are some twelve or fifteen Looking Glass and Picture Frame manufacturers in this city, employing a capital of about $50,000, doing a business of about $60,000 annually.

ARTIFICIAL TEETH AND DENTAL MATERIALS.

IN nothing has the astonishing genius of the present age more signally exhibited itself, than in the rapid progress toward perfection in the Dental Art. The many victories over seeming impossibilities which the genius of invention has achieved during the present century, have been the theme of philosophers, orators, and poets. In 1818, or thereabouts, some experiments were made in the manufacture of porcelain teeth. It was not until after 1830, that any considerable progress was made; all the teeth made previous to that time being very unsightly in color and shape, and unlike natural teeth. From that time to the present, the march of improvement has been steady. One after another, the difficulties in the way of imitation of the natural organs have been surmounted, until it would seem that in point of strength, beauty of finish and perfect resemblance to nature in form, color and surface, as well as in the almost endless varieties of shape and style, and the ease with which they can be adapted to the great variety of cases which present themselves, there is little to be desired.

Originally the human teeth were used, also calves, and sheeps teeth; next ivory, or teeth carved from the tusk of the Hippopotamus. Fifty years ago there was not a porcelain tooth made in this country. Twenty years ago not more than two hundred and fifty thousand were manufactured annually in the United States, and but a trifling number in Europe. Since then the demand has been rapidly increasing, owing in a great measure to the improvements made from year to year; and in the last ten years, it is said the consumption has increased more than one humdred per cent. The greater durability and cleanliness of Porcelain Teeth has caused all others to be discarded. The most extensive and celebrated manufacturer of artificial teeth, in the world, is Mr. SAMUEL S. WHITE, formerly of the firm of Jones, White & McCurdy, whose establishments were located at Philadelphia, New York, Boston and Chicago. The business is now continued by Mr. White, at all their former establishments. Mr. W. has had an experience of twenty-five years in the manufacture of Porcelain Teeth, and eighteen years of that time, has had the entire charge of the manufacturing department, with all the changes of the firms with which he has been connected. The

Porcelain Teeth manufactured by Mr. White, are celebrated above all others in Europe, South America, the West Indias, and in fact wherever the advancement of civilization has rendered the Dentist a necessity, large orders are received for these Teeth. He makes about two millions annually, giving employment to over one hundred persons, nearly one-half of whom are females. The amount of wages paid weekly, will exceed one thousand dollars.

The four Dental Depots of Mr. White, located respectively in Philadelphia, New York, Boston and at 102 Randolph Street, Chicago, are the most extensive and perfect institutions of the kind on this continent, and indeed it is doubtful if there is any thing in the civilized world which will at all compare with the Philadelphia House, in all its various departments, for the Dental Instruments manufactured by Mr. White are every where becoming the most sought for, not only for their beauty of finish, but their perfect adaptation for the various purposes required. For a period of eighteen years, Mr. White has devoted his whole time and talents to the development of this business. Every conceivable article of Dental Materials, in their most perfected manufacture, which the genius and inventive skill of man have devised, in both hemispheres, may be found at these Depots. Mr. White has received, in this country and Europe, THIRTY FOUR FIRST PREMIUMS.

The Chicago Depot was established about three years ago, under the superintendence of Mr. Bingham, whose affable manners, and high business qualifications, have made him pre-eminently popular with the leading Dentists of the North-West. They have been made acquainted with the fact that at this establishment they can purchase from first-hands, at the lowest rates, and the best goods, with all the modern improvements that can be had in any part of the world.

No. 102 Randolph Street, opposite the Matteson House.

BRUSHES.

FEW articles of manufacture admit so great a diversity of forms, sizes and qualities, or so wide a range of uses, as the productions of the Brushmaker; and of none does it hold more true, that the best article is the cheapest. From the delicate Pencil of the artist to the "Whitewash," or the "Scrub," the variety, in style and ornamentation, is exceedingly great. The manufacture in this city includes the usual variety of Hair, Paint, and the commoner kinds of Brushes. In this, as in other branches, our manufacturers have aimed at the production of substantial and reliable work. Of

Brushes and their manufacture, the same may be said as Liebig said of soap, that "the civilization of a nation may be estimated by the amount consumed." The free use of brushes is indispensable to personal cleanliness. In France and Germany, brushes are put to every manner of use, and all our finer brushes are still received from Paris. English brushes are noted for their durability, though not as tasty or elaborately finished as the French.

In all the Eastern States, every family is supplied with brushes for every conceivable purpose; while in our own families of the West, until quite recently, it was difficult to find even an apology of a Brush.

In the year 1850, a young man who had served a regular apprenticeship with one of the best manufacturers of Brushes in the city of Boston, emigrated to Chicago for the purpose of establishing a Brush Manufactory. He soon learned that cheap prison work was the only style of brushes which had hitherto been introduced into the country. Long did he toil, unceasingly, to introduce a superior quality of his own manufacture, and after years of effort, secured the coveted and long-sought-for reward — an extensive trade with the best commercial houses of the West. The price of Brushes, like all other manufactured goods, depends upon the quality of the material and the labor expended. In Brushes, it is mainly in the bristle, of which there are five distinct grades; the highest is Russian, and German, French and American, in different qualities. The Russian ranks first in quality, yet differs materially in grades and prices. The best are known as Okstha White; their length from five and a half to seven and a half inches, and is worth from $2.75 to $3.50 per pound. Next follows yellow, gray, and black, which latter are called whalebone. The other varieties are known as first quality; a good, straight, stiff bristle, from four and a half to five and a half inches long, worth about $1.50 per pound; and the inferior qualities are sold from thirty cents to $1.25. The above are peculiarly adapted for the manufacture of Paint and Whitewash Brushes. There are many varieties of German and Polish bristles imported; but for the finer grades of Brushes, the French bristle is superior to all others, being whiter, and of a soft and silky nature, produced by the climate, and the superior breed of animals; varying in price from ninety cents to $1.50. Our American bristles are of an inferior quality, crooked, shorter, and with a wiry and coarse flag, which renders them unfit for the finer quality of Brushes. A substitute for cheap brushes has been found in an article known in commerce as Sisal Tampico, a vegetable product found in Mexico. It is nearly white, but dyed black for Scrub and other Brushes, and is an excellent substitute.

The amount of Bristles imported into this country is not far from $1,000,000 annually; and the demand is rapidly increasing, while the price steadily advances.

Of the fine Artists' Brushes, such as Camel, Sable, Fitch, Hair, etc., large quantities come from France, where they are made cheaper than can be produced in this country. The best qualities of Brushes are manufactured in this country. The Manufactory of George E. Gerts & Co., No. 204 Randolph Street, is a noble example of perseverance and integrity in commercial transactions. When they commenced business on Wells Street in this City, some twelve years ago, they might have carried all their stock in trade on their back. Now they represent one of the most reliable and extensive Brush Manufacturing Establishments in the West. They employ only the best workmen, keeping first-class work. During all the financial reverses which have swept over Chicago, they have moved steadily on, meeting promptly all their obligations; doing no more business than their capital would allow to do safely. In addition to their own manufactures, they keep a full supply of all Imported Brushes. The amount of Brushes manufactured annually in Chicago, will probably exceed fifteen thousand dollars; and the demand is rapidly increasing.

TYPE-FOUNDRY AND STEREOTYPING.

A VERY large proportion of the book printing now done through the world is from stereotype plates. Every book that is intended for a second edition is stereotyped in the beginning. The process is simple and easy to be understood. A page is set up with movable type; an impression is taken from it in plaster, and the type metal run into the mold where the entire page is cast, which with the proper cleaning up, remains for future use. All the delay and expense of re-setting type is saved, when a new edition is called for. The art of stereotpying is by no means so modern as is commonly supposed. In the first era of printing, solid blocks of wood, in which a whole page of words was carved out, were in common use. Next follows the process of type-founding, or casting the letters separately in molds, which enabled the printer to set up any page he pleased in a short time. In the beginning of the last century a Dutchman, named Van de Meyer approached very near the modern system of Stereotyping, by setting up the pages of a quarto Bible in movable type, which were converted into a solid mass by soldering them at the back. This was more expensive. Probably William Ged, an Edingburgh goldsmith, was the first to practice stereotyping as at present understood. He invented the process of casting whole pages, in 1725. He stereotyped Bibles and prayer-books for the University of Cambridge; but owing to the opposition of his compositors, they artfully introduced errors enough to bring the books into discredit.

Great credit is due in tracing the history of this important improvement in printing, to the exertions of Earl Stanhope, who furnished the means and encouraged extensive trials and experiments at his country-seat in Kent. Although the cost of stereotyping a work in the beginning, is nearly twice as great as that of merely setting the type, still it is considered best to stereotype a book; because, from the plates once made small editions can be produced whenever required, and less risk incurred in paper, printing, and binding, besides, at short notice a new edition of a work can be produced. It is supposed that the almost universal habit of stereotyping works in this country has reduced the cost nearly one half upon all works brought out by that process. Type-Founding, in this country, dates from 1735, when Christopher Sower established a printing-office in Germantown, near Philadelphia.—About 1790, Messrs. Archibald Bimy, and James Ronaldson made the first real improvement in Type-Founding since the days of Peter Schoeffer. Since then, the art has been brought to its present state of perfection, by a combination of inventive talent, so that one man is enabled to make eighteen or twenty thousand types in a day. The metal used is a mixture composed chiefly of lead, antimony, and tin, in proportions suited to the kind of type required.

During the last few years, the demand for Printing Presses, Type, Stereotyping, Electrotyping, and every article connected with the printing business, has increased to such an extent, that great establishments have become necessary to supply the rapidly increasing demand.

Nearly half a century has elapsed since White's Type Foundry was established in New York, the reputation of which has become favorably known wherever the printer, that herald of progress and advancing civilization, has gone forth.

In 1855 Mr. White was induced to establish, in Chicago, a branch of his New York house, to facilitate his extensive trade in the North-West, and for the better accommodation of his numerous patrons—the result of which is, that the "Chicago Type Foundry," as a central Depot, for supplying every article that may be required by the craft, throughout this section, has become a permanent institution.

The manufacturing department of the Chicago Depot, being under the supervision of persons trained to their several duties, is a guarantee as to the quality of the type made. The press of the North-West, everywhere, speaks of the type, presses, and material from this establishment, in terms of the very highest commendation.

The Chicago *Tribune* says, "We can endorse most cordially the resources of this Foundry in Type, Presses, Cases, Inks, and all the appurtenances of of a Printing Office. Their type is of a quality equal to any manufactured in this country, and their facilities are such as to meet any orders." This establishment is managed in a manner most gratifying to the entire printing craft of the North-West by Mr. H. A. Porter, whose strict business qualifications and gentlemanly demeanor are fully recognized by those who have any dealing with this House.

They are located on Washington, between Clark and Dearborn Streets.

SILVER PLATING.

A FEW years ago, the Russian frigate *General Admiral* lay at her berth in the harbor of New York, being thrown open for the inspection of the public, previous to her departure for the Russian seas. She was one of the most beautiful models of naval architecture afloat. Her cargo was an assorted one of great value. She was laden and furnished by one of the wealthiest and most extensive manufacturing firms in New York. Of her furniture, nothing was more calculated to attract the attention and admiration of the vast throng of people which visited her, than her table outfit of Silver, glass and porcelain, but more especially the Silver Ware; among which there were twelve cups, saucers and spoons, encircling a broad, massive *plateau* of pure silver, from which the *epergne* rose with its branching columns four feet, holding the vessel in its glittering recesses, separated by statuettes representing the Seasons; the whole surmounted by a classic urn — our eagle, (as over all the works of this house) with bended beak and hovering wings keeping sentinel.

The other table presented a sight, which at first glance made us think of some enchanted castle, built on a crystal mountain side by the Genii of the East. It cost $15,000. It looked like the *buffet* of an emperor prepared for a banquet of kings. It had two complete services of Silver of $4,000 each — two exquisite Tea Sets in the *antique*, one wreathed in the leaves and boughs of the "Old English Oak," the other in the *basket* style, now the *mode* — several Fruit Bowls — one for *ice*, ornamented with the polar bear, the reindeer, and other arctic emblems — Strawberry Bowls of fine workmanship, with wicker tracery of the vine and berry, embracing opal-hued glass, and many other things of taste and beauty. All these articles were thoroughly American, the workmanship of our own artists, ordered by his Imperial Majesty, the Czar of Russia. They had none of the air of servility about them: Europeans stopped to gaze on them — for they breathed the spirit of nationality. Among the number who lingered longest to gaze upon so much beauty in gems of Silver, was a young man, then a foreman in one of the extensive Silver Plating manufacturing establishments, located on John street. He had emigrated from one of the New England States. He drank in all their beauty; his Yankee soul was filled with a new ambition — a desire to reproduce the same amount of beauty at a price which would come within the reach of men of more humble resources. His purpose has been accomplished; and for the last few years that young man has been a resident of this city, carving out his own fortune, and seeking a worthy reputation for Silver Plating in all the latest and most perfected forms. He has accomplished his purpose; and W. K. Ingram stands without a rival in this domain of manufacture in this city.

It is a fact of moment to our progress, that the nations of Europe should be sending to our American manufacturers for their most costly and elaborately worked wares. In this respect, as in many others, it may well be said,

"Westward the star of empire takes its way!"

During the last few years, another, to us, important fact, is being developed — that "the star of empire" is fast wending its way westward across this continent. Its power is rapidly culminating here in Chicago, in Commerce, the Arts, and Manufactures.

The process of Silver Plating, or of electricity, on the base metals, such as Copper, German Silver, etc., is a result which very few persons in this country can, or do, accomplish. The process is done by the aid of the galvanic battery — one of those chemical and physical wonders which give to it much of the mystery of the supernatural. What galvanism is, we know not. We only know it is not electricity, it is not magnetism, it is not "spiritualism," it is not gravitation; we know not what it is any more than what the principle of life is. The process is, by filling large tubs, or vats, with a liquid holding pure silver *in solution*. In this solution the articles to be plated are suspended by a wire from a bar of silver, which, with the copper wires upon the ends of the tubes, forms the galvanic current medium. The batteries are then put in connection, and immediately the deposit of silver commences upon the articles suspended in the solution. This deposit would soon exhaust the metal held in solution if there was not a constant supply given in its stead. This is done from thin plates of pure silver, suspended in the solution also, which are passed by the galvanic current into the solution to keep up the strength of the precipitate upon the plating articles After coming from the tubes, the articles are in an unfinished state, though very white They are then sent to the burnisher, under whose quick touches they are readily fitted for the show case, or the purchaser.

Every imaginable article can be plated; steel, iron, copper, composition metal, German silver, britannia, zinc, etc. The best plate is that upon German silver. A good, first-quality deposit on this metal is, in all necessary qualities, just as good as the solid silver, and costs only about one-quarter as much. There are four establishments in this city, which nominally profess to be able to do Silver Plating; but Mr. W. K. Ingram, located at No. 194½ Clark Street, stands at the head of his profession, and may be relied on as being fully competent in all its details.

MACHINERY DEPOT.

THIS, of all the ages, is the most remarkable for new inventions. Old industrial methods, and the rude tools of handicraft, are passing away, and new processes, original devices and curious machines that have no sweat upon their brows, are taking the place of the toiling, perspiring workers of the past ages, or are putting the hand-workers into the position of the head-workers, and making them guides, overseers and thinkers. It is the mission of man to hold the earth and its waters in subjection by machinery. By machinery he is destined to lighten the drudgery which at the dawn of creation fell upon his race. To accomplish this, he has been endowed with genius and inventive power; and where the force of a thousand giants would be fruitless, these triumphantly prevail. We are living in a wonderful age. Truly, the race of invention is the race of progress. Our own country is contributing her full share to this material progress of the race, and the hope begins to dawn, that we shall be able to obviate the sternest difficulties the genius of invention has had to contend with. Our own City of Chicago, too, is contributing her full share to the mechanical arts. Here we have inventive geniuses, who are scattering their rich gifts among us, multiplying luxuries and creating innumerable comforts. Here, also, we have business firms, whose enterprise prompts them to search out every valuable invention and offer them to the public. Among such firms we would refer to Messrs. WALWORTH, HUBBARD & Co., who are the manufacturers of Steam Engines, Gas Fittings, and everything pertaining to Steam and Gas they make a speciality; and whatever there is of the production of inventive skill, and of utility, pertaining to these two branches of manufacture, will be found at this establishment.

Who shall dare say that the Steam Engine is perfected? Every day produces some new improvement in this potent Motive Power. One hundred and twenty years before the Christian era, a wheel driven by steam revolved in the Egyptian Capital. More than nineteen centuries succeeded, making their deep furrows upon the broad face of creation, before this whirling toy ripened into the mighty Steam Engine, now so familiar to our race. At the end of the eighteenth century, this power appeared and assumed a form which enabled it to drag heavy burdens upon land and sea; and then the globe seemed contracted to half its former size. In strength, it was mightier than any moving thing, and in speed it rivaled the birds of heaven. It has become the strong carrier and the fleet racer. Its unearthly shriek troubles the air, and its rolling tramp shakes the earth. It impels huge ships, that spread our commerce over every ocean; defying the hurricane and mastering the storm. It digs the ore, blows the furnace, wields the heavy hammer, and turns the spindle. It toils in the workshops, it toils in mid-ocean, and it toils as it bounds along upon its iron track. Its years have been few; but in this short period of time, it has stamped new and everlasting characters upon the history of mankind. Human speculation fails adequately to estimate its influence upon the social and commercial relations of men and of nations. The end to its improvements and appliances is not yet.

Every new improvement, every floating fragmentary idea on the subject, is sought for and crystalized by Messrs. Walworth, Hubbard & Co., for the benefit of the people of the North-West.

They are extensive dealers in, and manufacturers of Boiler Flues, Valves, Cocks, Gauges, Pumps, Steam and Gas Fittings, Steam Boilers of all kinds, made of superior Pennsylvania Charcoal Iron, manufactured expressly for their use; Patented Stretched, Cemented and Riveted Leather Belting; also Boston Belting Co.'s celebrated Rubber Belting, Packing and Hose.

They are agents for Worthington's Steam Pumps — Ashcroft's Low Water Detector — Campbell, Whittier & Co.'s Steam Engines; also those manufactured by Mr. George H. Corliss, of Providence, Rhode Island, etc., etc. Perhaps no improvements have been made which correspond in extent, or value with those of Corliss'. His improvements are two-fold; first, a peculiar device for moving each steam and each exhaust valve, with a distinct and independent motion, by means of a crank-wrist. There being a series of crank-wrists attached to a common disc, secured to a work-shaft, connecting with the main eccentric, all the valves are moved at the right times, and with complete effect. This saves much power that is injuriously expended in the common engine, in moving the closed valve, and prevents the waste of the expansive force of steam. The second improvement consists in a perfect automatic regulation of steam in its passage into the cylinder; so that by means of a cut-off at the steam-valves the entire expansive or motive power of steam is saved, and applied directly to the machinery.

There is a most delicate sensibility displayed in the action of all portions of the machinery, through the agency of stops or cams, with the catches that liberate the steam valves, for the purpose of cutting off the flow of steam into the cylinder; which makes the observer, who understands the operation of machinery, feel that he is in the presence, not only of a high mechanical power, but of a moral and intellectual one —since no volition of the clearest intellect could will a more even, sensitive, self-adjusting, equalized, and perfectly-balanced operation. The saving effected by these improvements in fuel alone, is so great as to interest the entire public in the universal introduction of it. They have recently placed one of these engines in the Sherman House.

Within a few weeks past several cases in this city have come under the notice of physicians where persons have been poisoned from using the water which has been allowed to remain over night in the pipes attached to hydrants. If galvanized iron pipe were used, such as Walworth, Hubbard and Co. manufacture, it would not only effect a great saving in a pecuniary way, but the health of the citizens would not suffer from the injurious matter which collects in leaden pipes.

THE STRUGGLE FOR SUPREMACY.

THIS is an age of electric progress, especially in the mechanic arts. The introduction, and application of the Sewing Machine, forms one of the most wonderful chapters of industrial history of modern times. There is no nation on the face of the earth, where mechanical inventions are brought to such a perfection, and adapted to so many purposes of utility, as in the United States. This arises partly from the inventive genius of our people, which has out-stripped the world in many important departments of the mechanic arts; and partly because of higher talent and intelligence here, having devoted themselves to this business. The inventive life of this continent is only just dawning. Our poorest mechanic, now, has access to libraries, from which he devises plans and designs in mechanism, which he could gain in no other way;

the result of which can be measured by no man, for they will stretch on, mingling with the ceaseless stream of human ingenuity that flows on from age to age. Since the invention of the Steam Engine, the Printing Press, and the Telegraph, three of the mightiest material agents God has given to man, no other one invention has become of so much importance as the Sewing Machine. The introduction of this wonderful invention is revolutionizing the age in which we live — it is bringing order out of chaos, and woman's power over the force of nature, by placing in her hands the sceptre of the material universe, through which she is asserting her importance in the scale of human greatness.

Great men beget great ideas; they are not often able to carry them out, the activity of invention out-stripping the means of execution. Thus it was with Elias Howe, Jr., of Cambridge, Mass., who, in 1846, secured a patent for the first practical Lock Stitch Sewing Machine, but imperfect in all its practical bearings. It remained for Mr. Isaac M. Singer, of New York, to perfect this most wonderful invention of the age. In August, 1860, he placed it before the public, and from that time to the present, has continued to improve it, until it now is without a rival in the domain of Sewing Machines.

To I. M. Singer belongs the honor of inventing the straight needle, perpendicular action Sewing Machine. The herculean efforts of this man convinced the world that Sewing Machines were invented by the Creator to take from the labor of the needle its drudgery and make mechanism execute the graceful conceptions of a planning brain. The world will not soon get tired of hearing about I. M. Singer, the man who is believed to have done more to perfect the Sewing Machine than any other man living. In speaking of Sewing Machines, we can truly say the genius of art has invaded the household. It is doing, in one department of house-wifery, what the steam engine, the telegraph, and other inventions have done, and are doing for man. The care of the wardrobe has been one of woman's chief employments, probably one half of the efficient female force in this country has been devoted to it. It is not the expenditure of that time that is to be regarded; it is the deadening effect of the employment on the mind and body, the monotony of continual employment in stitching, the minute attention required, the strain upon the eyes, the confined and unhealthy position, that have told with terrible effect upon the minds and bodies of women.

The Sewing Machine changes this, and renders sewing a healthy and inspiring employment. A woman accustomed to the use of the machine, would no more be content with the hand needle, than would the business man at the present day, with the facilities of the past century. What the steam engine proves compared with horse power, this beautiful machine is, when set in operation, to the slow, patient progress of the ordinary needle. It may require a little care, a drop of oil now and then, touched to the delicate mechanism, and then you have the power of fifty seamstresses, doing ornamental duty in your parlor, while out of active use eating nothing, and never singing Hood's mournful Song of the Shirt,

"Stitch, stitch, stitch."

There has been no machine able to achieve more good for saving labor and making money for those that work them than Singer's, owing to its great adaptability to all kinds of work from the heaviest pilot cloth down to the finest piece of cobweb muslin. Wherever we have visited cities or large towns on this continent, we have seen or heard of Singer's Sewing Machine.

Singer's letter A Machine, is probably the best Sewing Machine in the world, for family sewing and light manufacturing purposes. It is only of late that the public began to learn that the essential element of a machine best adapted to the heaviest work, would also be the elements to be embodied in a family machine; while they will sew the most delicate material to perfection, they are also adapted to light manufacturing purposes.

Singer & Co. have made considerable reduction in the price of their machines, with a view of placing them in the reach of the masses. Their capital is very large, and their facilities enable them to produce a better machine, for less money, of their valuable invention, than any other manufacturer, of any other machine. It is only by doing a great business, and having extensive manufacturing establishments, that good machines can be made at moderate prices. The qualities to be looked for in a good machine are: certainty of action at all rates of speed, simplicity of construction, great durability, and rapidity of operation, with less labor. Singer & Co. may well be called public benefactors, for they have, through the medium of their invention, contributed, in no small degree, to the industrial prosperity of the nation.

The Chicago Agency is located on Clark Street, opposite the Tribune Office, occupying one of those elegant stores in the Sherman House.

BILLIARD TABLE MANUFACTURE.

TO America belongs the honor of constructing the only perfect Billiard Tables made in the world. This is the more remarkable, as it has been pretty satisfactorily demonstrated that the game was in vogue among the Romans, and particularly cultivated by Consul Lucullus, that elegant and accomplished Roman epicurean, who devoted his colossal fortune to the graces and accomplishments of refined and polite life. Some have referred its introduction to the Emperor Caligula. We have never

Great Western
BILLIARD TABLE MANUFACTORY.
Nos. 74, 76 & 78 Randolph St.
Between Dearborn & State.
CHICAGO ILL.

leaned to this conclusion, because it is hard to believe that so hard-hearted a wretch should have had any agency in introducing so elegant and generous an amusement among his countrymen. There seems to be little doubt that the game of Billiards was known to the Romans; and we think it would not be difficult to prove that every hospitable and elegant palace of the Roman citizens had a room devoted to this glorious and inspiring game. Billiards were introduced into France as early as the first crusade, which occurred in 1090. During the reign of Henry III., one of the most luxurious of the French monarchs gave to this amusement the epithet of "the noble game of Billiards." With this royal sanction, its fascination soon enthralled all the elegant circles of Europe, and before a quarter of a century had passed, Billiards became the favorite amusement of the nobles and principal classes of England, Germany, Italy and Spain. The game was introduced into this country by the cavaliers of Virginia and a few gentlemen of Holland, who became the early possessors of Manhattan Island, then called New Amsterdam. It was cultivated before the revolution by the most illustrious, intelligent, and best educated classes. General Washington devoted to it as many moments of leisure after dinner as the serious occupation of his life allowed. John Quincy Adams, while President, had one in his house, as one of the luxuries which his hospitality provided for the after-dinner hours of Lafayette.

There is much to be said on the subject of innocent and exhilarating amusement. Physicians and surgeons of the highest rank among all nations have prescribed Billiards as the most exhilirating and the most beautiful of all games. Chess is too sedentary; and, besides, it turns out to be too irritating. To be well played, it taxes the intensest powers.

Billiards can be played as a relaxation; It becomes an intense and exciting game only when the mind throws all its energies in that direction, and then it is full, often, of the spirit of heroism. Sir Astley Cooper attributed to the practice of this game, among the families of the English aristocracy, both male and female, their admitted superiority of health, beauty, and physical development, over all other races on the earth.

The demand for Billiard Tables in the West and North-West became so great, that three years ago, Messrs. E. Brunswick & Co. established a manufactory in this city, for the better accommodation of the many applicants for their celebrated Tables. The best players in this country resort to them for Tables, Balls, Cues, and all the apparatus of the game. They receive orders from men of taste and fortune, from every quarter of the North-West. They doubtless construct them with more care, and superintend the manufacture of each one with more earnest personal attention than any other manufacturer.

Not a Table is allowed to leave their manufactory that does not first pass the scrutiny of their eye. They have devoted the energies, talents, and experience of life to the gradual perfection of Billiard Table manufacture. Billiard players seek these Tables in preference to all others.

Their Salesroom and Factory are at Nos. 74, 76, and 78 Randolph Street — the manufactory occupying one entire floor. Their Office and Sales-room are on the first floor. They employ a capital of about $20,000 — from twenty-five to thirty men; and furnish from ten to twelve tables per week. These Tables are made of Rosewood and Mahogany, with Slate, Marble, and Wooden Beds, and cost from $225 to $1,500.

PHARMACY AND CHEMISTRY.

MEDICINE is known as the art and science of curing disease. The practice of medicine must everywhere have arisen from the accidents and infirmities to which mankind are liable. In Greece, as elsewhere, the early history of medicine is involved in darkness. We know, however, that the temples of Æsculapius were, from an early period, the resort of the sick, who submitted themselves to the regulations of the Asclepiadæ, the priests of the temples, and that these priests must thus have had large opportunities for the study of disease. But the temples of Æsculapius are not the only source to which the origin of scientific medicine is to be traced. In the schools of philosophy, some attention was always paid to the healing art, as a branch of education. At this period, it seems there was still another class, the Charlatans, who, without any pretension to education, offered their nostrums for sale in the market place. Besides the temples of Æsculapius and the schools of philosophy, there were other sources which undoubtedly contributed to form the early physicians. In these various ways, medicine had already made sensible progress, when Hippocrates (born in Cos, about 460 B. C.,) collected the scattered knowledge of his time, and added to it by his own genius and observation.

For six hundred years, according to Pliny, Rome had no physicians — not that no attempt was then made to cure disease, but that these attempts consisted mainly in superstitious observances. Thus, according to Livy, pestilence was repeatedly stayed at Rome by erecting a temple to Apollo; by celebrating public games, or by the dictator driving a nail into the Capitol; and Cato the Censor, trusted to simples, with charms and incantations. Galen, who was born A. D. 130, had a far wider share of renown than other physicians; for more than twelve centuries his authorities reigned supreme in the schools; even a fact was disputed if it was against the authority of Galen. From the time of Galen, medicine began to participate in the decline which had already overtaken art and literature.

While the Western empire had sunk into barbarism, and the Eastern, sadly limited, was struggling for existence, medical science found refuge for a time among the Arabians. As order again began to emerge from the chaos of barbarism which succeeded the fall of the Western Roman Empire, monks and priests became the principal physicians, and a little medicine was taught in the monasteries. From the ninth to the thirteenth century, the Jews became celebrated as physicians, and by administering remedies, obtained access to the courts, and even to the palace of the Roman Pontiffs.

In the last sixty years, practical medicine has made greater advances than in any other similar period. This may be attributed to many reasons; among which are the brilliant discoveries which have rendered Chemistry a new science; also the discovery, by Pharmacutical Chemists, of the active principle of various drugs, which has not only rendered the active use of these drugs more certain, and less nauseous, but has enabled them to exhibit necessary doses, which the stomach otherwise would be unable to retain. Pharmacy is intimately allied with several of the natural sciences, and its successful cultivation demands an extensive knowledge of Chemistry, and familiarity with chemical manipulations, and with the physical properties of medicine.

The various operations of Pharmacy have for their object, to render medicine more effective, and less repugnant to the taste and stomach.

In no article of commerce, perhaps, is there greater and more frequent adulterations than in Drugs and Medicines. At a Pharmacutical Convention held in Boston in 1859, a committee which was appointed the preceding year to consider the subject of adulteration, submitted an exceedingly able, interesting and valuable report. They give a most formidable list of adulterations which are known in the trade, and manfully acknowledged it to be their high duty to purge their profession of the disgrace which their dishonest brethren bring upon it. A long catalogue of drugs were furnished, which have been taken from shops, and which are adulterated in every conceivable way. Five different methods of treating the Para Balsam Copaiva are enumerated. Cream of Tartar, which is so largely used, both as a medicine and an ingredient of of food, is a favorite article for adulteration.

Every city and town may have its dishonest druggists, who resort to adulteration. As a general thing, if the public are imposed upon it is their own fault. In every city like Chicago, there are Druggists whose reputation in this respect is without reproach — those to whom physicians invariably direct their patients for prescription; not only for compounding and selling none but pure medicines, but for their thorough knowledge of Pharmacy and Chemistry.

Among this latter class of Druggists, who enjoy the highest confidence of the public, and the medical faculty generally, we may mention Mr. E. H. SARGENT, whose elegantly fitted up Drug Store is located on the corner of State and Randolph Streets. Mr. Sargent has been thoroughly educated in Pharmacy and Chemistry, having been uninterruptedly engaged in it, in all its details, for nearly twenty years, enjoying advantages rarely conferred upon others. His store is supplied with all the modern pharmaceutical preparations, new remedies, etc., accredited by modern Chemistry and science. Extracts, perfumes and toilet articles of the choicest foreign and domestic production, may be found here in great variety. Among other things, we noticed a fine assortment of brushes, manufactured in Paris for this house, Mr. Sargent's name marked upon each by the manufacturer.

Their facilities for obtaining goods from first hands enable them to supply the trade or the consumer at greatly reduced prices from ordinary rates. No representation will be made by this house that will not be most fully substantiated.

FURS.

COMMERCE has brought the luxuries of all countries and the refinement of all ages to our American homes. Ages ago Europe's kings and nobles were wearing furs which were then restricted to the royal families, and served as distinctive marks and badges of rank, and were for this purpose, introduced into armorial bearings. But that age has gone by. Democracy has revolutionized the world — it has lifted the veil and opened an earthly paradise on this continent to the long toiling millions who have fled from the crumbling despotisms of the old world. Here they find an empire under a Republican form of government, reared on democratic principle, of "the greatest good for the greatest number"— and opulence has drawn around us curtains of silk and gold. Here we can enjoy, undisturbed, the luxuries of both hemispheres. All these elegant furs, once restricted to the privileged few, can now be enjoyed by every honest, upright and industrious man. A brief account of the sources from whence these furs are obtained may not be uninteresting to the reader.

In Siberia an annual fair is held in Kiakhta, near the Chinese frontier, which is the great emporium of the trade between Russia and China. Here Rusisan furs form the leading article of trade. Large caravans of Russian and Chinese traders meet every year in December at this fair, which has existed since 1720, and has powerfully contributed to promote the commercial intercourse between the two nations. Here the valuable furs of the Cossacks are brought for barter. The word Fur indicates the thick, warm covering of certain animals, especially such as inhabit the lands and waters of cold countries, distinguished from hair by its greater fineness and softness; most generally the skins of such animals are dressed with the fur on. Before being dressed the skins are known in commerce as peltry. Fur is used especially for winter clothing, for which it is well adapted, not merely by reason of its important qualities of warmth and durability, but also on account of its great beauty. In all cold climates, man has availed himself liberally of the warm covering with which nature has clothed the animals around him; but the wealth of the most favored nations has drawn to them the most beautiful furs, in whatever part of the world they are procured. Skins of animals were among the first materials used for clothing. Before Adam and Eve were driven from the garden of Eden, they were furnished with coats of skins. The ancient Assyrians used the soft skins of animals to cover the couches, or the ground in their tents; and the Israelites employed badger's skins and rams' skins dyed red, as ornamental hangings for the tabernacle. The ancient heroes of the Greeks and Romans are represented as being clothed in skins; Æneas, wearing for an outer garment that of a lion, and Alcestes being formidably clad in that of the Libyan bear. Plutarch speak's of the Persians reclining upon soft furs. The fur of the beaver was in use in the fourth century; the animal was known as the Pontic dog. The sable of the far-off regions of Siberia, was not known till many centuries later; but it was the production of that region in furs that chiefly prompted the Russians to its definitive conquest. In the early periods furs appear to have constituted the whole riches of the northern countries—they were the principal if not the only exports; taxes were paid with them, and they were the only medium of exchange. So it was in our own western territories in the latter part of the last century, and still continues to be among the Indians. In the eleventh century furs had become fashionable throughout Europe. In the history of the Crusades, frequent mention is made of the magnificent displays by the European princes of their dress and costly furs before the court at Constantinople. In those times the use of the choicer furs, as those of the Ermine, Sable, the Vair or Hungarian Squirrel was restricted to the royal familes and the nobility. These privileged persons applied them lavishly to their own use — the extravagance had grown to such a pitch, that seven hundred and forty-six ermines were required for the lining for a surcoat for Louis IX; the fashion extended to the princes of less civilized nations. The early settlers of the northern provinces of North America soon learned the value of the furs of the numerous animals which people the extensive rivers, lakes and forests of the vast territories.

In this county we procure most of our furs from the semi-annual sales held in Leipsig, known as the Eastern Fair, which is attended by purchasers from the continent, from the United States and other parts of the world.

In 1855, many choice furs were received in New York from the Russian American company at Sitka; it being thought more prudent to send them there, than to risk their reaching St. Petersburgh. Among the packages, was a camphor wood box of about three feet in length, bearing the stamp of the Russian government, and containing four hundred small skins which were valued at $14,000. The highest price were those almost black, which were rated at fifty or fifty-two dollars each. A cape of full size would require from twenty to twenty-five of these skins. Among the furs and skins from the United States, and the Hudson Bay Company in British America, which are usually on exhibition and offered for sale at the great Eastern Fair, we may mention the following:—Muskrat, Beaver, Otter, Fisher, Silver Fox, Red Fox, White Fox, Martin, Mink, Sea Otter, Lynx, Black Bear, Brown Bear, Gray and White Bear, Raccoon, Wolf, Wolverine, Skunk, Wild Cat, and Opossum.

Beside these furs of American origin, the principal ones are the *Russian Sable*, everywhere esteemed as the most beautiful, costly and useful Fur the Artic zone produces; the *Baum*, or *Pine Martin*; the *Stone Martin*, more valuable for the excellent quality of its skin than the beauty of its fur; *Ermine*, a Siberian and Norwegian Fur, the whitest known, though in summer the animal is a dingy brown; the *European Fitch*, or *Polecat*, a Fur remarkable for durability and smell, which it is difficult to counteract; the *Tartar Sable*, of which the tail is used exclusively for artists' best pencils; *Nutria*, a fur used exclusively for making hats, and having considerable resemblance to Beaver; *Hamster*, a German fur; European *Gray Hair*, and the *Chinchilla* a native of South America.

The skin that is probably the most extensively used is that of the *Siberian Squirrel*. Of these little animals, not much larger than our common red squirrel, fifteen millions, it is said, are every year captured in Russia. Their color varies from a pearl-gray to a dark blue-gray.

The principal Fur trade in the United States is confined to comparatively few dealers, considering the immense capital invested. Among one of the leading firms established in the city of New York, as early as 1832, is that of the celebrated house of F. W. Lasak & Son. For many years they were located at No. 19 John Street. Few persons who may have passed through that street will fail to remember Lasak's Fur store, at the sign of the *Golden Lion*, and the great *White Polar Bear*; the former standing over the entrance way, erect, in all his native pride, keeping sentinel watch;

the latter filling the entire space of a great window, before whose translucent French plate glass, many a pedestrian, of either sex, has lingered for a moment.

Lasak & Son purchase Furs in Europe at the Hudson Bay Company's sales, held in London — in Paris and at the Easter Fairs in Leipsig; and also all the American Furs. Their capital invested in the business is large. Their sales to manufacturers in New York, and throughout the United States, in Canada and the British provinces, are very extensive. They are now located at 520 Broadway. In 1862, Mr. Lasak established a branch of the New York house in this city, at No. 107 Randolph Street, under the firm of T. B. Morris & Co, where every article in Furs may be had of the very best quality, and at the lowest rates. Every article sold will prove just what it is recommended. Mr. Morris was for many years with Mr. Lasak in New York, and is most thoroughly master of his business. They have connected with their Fur trade, Hats, Caps, Gloves, etc.

Look for the "John Street *Polar Bear*," at No. 107 Randolph Street.

LEATHER AND ITS MANUFACTURE.

THE manufacture of various kinds of Leather is considered a leading pursuit in Chicago. The abundance of bark, the abundance and low price of hides and skins, have facilitated and rendered profitable the business of tanning. The two principal processes for the manufacture of Leather, it is perhaps needless to remark, are denominated *Tanning* and *Currying*. The latter is mainly a mechanical process, and the former a chemical one, though requiring more or less manipulation in order to facilitate the chemical action. There are several firms engaged in the business in this city — one very extensive, that of the "Chicago Hide and Leather Company," organized in 1854, with a capital stock of $125,000, W. S. Gurnee, President, and C. C. Chase, Secretary. The sales of this company amounted, in 1861, to $50,000, more than the entire product of the whole State in 1840. They manufacture twenty thousand hides and ten thousand skins annually; employing an average force of sixty hands, using twenty-five hundred cords of bark; their sales amounting to over a quarter of a million of dollars per annum. They manufacture Harness, Bridle, Collar and Sole Leather, Kip and Calf Skins.

They also keep on sale, Spanish and other Sole Leather, of the best New York manufacture. The reputation of their Leather is superior to any in market, and it is sought for by consumers over all other manufactured in the West.

It would be interesting, did our space admit, to note and trace the *modus operandi* of the process of manufacture, also the effects of the various improvements which have been made by mechanical means in the manufacture of Leather. The steam engine has been generally introduced into the factories of Leather dressers and tanners, and is now used in grinding bark, for softening hides, and in giving motion to many machines for washing, glazing and finishing Leather.

The skins of various animals, in their fresh state, are flexible, tough, and elastic, but in drying, they become hard and horny. The art of restoring the supple qualities to skins, and rendering them durable, appears to have been discovered at a very early period, and the word leather, from the Saxon lith, lithe, or lither, indicates the quality of suppleness. Leather is formed by the chemical union of the cutis, or true skin of the animal, with an astringent vegetable substance known as tannin, or tannic acid. Leather may, however, be preserved by impregnating the skin with alum, oil, or grease. In the animal hide, or skin, the outer part, which is covered with hair or wool, is called the epidermis, or cuticle, below which is the reticulated tissue; and then, in contact with the flesh, is the dermis, or true skin, which is the only part which admits of being tanned, and varies in thickness in different parts. When the tannin, which is soluble in water, is applied to the hides of animals, from which the hair, epidermis, and any fleshy or fatty parts adhering to them are removed, and which hides thencon sist wholly of gelatine, also soluble in water, these two soluble substances so unite chemically as to form the whole insoluble substance called Leather.

Of the ox-hides which are converted into Leather, those supplied by bulls are thicker, stronger, and coarser in the grain than those of cows, while the hides of bullocks are intermediate between those of the bull and the cow. Such leather is employed for the soles of boots and shoes, for many parts of saddlery and harness, for making leather trunks, buckets, hose for fire engines, pump-valves, etc.

Most of our readers, it is presumed, are acquainted with the old method of tanning, which is not yet entirely abandoned. The process has been expedited by the use of a concentrated solution of bark, instead of mere layers of bark in water. The variations of practice among different tanners extend to the substances used as astringents, as well as to the manner of applying them.

The various substances used are, oak and hemlock bark, valonia, catechu, or terra-japonica; also several other patent and secret combinations — substances which are used either individually or in various combinations.

The quality of the Leather depends upon the material made use of as well as the manner of manufacture. The difference in quality is as great as the number of manufacturers. Therefore, it is advisable for purchasers of Leather to know the reputation of the manufacturer, and the character of the house with whom they deal. In speaking of the Chicago Hide and Leather Company, we have but a word to add, that anything that Walter H. Gurnee is connected with can be relied on — for it bears the seal of public confidence. This company have been doing business in Chicago for the last eight years, and wherever their products go throughout the North-West, they carry with them a "tower of *strength*." Their Office and Salesroom is located at No. 45 Wabash Avenue, in Burch's Building.

CAPARISONING.

THE horse has always been regarded as the noblest of the brute creation, and he has from the begining, vindicated his claim to the affection of man. He has mingled with the sympathies, and affected the fortunes, of the greatest and the best of men. So matchless is he in his proportions, so undaunted in his courage, so lofty in his bearing, so firm in his love, so defiant in his pride, and so sublime in his power, that he seems to impart to man, when he bears him on his back, a glory man cannot impart to him. No wonder he has been thought worthy of being richly caparisoned. From the early periods of the ancient world, all nations have been proud of clothing the horse in rich attire; and every man of true dignity and appreciation would spend his money with greater pleasure in putting a fine harness upon his noble steed, than he would in putting a fine garment upon himself. Through all languages, in all literatures are strewn the records of the wonderful achievements of this companion of man, who seems to have been created especially to be worthy of rendering him the highest service, and commanding from him the most endearing affection. On the art of caparisoning the horse, the attention of every age has been bestowed. The conquerors of nations, and the builders of empires; the chieftains of state and the masters of art and poetry have considered this subject worthy of their best attention. Alexander rewarded the man who caparisoned his Buchephalus appropriately and well, with his treasure and his love. Cæsar gave a farm to the Roman artisan who had made trappings for his horse that went through the campaign of Gaul; and Washington wrote grateful letters to the man that made the saddle in which he rode through so many battles. The art of saddlery is not an ignoble one; and the man of generous qualities looks with pleasure into the windows of a saddler's shop, and on the art of clothing the horse, for the road or the battle-field. The manufacturer of saddlery in this country is distinguished from that in any other part of the world by the immense variety of styles and qualities which are produced. We are informed by a leading manufacturer, that of *Saddles* there are probably not less than five hundred various styles and qualities, with a proportionate quality of Bridles, Bridle Mountings, Martingales, Girths, Circingles, Stirrups, Leathers, Saddle Bags, Medical Bags, etc. Of Harness for Coach, Gig, Dearborn, Sulky, Stage, and Omnibus, there are perhaps three hundred styles and qualities; while in coarse Harness, for Carts, Drays, Wagons and Plows, there is also great diversity.

In the manufacture of these articles, Chicago is justly proud of the house of Messrs. Turner & Sidway, located at No. 49 Lake Street, who represent the largest and most reliable firm engaged in this business in the North-West.

Previous to the opening of their establishment in 1858, there had been no attempt made to manufacture Saddles in Chicago for the wholesale trade. The dealers here depending on manufactories in the east for their supplies, were unable to offer to the trade sufficient inducements either in price, variety or quality of goods to draw more than a very small part of that business that naturally belonged to Chicago, and among the large buyers in the country, hardly any one thought of coming to Chicago to make his principal purchases; consequently the trade had to be attracted here from other points, and although times were hard and money scarce they soon succeeded in getting a paying trade.

Confining themselves to Saddles, Horse Collars, Blankets, Whips, Bridles and Patent-Leather work—making no Harness—they were enabled to keep ahead of competition from those whose attention and capital were less concentrated than their own, as they generally afforded better goods for the same price, than could be by those who sold eastern goods.

From season to season business increased until the spring of 1861, when the breakin out of the war prostrated all business, until there was a demand for army goods, when Messrs. T. & S. were among the first to receive orders from Quartermaster General Wood, for Knapsacks, Haversacks, Gun accoutrements, etc., and when the call for cavalry was made they received the first order given for equipments, which were for Capt. Barker's Chicago Dragoons — now Gen. McClellan's body guard. This order was soon after followed by one to equip Capt. Shambeck's company, the Hoffman Dragoons. The quality of these goods, the reasonable price, and the promptness in furnishing them, soon gave them an enviable notoriety, which resulted in orders pouring in on them from all sections, until the middle of August; orders were received for thousands of cavalry equipments that they could not supply, although at the time they were making from six to eight hundred per week.

Several commanders of regiments coming to the city and remaining for days trying to induce them to undertake the equipping of their command; but an understanding with Quartermaster General Wood, that the State of Illinois should receive their supplies in preference to all others, prevented; although the prices offered were generally larger than those paid by the State, and in many cases payment was offered in gold on the delivery.

This rush of business continued until January, 1862, most other manufacturers having stopped in October, November, or December. Messrs. T. & S. keeping constantly employed from two to five hundred workmen, and making in all about fifteen thousand complete sets of Cavalry equipments; ten thousand Knapsacks; forty thousand Haversacks, six thousand Gun accoutrements, Cartridge boxes, Belts, etc., etc., which in the aggregate amounted to about $600,000, being much the largest business, in this line, ever done in the United States in the same length of time.

The business of army supplies being over, they have resumed the business of manufacturing Saddles, Horse Collars, etc., for the trade, at No. 49 Lake Street, with increasing facilities, and intending to make it better for dealers in this line to buy in Chicago than any other place east or west.

DRY GOODS.

THE establishment of Cooley, Farwell & Co., at 42, 44 and 46 Wabash Avenue, is the oldest Wholesale Dry Goods Jobbing house in Chicago, and enjoys a reputation for honorable dealing, and every other requisite to make up a successful and popular house, which is not surpassed.

The cut, on the opposite page, represents their ware-rooms, which are constructed of Athens marble, covering a space of 60 by 120 feet, and six stories in height. Altogether, it is one of the most elegant and convenient structures for a dry goods jobbing business West of New York.

There is but few houses in New York which is now selling a larger amount of dry goods than Cooley, Farwell & Co., which is a very significant fact, both as regards the business ability of this firm, and the growing preference among Western merchants for buying goods at home. The probable secret of this, is, that they buy and sell for cash, and have their senior member of the firm constantly in the market to secure the best bargains.

The West has been burdened beyond endurance, in past years, by the abuse of the credit system, till experience as well as necessity has taught them that John Ran-

44
12
46
COOLEY. FARWELL & Co.
DRY GOODS AT WHOLESALE
COOLEY FARWELL & Co.

dolph's "philosopher's stone"—"*pay as you go*"—is the only sure guarantee for commercial prosperity.

We learn that this firm quite recently purchased the entire production of one of the largest print works in New England, for cash. Such facilities, in a financial view, will at a glance show any thorough-bred merchant, that they deserve the wide-spread reputation they have so well earned in the past, as successful merchants, and mark their house as the leading dry goods firm of the North-Western States. While the cash system is adhered to strictly in buying goods, we are informed that in fancy goods, notions, woolens, etc., short time is given for approved paper.

We see no reason why such houses cannot sell goods as cheap as any in New York. Expenses are much lighter in Chicago, and freights on small bills are always higher than for large consignments; so that the retailer, in widening the distance between him and the source of his supplies, must necessarily increase the cost of his goods, when the home market is represented by merchants equally competent to command goods at the lowest prices from the manufacturers.

As before stated, the fact that they are making such large sales, is conclusive proof that buyers are satisfied that Cooley, Farwell & Co. occupy that position, and are determined to improve it in a practical way. Chicago, in a commercial point of view, by the energy and public spirit of such houses, is fast becoming what nature has destined her to be—the metropolis of the North-West. Western States and Western men are beginning to feel a just pride in her prosperity, and patronage naturally follows such a state of feeling in the minds of all who hold commercial relations with her. This must continue to increase, as the untold natural resources, with which she is surrounded, (in a vast country, with a soil and climate of unsurpassed richness and salubrity, held firmly in its embrace with iron bands, radiating in every point of the compass), shall continue to be developed by the gathering millions that are seeking a home among us.

HOOP SKIRTS.

NO Business better illustrates what ingenuity and enterprise can do for it than the manufacture of Hoop Skirts. From the first Crinoline worn by the Empress Eugenie down to the elegant skeletons of the present day, the demand for expanding petticoats has been steadily increasing. The improvements, too, both in the article itself and in the processes of manufacturing them, have kept pace with the demand, until now there seems none left to be desired. So prolific has been American ingenuity in this line of invention, that the Patent Office exhibits nearly as many models in this department as in any other.

These improvements made, with the active competition among manufacturers, have reduced both the price and the profits to the lowest point of a paying business. The effect has been to bring it into the hands of a few leading firms, whose superior facilities and large capital enable them to compete successfully with each other.

Their enterprise, under the lead of fashion, has pushed forward the business until their sales amount to millions yearly, and extends all over the civilized world.

Among those who engaged in the business at its first introduction, and who have kept pace with its growth, none have taken a higher position, or done more for its advancement, than Messrs. H. De Forest & Co., of Birmingham, Conn.

Their Skirts have from the first had a high reputation for elegance and style, and for the superior quality of the material used.

They were the first to introduce those elegant Skirts, now so popular, made with from thirty to fifty light elastic springs.

The other manufacturers had confined themselves to making skirts with a few heavy, rigid hoops, clumsily put together, until they brought about this desirable change. For a long time they supplied the celebrated house of A. T. Stewart & Co., of New York with this improved style, and by their extended sales became known throughout the Union.

They are also the inventors of several valuable improvements in Skirts and in the machinery required in their manufacture, enabling them to produce a more durable and elegant article at a less price.

The various operations performed on the material before a complete Skirt is produced, with the improvements they have made in that direction, are highly interesting and worth a visit to see them.

To accommodate their Western trade, they have established a depot and branch manufactory, for supplying dealers only, at 84 Lake Street, opposite the Tremont House, under the management of one of the firm, Mr. C. T. Morse.

They will at all times keep a large stock there, of every kind of Ladies' and Misses' sizes, enabling dealers to select those styles best adapted to their trade; and should any customer desire a style peculiar to his market, he can have them made up without delay. These are opportunities hitherto not to be found west of New York City.

With the facilities which they possess at both places, and from their long experience and reputation as manufacturers, we can assure our readers that they will be able to purchase of them on as favorable terms as in the Eastern market.

By purchasing their Skirts nearer home, dealers will have the advantage of selecting their goods often, and run no risk of accumulating bad styles. This remark will apply as well to all purchasers of dry goods

We bespeak for the firm and their gentlemanly representative here the patronage of our readers, assuring them that they will be honorably and liberally treated.

FANCY LEATHER GOODS.

THIS is a branch of business which may be regarded as yet only in its infancy in Chicago; but destined to become one of considerable magnitude at no distant day. Considering the rapidly increasing demand for these goods, it is gratifying to know Chicago is actively leading in an enterprise which must aid in eventually rendering us independent of Eastern markets. Large quantities of these goods find a ready sale in this city. They enter into almost every department of trade — the druggist, the jeweler, the banker, the dental and surgical instrument maker, the daguerrean case and cigar case manufacturer — they are kept on sale by the fancy goods dealer, the stationer, and in almost every branch of trade.

Formerly these goods were mostly manufactured in Germany; for several years past, extensive manufactories have been established in New York and Philadelphia. In 1849, Messrs. STROBEL & BROTHER, two young men from Germany, commenced business in Cincinnati, for the manufacture of Fancy Leather Goods. During the last two or three years, the demand for this class of goods has increased to such an extent, and especially from the North-West, that they were induced to open a branch establishment in Chicago. One of the brothers devotes his whole interest in the managing of this house, which is rapidly becoming a representative business We found, on looking through their stock of goods, almost every article of utility and beauty that art and genius could devise, among some of which we may enumerate, Pocket Books, in every conceivable style and size, Portmonnaies, Note Cases for bankers, Trays for Show-cases for jewelry, Morocco Boxes, for silver-ware, etc.; Dental, Surgical and Toilet Cases. We were also shown beautiful specimens of imported fancy Leather Goods, such as Ladies' Purses, Traveling Bags, Card Cases, Workboxes, Dressing Cases, Cigar Cases, and every article manufactured in this line of goods.

Messrs. Strobel & Brother are extensive Importers of many articles in this line, all of which they claim can be sold for less prices in Chicago than they can be purchased for in Eastern markets, including charges for freight, etc. One reason that they have for entertaining this opinion is, that expenses for conducting business are less than in most Eastern cities. For many reasons, which we have not the space here to cite, it would seem evident that a merchant or manufacturer in Chicago can afford to sell at a percentage of profit which, on the same amount of business, would not pay under greatly increased expenses elsewhere. These are the deductions of reason and common sense — the laws of trade and commerce. Hence it is obvious that a purchaser of a miscellaneous stock for the North-western trade, can purchase at less prices at the fountain head, where goods are as yet in first hands. If there be an atom of truth in that principle of political economy which demonstrates that the nearer the place of production the cheaper the price, they will discover, as thousands of North-western merchants have done, that Chicago is the *cheapest seller and natural distributor of merchandise adapted to the wants of the North-west.*

Messrs. Strobel & Brother have located their manufactory here, that they may fully demonstrate this fact to Western dealers. Their Store and Salesroom is located at No. 76 Dearborn Street.

THE ART OF BOOK-BINDING.

ANCIENT books seem always to have been preserved in rolls. They were merely groups of leaves in thin skins, or some kind of vegetable membrane. The book-binder's art was a very primitive one. He had only to paste or glue the leaves together, thus forming an extended sheet, to which he attached a cylinder, around which the scroll was rolled. Even in our times it is customary, in oriental countries, to write on strips of vellum, sewed together in one continous sheet, with rollers at each end, clasped with silver and gold. The square form of binding, which was so great an improvement, was not adopted until after the Christian Era. Long before the art of printing was introduced, book-binding had reached perfection, and very many illustrated missals and MSS. of the Middle-Ages are still preserved in the great libraries of Europe, in binding which has never been surpassed in durability, artistic finish and taste. It is only within the last few years, that the art of book-binding has been carried on in its most advanced and beautiful forms in this country; but the display which is made in the leading American book-stores and libraries, is fully equal now to the same sights in Europe. With the growth of the business, the art has not only advanced in every department, but the cost of book-binding has been very materially reduced, while the process of the work has been greatly shortened. In this city, men of wealth and taste can procure their rare volumes bound in accordance with the true principles of the art — that is, to adapt the style of the covering to the contents of the volume.

As a manufacture, modern book-binding is distinguished for the extent to which machinery has been employed, and the consequent rapidity of production. Mechanism is applied to block-gilding, blind-tooling, and embossing; hydraulic presses are used instead of old wooden screw presses; cutting machines of modern manufacture, supersede the plow; cutting tables with shears are now used for squaring and cutting mill boards for book corners; and machines have recently been invented for backing and finishing. The binding of BLANK BOOKS is a distinct but important branch of the general trade. In the manufacture of Account Books, foreigners acknowledge that Americans excel all others; and those who are conversant with the best workmanship executed in this city will acknowledge that our makers are not surpassed by any. Every variety and description of Blank Books for merchants, and blanks for public offices are made here, from the cheapest to those distinguished as *indestructible*, which are bound in Russia, paneled, and edged with brass. The leading establishments employ the most improved machinery, and no expense is spared to expedite and cheapen the process of manufacture.

Mr. CYRUS J. WARD, has at No. 136 Lake Street, the largest and best conducted establishment in Chicago. There are none where more volumes are turned out, none where the work is done more substantial, or in finer taste. His facilities are such as to embrace every kind of binding, from the plainest muslin to the richest and most elaborate styles, while in his Blank Book department none excel him, as his conveniences are such that he can equal, if not exceed, any other establishment in the binding of all kinds of Railroad Blanks, County and Mercantile Blank Books, of every description.

He is master of his business, devoting his whole time and best talent for its development, and making prices to suit the times, his manufacturing rooms present a scene of busy life. This is one of the expanding arts now, in all countries where the Press is unshackled. With the perfect liberty it enjoys with us, the increased number of volumes to be bound every coming year will amount to millions. The increasing taste and demand for schools, private and public libraries, the increased number of readers for every volume, and the rapidly growing taste for reading and intelligence, will call for a constant improvement in the art of book-binding, to meet the exigencies of a great and well educated people.

The binders of this city have peculiar advantages in being able to procure many of the requisite materials direct from manufacturers in our midst; except book-binder's muslin, which is made only by one house, Messrs. N. M. Abbott & Co., New York city. The very best Morocco that can be obtained, and Marble Paper are made in Philadelphia, and Tar boards are supplied from New York.

The business of account Book-binding and Ruling in this city amounts to about $175,000, while the entire Book-binding including Blank Books, exceeds $350,000 as nearly as we can ascertain.

THE GIFT OF THE GREAT SPIRIT.

FROM the "Counterblast to Tobacco," by King James, down to the latest Modern Reformers, everybody who has been ambitious of parading before the world his claim to exhalted virtue, has been ranting against Tobacco. By the naturalist and the man of taste, it is considered among the choicest and most luxurious gifts. Like the New World itself, it was not revealed to a knowledge of mankind, until the later periods of civilization. One of the most characteristic and beautifully executed designs we have ever seen, represented a scene in the primitive life of the aboriginal lords of our forest, when they received the tobacco plant from the Great Spirit, accompanied by its *pendant*, in which an Indian maiden offers the same boon to a cavalier of England, and they smoke the pipe of peace together. Tobacco has gone through the civilized world, and become one of those luxuries which, when once tasted, will be enjoyed forever. Pit against it, philosophy; bring whole regiments of chemists; parade doctors, arguments—and yet men will snuff, chew, and smoke.

Snuffing is considered, in Europe, rather an elegant and courtly accomplishment. Snuff abounds in courts. Kings take snuff; emperors, popes, and above all, diplomatists. It is doubtful whether any important diplomatic question has been settled in Europe, for two centuries, without a cross-fire over a pair of snuff-boxes. So, too, they smoke; not in *salons*, where ladies are present — always excepting Holland and the entire Dutch world, where a whole country is saturated with smoke — and very bad tobacco smoke at that—and where they persist in smoking, without regard to sex, circumstances, or occasion. The manufactures of Tobacco in Chicago are limited to cigars, snuff and smoking tobacco. Chewing tobacco is made in the neighborhood of the plantation; and the reason that so much inferior quality is made, is that the demand exceeds the supply. All the first quality grown is required for wrapping the frost-bitten, unripe, and otherwise injured leaves, which are deposited in the center of the plug. About one-third of the leaf tobacco, for making cigars, is obtained from Cuba; the rest is of American growth. The Cuban is of course used for the superior qualities. The best cigars are known by their pure color and the white solidity of the ashes. The best cigars made in Chicago need only the foreign brands, and custom-house marks, to sell as real Havanas. Machines have not as yet been found to work well. A Liverpool house is said to have a patented machine in operation, which will make five thousand cigars per day; and in Prussia, machines are extensively used, which is one reason why German Cigars are so cheap, and so badly made that few will smoke.

The introduction and use of Tobacco form a singular chapter in the history of mankind. At the time of the discovery of America, Tobacco was in frequent use among the Indians, and the practice of smoking was common to almost all the tribes; and by it they pretended to cure a great variety of diseases.

All the Sovereigns of Europe, and most of them of other parts of the world, derive a considerable part of their revenues from Tobacco. Its use has vastly increased in France since the last Duke of Orleans set the fashion of smoking in the streets. The profit the government derives from this source is said to exceed a hundred million francs.

We are acquainted with no man in the West, who, as a merchant and a student of this delicious weed, has mastered it so thoroughly as Mr. JAMES DUFFY, the gentlemanly proprietor of the popular Tremont House Cigar Store, and also the favorite establishment on Clark Street, where the *best Tobacco* in *all its forms* may always be found. These two establishments are known by every consumer of the delicious gift of the Great Spirit, who seek their supplies in this market, either for private use, or to re-sell. Mr. Duffy has been a resident of Chicago about fourteen years. He found the merchandise of Tobacco in this city in the hands of adulterators, tricksters, deceivers, and impostors. He took it out of their hands; he became the master of the business; and now everybody who knows enough to do it, or who cares anything for his life or personal comfort, goes to Duffy for Tobacco in all its forms, with the absolute certainty, that what bears the mark *he* puts on it, is the thing it pretends to be.

His establishments are, No. 4 Tremont Block, and No. 37 Clark Street.

MILLINERY GOODS.

SOME one says, "Commerce is King." Not so — Fashion is King. Fashion is King everywhere; from policies of princes down to the circumference of hoops, the number of flounces on a woman's dress, or the bonnet she wears upon her head. Trade, commerce, agriculture, science, art and literature, are all conducted after a fashion. A man or woman is clad from head to foot after a fashion. No matter what is comfort or necessity, everything must have a degree of fashion. "To be out of the fashion is to be out of the world," is no joke. We are all governed by omnipotent fashion — a fashion that has exemplars and imitators. Fashion is a most imperious ruler; and the only way to get justice is to follow the fashion. Fashions, like politicians, keep "bobbing around" in such a metamorphosis, that it is difficult to keep consecutive trace of their changing hues and forms. Fashions range through three circles — the offensive, the absurd and the admirable. In the offensive, among other things, they filthily descend to street sweeping. In the absurd, skirts swell interminably over hoops, or are lost in flounces, while bonnets are hung upon balls of hair at the back of the head. In the admirable, woman appears the "visible angel" that she always should be, fragrant and smiling, like a beautiful flower, whose costume and color God has given in harmony with its character and sphere. In the empire of fashion, the leaders, high-priests and oracles — are few; but their influence how potent!

The Empress Eugenie says to herself, "Let the world of women put on a new bonnet." And forthwith the Queen of England, the Empress of Austria and Russia, and the Queen of Prussia, (all of whom look upon the *parvenue* Empress with mingled feelings of aversion, fear and contempt) bend in this matter to her authority. And not only they, but without the aid of government couriers to circulate it, heralds to proclaim it, or officers to enforce it, the silent edict is borne by steamboat, by railroad car, by stage coach, by pone express, to all parts of the earth; and all women, from the wives of our merchant-princes, who recognize no one for mistress, who are not the subjects of any, and who have never looked upon a superior, to the thousands who never heard of the name of Eugenie, hasten to render it prompt and willing obedience. Ladies' bonnets are very interesting things — not only to the dear creatures who wear them, or the lovers who glance under them with such bewildering anxiety, but also to the fathers and husbands who pay for the wonderful fashions.

There are inventors *des modes*, among all classes and trades, yet only a few in each branch who are capable of being leaders. There is, perhaps, no department of commerce in which fashion is more imperious than in Millinery and Dress-making. Among the leaders in this branch of industry in Chicago, there is none who is consulted more by the *elite* among our citizens than Mrs. CARY, at No. 90 Lake Street. Her importations are of the latest styles, her arrangements are such with leading establishments in New York, that every new article in her line, and every change in the fashions reach her within thirty-six hours after their arrival from Paris. Among some of the leading articles to be found at Mrs. Cary's we may mention, Straw Goods, Bonnets, Ribbons, Flowers, Laces, Velvets, Silks, Head-Dresses, Hoop Skirts, Superfine made Corsets, Dress Patterns in every variety, for ladies and children. Mrs. Cary keeping a large stock constantly on hand, is enabled to supply the trade with many articles at New York prices.

Mrs. Cary has recently had her store enlarged, and elegantly re-fitted up for the better accommodation of her rapidly increasing patrons.

In Chicago, there are about sixty Millinery establishments, employing about three hundred hands, and requiring a capital of about $175,000.

We have no extensive manufacturers in Chicago of Straw Goods, Artificial Flowers or Bonnet Frames; these are principally made in eastern cities. Many of the Bonnets sold in this city are those which have been made in eastern cities, there offered for sale until the fashion had changed, or about changing, and then sent to Chicago and other western cities and towns, and palmed off on the public as the latest styles. Ladies in purchasing Millinery articles should always consult some reliable dealer. The lady who wishes to dress fashionably, does not ask what *was* worn, but what *is*.

Mrs. Cary enjoys the fullest confidence of the public, and it gives us pleasure in making reference to her as the leader in fashion, in Millinery and Dress-making.

AMERICAN PROFICIENCY IN ILLUSTRATION.

WOOD ENGRAVING is an ancient art—long preceding the art of printing. The discovery—or invention shall we call it?—of the art of printing had already been anticipated by the Wood Engraver's art. Indeed, it may be said it was the Engraver who first suggested the use of wooden letters, as well as wooden blocks, in multiplying figures; for Faust called the Engraver (already in existence) to his aid in manufacturing his first "font" of types. It was not long after *book* illustration commenced ere the Graver's art became an art feature of each generation. For many years the *wood cut* has acted a most important part in art and literature, absorbing in its design and engraving, some of the best artistic and mechanical talent of the generations past; while for the present, it is its own best exponent. At this time some of the most unquestionable art genius of the age is laboring in this department, as their achievements fully attest.

"Illustrated *books*" and "illustrated advertisements" are as necessary as books themselves, or capital for conducting business successfully—for in many cases they are capital, and if expensive, are growing in popularity from day to day. It is no longer a question—will it add to the interest and value of a book to illustrate it well? —will it add to the value of an advertisement to be illustrated? That it will, is regarded as a matter of fact. In this city there has sprung up, during the last few years, a demand for a superior style of Wood Engraving, which called for the best powers and developed the highest capabilities of the art. Mr. Baker, in a grea degree, has supplied that demand, and as it increases, he is extending his facilities, until he has at the present time one of the most efficient establishments in this city.

His orders are received from every quarter of the North-West; for his reputation as a Wood Engraver is everywhere acknowledged.

The highest and most difficult range of Wood Engraving consists in landscape scenery, and historical pieces. Wood is capable of developing any effect which can be brought out of steel or copper, with the single exception, perhaps, of the mezzotint, which is neither prized nor appreciated, except by a practiced artistic eye.

Wood-Engraving is superior to a lithograph, or a work on copper or steel; first in the greater rapidity and economy with which they can be transferred, stereotyped, and put in various forms by which they can be multiplied *ad infinitum*, preserving the original work of the artist, which is never destroyed. Mr. Baker is one of the most enterprising and best Wood Engravers in the North-West. For several years, in this city, he has made himself a reputation for Wood Engraving second to no other artist.

His rooms are located on the north-east corner of Clark and Randolph Streets, opposite the Sherman House.

WHOLESALE GROCERIES.

THE wholesale Grocery business is now one of the most important branches of trade in this city. It dates its commencement about the year 1842. A great impetus was given to it by the opening of the Illinois and Michigan Canal in 1848, and it has steadily increased with the extension of the various lines of railroads into the interior, until it has now some thirty-five firms engaged in the business, (most of them on South Water Street,) doing a business amounting to probably over ten million dollars.

All goods in this line are sold at very low figures; no branch of trade in this city sells their goods at so small a margin over eastern prices or cost of manufacturing them as do the wholesale Grocery trade. The merchants engaged in this business are among the most reliable, active and enterprising men of our city; most of them have built themselves up from small beginnings, and have done much to enhance the welfare and prosperity of the community and state in which they live. A large capital is invested in this business, and the leading houses buy their goods for cash: this with the facilites they have of getting their freights from the sea-board at the lowest figuers at all seasons of the year (often as low as fifteen to twenty cents per one hundred pounds) enables them to lay down goods here and sell them at prices that will defy competition in any market.

Among the leading houses in this line of business stands the well known firm of Williams, Smith & Co., No. 45 South Water Street. This old and popular house has gained a high reputation with the trade, for its fairness and candor in dealing. The firm is composed of John C. Williams, Washington Smith, and Samuel Bliss, the senior partners being old and well known merchants in Chicago. The house was established by Mr. Williams, whose name stands first in the firm, in 1843, over nineteen years ago, and is now one of the oldest Grocery houses in the city.

They keep an extensive stock of both staple and fancy Groceries, comprising a greater variety than is usually found in wholesale houses. For the successful management of their large and increasing trade, they occupy the whole of one of the largest-class stores in the city, measuring one hundred and fifty feet deep, twenty-seven feet wide, and five stories high, with a cellar, making six entire floors, which are constantly filled with the various kinds of merchandise in their line. Their ample means, and long experience in the trade as buyers, enables them to compete with any house in the west; and the straight forward, honorable course in which they conduct their business has gained for their establishment the high and wide-spread reputation it sustains of *a first class house.*

They buy their goods for cash and sell them for cash, or on short time prompt pay. They give particular attention to the sale of Teas, and are the agents of the celebrated Joseph Allen's German Olive Erasive Soap, of which they sell large quantities, and is known for good in the household, throughout the west; and are also agents of Wolsey's English Saleratus, which for purity and strength takes the lead wherever it is once introduced. Merchants through the west can fall into no better hands than Williams, Smith & Co. in sending their orders by mail, or making purchases when in market themselves.

PAPER BOXES.

As civilization advances, and commerce extends her boundaries, just in proportion do the wants of the people increase for articles of luxury and utility. Only a few years ago, all the small articles in the Dry Goods, Millinery, Druggist and Fancy Goods business, were put up in paper packages. At the present day, if the manufacturer would compete with his rival in the same line of business, he finds it necessary to procure neat, and in most cases, elegant Boxes, in which to place his goods before the public for sale.

The demand for Boxes, for all purposes, renders the variety seemingly unlimited—Boxes for Fancy Hosiery and Gloves, Shoes and Parasols; Boxes for Shirts, Bosoms and Collars; Boxes for Artificial Flowers, Ruches and other Millinery goods; Boxes for Brushes and Combs; for Perfumery and Fancy Soaps; for Envelopes, Pencils and other Stationery; Confectionery Boxes, Jewelry Boxes, Pill Boxes, and Boxes for almost every fancy article that is presented to the public for sale. For any person who may have visited that gay Capital of the old world, to stroll through the shops and fancy stores on Lake street, might almost imagine they were again on the "Boulevard." All these different descriptions and varieties, from the commonest and cheapest up to the most elaborately ornamented, are made in this City, by Mr. Frederick Weigle, at No. 103 Lake Street, who served his apprenticeship to the business in Europe, and consequently is master of it. There are two or three other establishments in this city engaged in this business on a limited scale.

A description of Mr. Weigle's will illustrate the manufacture of the business. It consists of three floors in all; each one is appropriated to its own peculiar, separate and distinct operations. The first floor of this establishment, which is up one flight of stairs from the sidewalk, is chiefly occupied as a warehouse, counting-house, etc. On the next floor, the large Boxes, which require sewing, are made up and finished. In this, and in other rooms, are shears of various sizes and patterns, and machinery for cutting, with rapidity, pasteboards into the lengths and widths required. The next story is devoted to another description of work, and has machinery for a variety of purposes; such as cutting boards into circular pieces for tops and bottoms of round Boxes, machinery for scoring and cutting out the corners, preparatory to making square Boxes, etc.

The cheapness with which boxes can be made is remarkable. Some, of very neat appearance, can be made for about twelve cents per dozen; and yet each is made of several separate pieces, and each has to be many times handled, colored or fancy paper, labelled and packed; although most of the manipulations must be done by hand, yet within the last few years a great variety of machinery has been invented for the purpose, which gives increased facilities to the operations.

The Pasteboard is mostly obtained from New York and Pennsylvania, and costs, upon an average, sixty dollars per ton. The glazed and fancy papers, of which the consumption is considerable, are principally imported.

Mr. Weigle makes every description of Boxes, and not only supplies in part this City, but executes orders from other cities and towns in the West. Whenever a large order is given by our merchants and manufacturers for Paper Boxes, Mr. Weigle is the man sought for, on account of his facilities for producing, and integrity in business transactions. The whole business employs about twenty hands.

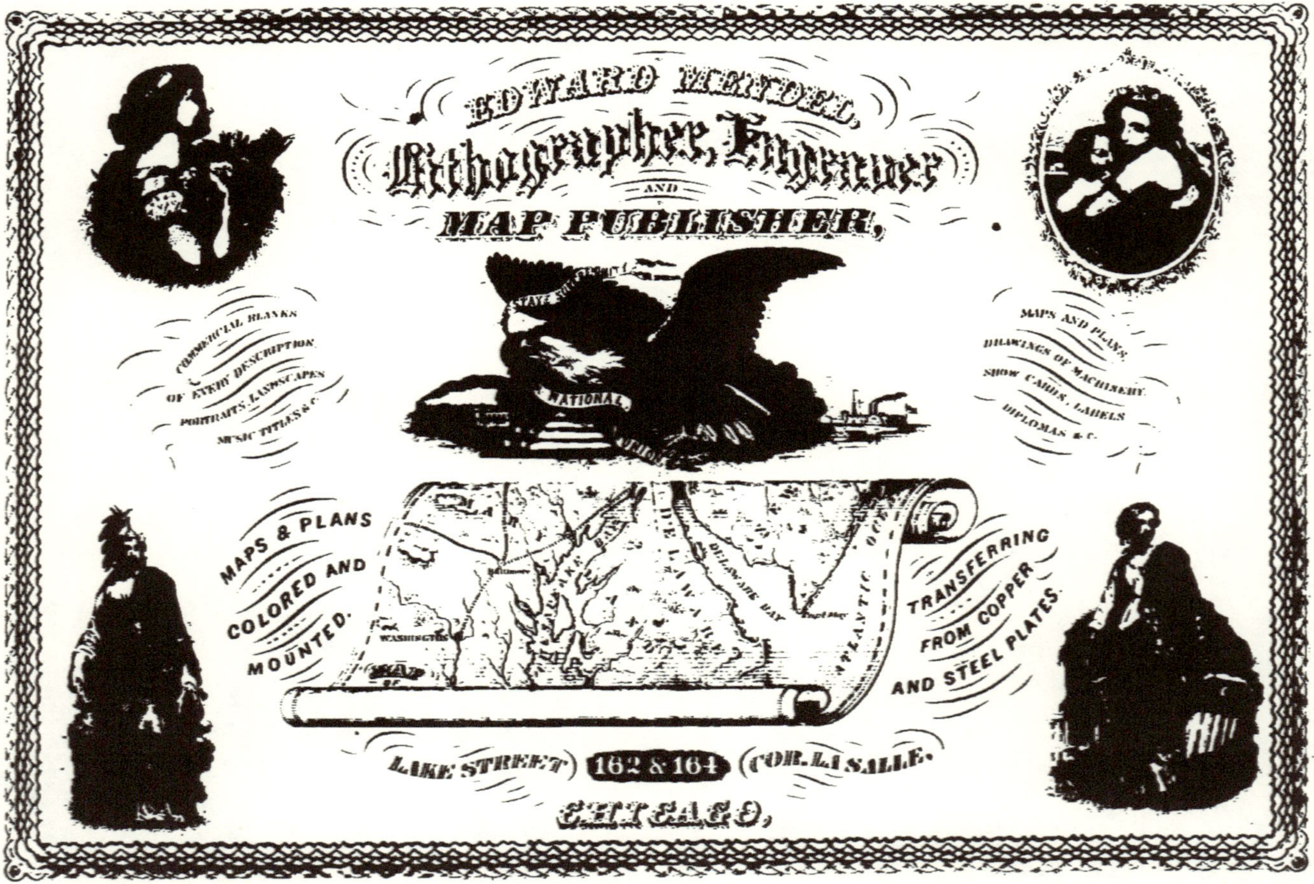
EDWARD MENDEL,
Lithographer, Engraver
AND
MAP PUBLISHER,
COMMERCIAL BLANKS
OF EVERY DESCRIPTION
PORTRAITS, LANDSCAPES
MUSIC TITLES &c.
NATIONAL
MAPS AND PLANS,
DRAWINGS OF MACHINERY
SHOW CARDS, LABELS
DIPLOMAS &c.
MAPS & PLANS
COLORED AND
MOUNTED.
DELAWARE
DELAWARE BAY
WASHINGTON
ATLANTIC OC
TRANSFERRING
FROM COPPER
AND STEEL PLATES.
LAKE STREET 162 & 164 COR. LA SALLE.
CHICAGO,

LITHOGRAPHY IN CHICAGO.

THE discoverer or rather inventor of this beautiful art was SENEFELDER, an actor at the Theatre Royal, Munich. This ornamental art, of so much service to the useful arts, is so nearly allied to engraving, that it might be treated as a branch thereof — being, in fact, engraving on stone, or surface engraving. The stone used, possesses in a high degree, calcareous qualities similar to limestone, and absorbs to a certain extent the only substances that are used to give the drawings sufficient adhesiveness to resist the friction of printing. These are Lithographic chalk, and Lithographic ink. They are composed of tallow, virgin wax, soap, shellac, and colored with lamp-black. The principal styles in Lithography, are *Linear and Crayon drawings, transfers on Stone from Steel or Copper-Plate engravings, Wood cuts, or from Lithographic drawings themselves.*

The art of Lithography has in no portion of the world been brought to greater perfection than in the United States, or perhaps we might, with perfect propriety, say in Chicago. This we owe in a great extent to Mr. EDWARD MENDEL, whose establishment occupies the two upper floors of Burch's Bank building, corner of LaSalle and Lake Street, who has executed some of the most impressive, beautiful, bold, and artistic works that have ever been produced by this process.

This establishment has been in operation in this city for the last twelve years; and is perhaps one of the most complete in all its departments on this continent. Mr. Mendel employs a capital exceeding $50,000, including presses, material, etc., furnishing employment to some forty or fifty hands in the several departments. They produce every description of printing, in colors and plain, Show Cards, Music, Title Pages, Landscape views, Lakes, Portraits, etc.; also, all kinds of Commercial Blanks, such as Notes, Drafts, Certificates of Stocks, and Deposits; Railroad, County and State Bonds, Diplomas for Agricultural Societies and Colleges, in fact everything pertaining to the art, may be found in process of production in this representative establishment of Mr. Mendel's. Having always employed the best art-talent in this department, he has produced work that has given to his name a popularity with Bankers, Insurance and Railroad organizations throughout the North-West, that is everywhere acknowledged and duly appreciated.

The great variety of specimens of Viguettes, and other embellishments, for every kind of bank and commercial purposes, renders it an easy matter for any person to select designs suitable for their purpose. As the cost of procuring new designs is expensive, it is a matter of consideration to have a choice selection to choose from, in point of expediency and economy.

There is, perhaps, no art which embraces within its range so great a variety of styles as Lithography. The productions of the pencil, the crayon and the graver, are all represented in the various methods of this useful and beautiful art. The word Lithograph, signifying writing upon stone, is a general term, including processes so entirely dissimilar as to require the employment of artists especially educated for the different branches or departments of the business; thus in the production of Commercial Blanks, the lettering, vignettes and other embellishments, are cut or engraved upon the stone by much the same process that is employed on copper and steel plate. The lettering for Maps is usually done by the same process. Other varieties of work are wrought upon the stone with a peculiar kind of pen, designed for the purpose; while large Pictures, such as Portraits, Landscapes, Views, and other varieties, are drawn with crayons upon the stone, and subseqnently so affixed by a chemical process, that impressions of the designs are obtained with the same facility as from an engraved surface. The designs for subjects requiring a variety of colors, are sometimes produced in this way; although in the finer class of color work, the design is wrought with the pen. Impressions are produced by a peculiar kind of press, designed especially for this purpose. Our limited space will not allow us to enter into full detail of all the various processes employed in the art, which rivals in one department the best efforts of the pencil and the crayon; and in another, bids fair to contend for suremacy with the proudest creations of Steel Plate Engraving, at a great reduction of cost.

A visit to the rooms of Mr. Mendel, by those who may be interested in these matters, will make them acquainted with all the facts pertaining to this art of so much utility and beauty.

SAIL LOFTS, ROPE, CORDAGE AND TWINE.

FEW great cities present such commercial attractions as Chicago, and few commercial houses represent so great and important an interest as the one of which this article will illustrate. Chicago is the commercial centre of the North-West, with a population, to-day, of more than nine millions of souls, which has sprung into existance, and developed the proportions for an empire, since the war of 1812, situated at the head of a vast chain of inland seas, upon which floats a marine of more than fifteen hundred vessels, with an aggregate of nearly four hundred thousand tonnage, employing more than eighteen thousand men. At the present time there are sixty-five more vessels on the stocks in process of building, many of these at the different ports on the shores of lake Michigan, and most of them, as is the case with most of the ship building on this lake, are supplied with their tackling by the leading commercial houses in this city. The principal and leading one is that of Messrs. GILBERT HUBBARD & Co., who occupy that massive iron structure of architectural grandeur, which will defy the desolation of time and the spoil of ages, located on the corner of South Water and Wells Streets. If the reputation they have already attained, for sagacious, careful and honorable merchants, shall continue as unsullied by the hand of time, as the iron building they occupy, long will they be proudly numbered with merchant princes. The importance of a great house of this character located in Chicago, and the extent of their trade is significant of the rapidly developing marine interest of our inland seas.

This house have the largest and best selected stock of all the various articles in their line, of any establishment in the North-West, which they furnish the trade at prices comparing favorably with New York or Boston houses.

Among other articles may be found, Twines, Cordage, Manilla and Tarred Rope, Sail, Duck, Bags, Bagging and Burlaps, Wool, Seine and Gill Net Twines, Nets and Seines, Oakum, Tar, Pitch, Paints, Oils, Chains, Anchors, Tackle Blocks, etc., etc. Coal-Tar, Roofing-Pitch and Felting, Awnings, Banners, Flags and Ensigns, always on hand, and made to order.

Their long experience makes them masters of the business in all its minute details, as most of the sailing masters of the upper lakes can attest; their large capital enables them to produce the best articles at the lowest price.

The term Cordage usually comprehends all the various sizes of rope, cords, twines, lines, etc. The materials of which they are manufactured are Manilla, Russian, Italian and American hemp; and for fishing cords, and twines, cotton, flax, and the best qualities of Linen thread. Manilla hemp is the fibrous inner bark of a species of plantain, growing in the Phillipine Islands, whence it is imported into this country. The American used, is grown chiefly in Missouri and Kentucky. A considerable amount of Russian hemp is also used, and *Jute* is now employed to a considerable extent, in the manufacture of cords, bagging, etc. This firm represents every article of cordage, from the finest fishing line to the largest cable used, and every conceivable article used in the rigging of a vessel. During the last few months they have been giving employment to one hundred hands, in manufacturing Tents, Camp Bedsteads, Flags, Banners, and other camp and naval articles, for the armies of the West, and inland navy. Many of the articles in their line are manufactured in the eastern states.

CONFECTIONERY.

THE word Confectioner and the term Confectioneries occur in the Scriptures in a form denoting that the making of sweet preparations was an established art in the time of Samuel. The business of preparing them, however, it seems, was then and until two centuries ago, confined to Physicians and Apothecaries, who used honey or sugar, principally for disguising disagreeable medicines, and pharmaceutically in making syrups, electuaries, etc. We presume that the separation which has taken place between the arts of preparing the conserves and the compounding of drugs, was originally instigated by the ladies or the juveniles, both of whom, like saucy boarders, prefer their flies on a separate plate.

The manufacture of Confectionery, in its modern development, as practiced in England and the United States, bears the distinctive artistic characteristics of French ingenuity and invention. In no other country does the preparation of sugar, as a luxury, absorb so much mental attention, and afford a livelihood to so many persons. In Paris more than two thousand persons find regular employment in making confectioner's fancy boxes, the most of which are distributed on New Year's day.

The manufacturing of Confectionery in Chicago, has become an extensive business. There are some twelve or fifteen wholesale manufacturing establishments. Of these, the firm of SCANLAN & BRO., No. 138, South Water Street, is one of the oldest and most extensive houses in Chicago. Their facilities are such as to enable them to keep always on hand a large supply and full assortment. In most instances they know who will probably be the purchaser of their candy, and therefore take pains to have it pure and first-rate in quality, regarding more their well earned reputation, than an excess of profit. There are nearly one hundred retailers of Confectionery in this city, most of whom are supplied by the few regular manufactories. There are a few that operate in the finer branches of Ices, Jellies, *Pieces Montees*, etc., to a large extent.

As our Chicago ladies, like all others of refinement, are emulous of whatever will lend enchantment to the personal charms, we will suggest to *them*, and also to the confectionery manufacturer, a preparation in great favor with the Turkish ladies, from its alleged property of developing those proportions of figure, which, in that refined country, are deemed a most essential attribute of female beauty. It is known as *Rahatlocoum*, and is of the most agreeable flavor, and composed of the following innocent materials; one part of wheat starch, six parts of sugar, and twelve parts of water, and formed into an elastic jujube-like mass; sometimes boiled Almonds are mixed with it.

The Messrs. Scanlan commenced the manufacture of Confectionery here several years ago. From the smallest beginnings, the business has grown into an extent and importance even beyond their most sanguine expectations. The cash system was adopted in the outset, and has never been departed from. It is found to work in all respects satisfactorily; enabling them to sell their goods at less price. Their establishment is at No. 138 South Water Street; it is five stories high. They give employment to twenty-five hands.

THE OIL AND LAMP TRADE.

THERE are few things in the industrial and scientific world at the present time, more remarkable than Petroleum, and the various uses of great utility it is made to subserve; and yet its multiform uses are just beginning to be developed. That great lakes of this valuable substance should have lain a few feet beneath the surface undisturbed for ages, is one among innumerable proofs, that the intelligence of civilization is required to enable man to bring to light and render available the natural resources of the planet which we inhabit. Petroleum has just begun to play the great part which it is destined to fill in the industrial arts. It produces the *whitest*, *best* and *cheapest* of all artificial lights.

Among the several firms in this city, engaged in the sale of Petroleum, or Kerosene Oil, we know of none who are devoting more attention to secure the best qualities, as well as the extensive Jobbing trade of Chicago, than Mr. JAMES F. GRIFFIN, who has recently removed from No. 165 Randolph Street, to that more central and eligible store, corner of Randolph and State Streets. Having a large capital invested, and unusual facilities for procuring the best Oils, he is thereby enabled to take the lead of this immense and rapidly developing business in Chicago.

Science and invention seem to be contributing more to the development of Kerosene as an illuminator than for any other purpose. The rapidly increasing demand for Kerosene as an illuminator, and the best arranged burner for using it, has called forth some of the best inventive talent, which has at last produced burners so arranged as to dispense entirely with the use of chimneys, burning the oil perfectly without smoke or smell, and producing an excellent light. This burner is of small expense, and may be readily adjusted to an ordinary lamp. It is sold by Mr. Griffin, to the trade or at retail. The greatest expense and trouble connected with burning

Coal and Petroleum Oil, arises from the frequent breaking of lamp chimneys. These are made of clear white glass, and are as brittle as a pipe-stem. By a recent improvement, they are now made of flint glass, which renders them durable, and of a different shape, which utilizes the light—producing a greater amount, without any additional consumption of oil. These, among many other improvements of recent origin, which we have not the space here to enumerate, that render Kerosene Oil the cheapest, best, safest and most brilliant luminator of all artificial lights, are to be found at the store of Mr. Griffin.

So great has become the demand for the various metal fixtures pertaining to Kerosene Oil Lamps, that dealers have been unable to supply the demand. Mr. Griffin has commenced their manufacture in this city, thereby adding another branch to our home industry. This house seems to comprehend the wants of the public, and possesses not only the capital necessary, but the enterprise, to strike out into new fields of discovery, to render this a leading representative business in Chicago, whose influence will be felt throughout the North-West. Those engaged in the trade will be enabled to order from this house at prices less than those of Eastern establishments. Their new place of business — the most central location in Chicago — affords facilities for conducting an extensive business. Every article pertaining to artificial light, embracing all the modern improvements, may be found here at the lowest prices, at retail or for the trade.

Since writing the above, we have been shown another article, just patented, and manufactured by Mr. Griffin, known as *Erwin's Patent Kerosene, Lard, or Sperm Oil Lantern.* It is the most important and useful Railroad Lantern yet introduced. Nearly all the principal railroads are adopting them as fast as they can be manufactured. This Lantern burns Kerosene, Lard, or Sperm Oil, with perfect combustion, without the use of a chimney; and cannot be extinguished by any of the usual railroad signal motions, or by a strong current of air or high wind. It is so arranged that whatever motion may be given it, the flame is always supplied with oxygen in sufficient quantities to prevent its smoking or being extinguished. This result is attained by horizontal and perpendicular flanges, placed in the air passage beneath the flame, to direct the current of air in such a manner as to produce the result claimed, of perfect combustion. The value of this Lantern for the great railroad interest cannot be over-estimated. It is the only lantern made that cannot be extinguished by any motion whatever. The price does not exceed that of a a first-class Lantern. The *Chicago Bell Hanger's Lamp*, manufactured by this same house, on the same principle as the Lantern, with the exception of requiring a small glass chimney, can be carried as a hand lamp from room to room, or even in the open air, without the least danger of smoking or breaking the glass.

Mr. Griffin has recently imported from Bohemia, and is now introducing in this market, a superior article of Lamp Chimney, possessing rare qualities for resisting heat and pressure, far more durable, and as cheap as the common American glass.

PAPER HANGINGS.

DECORATIVE Paper Hangings came into use about the middle of the sixteenth century, and are said to have been copied from the Celestials. The manufacture of them in this country, however, only dates about thirty years ago. The progress made in design and elaboration of workmanship, has been so rapid that now the importation of foreign papers is an unimportant item — said to be not more than five per cent. of the whole amount consumed, and confined to French goods of the first quality, which the French artists have brought to perfection.

Few persons are familiar with the extent of the manufacture of decorative Paper Hangings, and still fewer realize the power of their embellishment. For although most designs are only fragments of architectural drawings, yet there are those of high artistic merit, truthful delineations of nature. The walls of a house may be lined with statuary — with marble or with oak — may be embellished with pictures of landscape scenery — summer heat may be cooled with grand illustrations of Arctic scenery — winter's cold, warmed by the brilliancy of tropic vegetation — classic cartoons may surround us with the old Greek Gods and fables, at a far less expense through the craft of the paper-hanger, than from the artist's brush. The price of Paper Hangings vary from one cent to ten dollars a square yard, and form a part of the interior decoration of the humble cottage, as well as the palatial mansion. A few years ago wall paper was kept on sale only by Dry-Goods dealers, Oil and Paint establishments, etc. At the present time, it is a representative branch of commerce, and becoming a very important one.

A visit to the Paper Hanging establishment of Mr. E. G. L. FAXON, at No. 70 Lake Street, will give a fair representation of the immense scope of variety — the genius and labor that strikes the eye and kindles the fancy of this branch of luxurious commerce conducted by this house. Mr. Faxon commenced business in Chicago in 1855, since when his business has steadily increased, gradually extending over the entire North-West, until it has become the most extensive, perhaps, of any establishment in the valley of the West. The interior arrangement of his store has recently been remodeled — sky-lights introduced, and other improvements, with special reference to the convenience of visitors, and an artistic display of his goods. Neither the recluse scholar, the staid matron of a well ordered household, nor the radiant bride furnishing a new home, can call for a style or color, but it unrolls to the eye, as if it were summoned by the wand of enchantment.

The process of manufacturing Paper Hangings we will briefly illustrate, as we have not the space for a general detail of the process. The paper comes from the mill in rolls about twelve hundred yards long, and from twenty to thirty-five inches wide; costing from nine to fourteen cents per pound, the average being about eleven cents. The pattern first having been carefully drawn, is then pricked, and the outlines of the various tints are punched each on a separate wood block made of pear tree, mounted with pine. These blocks are pressed on the sieves of color and then applied to the paper, each block then following the other on the guide-marks left by the previous impression. An idea may be formed of the enterprise and labor required to produce decorative Paper Hangings, when we state that on a single one of these representing a chase in a forest, including the animals, birds, and attributes of the chase, exhibited at the World's Fair, twelve thousand blocks were employed.

In making *Flock Paper* the pattern is first printed in size, and then with a preparation of varnish or Japan gold size. When this is partly dry, colored flock, prepared from wools, is sifted on the varnish pattern, to which it adheres. When gilding is introduced, the leaf-metal is laid on the varnish pattern, or if worked in bronze-powder, it is brushed over with a hare's foot. The designs are principally original, and are largely supplied by the Female School of Design, which has made important contributions towards elevating the standard of correct taste.

The Window Shade department connected with this house, forms no inconsiderable part of its business. It has become an important department of art and commerce. We have reached a period of wealth and independence, and nothing which embellishes life, or adds splendor to its existence, is beyond the ambition or the taste of our people.

In the soft climes of the South, where sultry heats are enlivened by few breezes, the most delicate muslins are used to drape the doors and windows of habitations. In the frozen North, where the desolation of arctic winters comes down from the pole, they close up their windows, that even the eye may not rest always upon the chill, cold iceberg. But in our fortunate temperate zone, and especially in America, we have a drapery for our windows most appropriate for the seasons and most grateful to the fancy. The light and ornamented Window Shades now in universal use, soften most delicately to the eye, the intense light of our unclouded sun. They admit the air to breathe freely through every department; and while we shut out brick walls and heated pavements, with endless streams of rolling vehicles, they offer to the eye the sweetest scenes of nature, delineated in arabesque loveliness.

Mr. Faxon has recently added another very important branch of trade to his business — that of Mattresses and Bedding; being thoroughly versed in every branch of its manufacture. In looking through his show-rooms, we were shown a Spring Mattress of a new style of manufacture, so arranged that a child might handle it with ease, for adjusting and cleaning — obviating one of the greatest difficulties and objections hitherto found in handling heavy mattresses. They are *warranted* to keep in repair for two years, but with careful use, would probably last twelve or fifteen years. In connection with Mattresses, he makes to order and keeps on hand a full supply of fine Bedding, manufactured from the best materials. Mattresses of Hair, Spring, Cotton, Husk, Sea-Grass, etc; also Feather Beds, Bolsters, Pillows, Bed Linen, Comforters, Spreads, etc., in lots to suit purchasers, at Wholesale or Retail.

Mr. Faxon's Store is at 70 Lake, near State Street.

METAL WAREHOUSE.

IN no department of commerce is Chicago more favorably represented than in her rapidly developing Iron interest. The house of VANDERVOORT, DICKERSON & Co., represent one of the most extensive firms, probably the heaviest importers, of Tin Plate, Tinners' stock, and Sheet Iron Ware, in the North-West.

The house of Thomas Dickerson was established in this city in 1858, in Burch's Iron Block, corner of Wabash Avenue and Lake Street. The demand for metals became so great, that in the spring of 1862, Mr. Dickerson admitted as partners into the concern Messrs. P. H. and P. H. S. Vandervoort, when the business was removed to its present location, No. 199 and 201 Randolph Street, one of the most eligible and extensive warehouses in the city.

Few persons pass this store on Randolph Street without having their attention attracted to an elegant clock placed in a circular window in the second story, some five or six feet in diameter, erected by the liberality of this house, which is intended to be an infallible regulator of the time of this city; since, till the present hour, the city of Chicago has never been furnished with a reliable clock by the Common Council. This clock whose hands point infallibly to the hour and the minute, runs eight days. It is a Turret Regulator.

The business of this establishment has grown into an extent and importance that Chicagoans must recognize with pride and pleasure, while they award due honor to the integrity and business capacity of the men who represent it.

Tin Plate is extensively used in America, and all our supply is furnished by England. We are the best customers of tin ware which England has, consuming even more than all Great Britain. Tin-Plate consists of sheet iron rolled out to various degrees of thinness, and coated on both sides with a layer of tin, which forms with the iron an alloy uniting the useful qualities of both metals. The process of tinning iron is not the same in all establishments; some manufacturers affect a good deal of mystery upon the subject; still the methods pursued agree pretty nearly in all essential points. There are some twenty different qualities in common use, distinguished by certain marks attached to the boxes. This metal is worked up by the tin plate worker, into a great variety of articles of culinary or domestic use; within a few years a great revolution has been effected in the manufacture of tin-ware by the introduction of machinery. By the aid of Dies, Presses, Lathes, and other contrivances, the separate parts, or the whole, according to the degree of complexity of an article, are at once struck up in the required shape, plain or with devices, as may be desired, and the work of tin ware is reduced to the simple act of soldering or uniting the several parts. A great deal of work is done by stamping.

Few persons are aware of the enormous expense and difficulties attending the importation of Russia sheet iron into this country, and the quantity consumed. The uses to which this iron is applied are mainly in the manufacture of Stoves, the difference in its favor, in point of durability, being very great. The imitations that have been attempted in this country, have been hitherto so unsuccessful that a field of discovery lies still open in this department, in which some future inventor will yet, doubtless, realize a princely fortune. A large amount of *American* Russia Iron is sold for genuine, the imitation, in outward appearance, being so close, as almost to defy detection by any other than an experienced judge. Therefore the satisfaction in dealing with a firm of the established reputation of Vandervoort, Dickerson & Co. It is only necessary for them to say that an article is genuine, for the public to have faith in the quality. The imitation in this iron has been very complete, but the art of making it wear and not oxidize from exposure to dampness is still to American manufacturers a hidden secret. The indestructible quality of the Russia-made sheet iron is really extraordinary. We have seen stoves manufactured of it which have been in use for a period of thirty years.

This firm also represents the western agency of HOWE'S IMPROVED SCALES AND BALANCES. Messrs. Howe, of Brandon, Vt., claim to have no superiors in the manufacture of Scales, and they certainly enjoy a world-wide reputation, for their Scales are becoming everywhere popular. Eminence in this branch of manufacture, we are quite sensible, presupposes, in the manufacturer, very considerable mechanical skill, fidelity in execution, and taste, and accuracy in workmanship. Their manufactures comprise Mint Balances, Bankers' Scales, Jewelers', Druggists', Grocers', Confectioners' Scales, etc., in fact any kind required for weighing purposes. These manufacturers have recently invented some modification in their celebrated Scale, which adapts it especially to army use, rendering it exceedingly compact, holding its movable parts in a very firm manner, and boxing the whole very securely to prevent injury in camp or in transporting. It is now being introduced in the army and securing for HOWE'S SCALES that notoriety which is becoming world-wide. Messrs. Vandervoort, Dickerson & Co. are at No. 199 and 201 Randolph Street, opposite the Metropolitan Hotel.

MELODEONS.

ONE of the most powerful civilizers is Music. Let a house be ever so lonely, sordid, unhappy, and music will send the evil spirit away, and make smiles play upon the very walls. The world is all astir with music. Let a community be well supplied with Pianos or Melodeons, and a visitor requires no higher evidence of its high intelligence and excellence. That refined communities prosper, in a material point of view, more than those where the refining influence of music and education are less regarded, is a well-conceded fact.

We mention the Melodeon as a chief evidence of refinement, not that we underrate the piano, or the harp, o'er which the fingers of beauty sweep, but the Melodeon is now often found in homes of humble pretensions. Its more moderate price does not restrict it from many a home circle; and then its tones are so deep and solemn — so impressive — so organ-like — the peculiarity of its touch — the instantaneous speaking of each note, the moment the finger touches the key — being adapted to the more rapid execution of secular composition. It produces those grand effects which charm, bewilder, and answer to all our requisitions for musical expression and interpretation. It has thus come to be regarded as the most popular of musical instruments, and in its unique excellence, certainly is not likely to be superseded by any instrument extant.

The most deservedly popular instrument of this description, is that manufactured by Prince & Co., at Buffalo, N. Y. This establishment, which is the oldest in the United States, was established in 1848, since when they have manufactured twenty-seven thousand of these famed instruments, which have been sent to nearly every part of the civilized globe. They are to be found not only in America, but also in Europe, Australia, India, and even the islands of the ocean.

The Manufactory of Messrs. Prince, is one of the representative establishments of our country. The "Buffalo Commercial Advertiser" thus speaks of it: The building is a handsome brick structure, erected by Prince & Co., occupying nearly half an entire block, being five stories in height.

The lumber, prior to going into the shops, is thoroughly kiln-dried, a process insuring perfect instruments, and which will stand any climate. If there is a crevice in a board, it is cut out and jointed up. Outside, there are piles of lumber in the open air and under sheds. The woods used are principally ash, maple, cherry, white and basswood.

There are usually two hundred men employed in this, the largest and finest Melodeon manufactory in the world, whose business extends to the extremes of civilization, wherever music is known and instruments are desired to produce harmonious sounds.

When the reeds come from the factory, they pass into the hands of the tuners, who file them to the proper tone and fit them to the instruments. They make eleven sizes of instruments, ranging in price from $40 to $350. The cheapest instrument is just as well finished as the best, the difference being simply in their capacity. In volume and purity of tone, they have no competitors, and at the various exhibitions of industrial products, have invariably taken precedence and the prizes.

Steadily this enterprising establishment have continued on their course, increasing their facilities to supply the rapidly increasing demand, adding new improvements from time to time, until Prince & Co.'s Melodeons are of world-wide reputation.

The latest improvement in their Melodeon, is the "IMPROVED VALVE, OR PALLET," being a combination of cloth and leather, prepared expressly for the purpose. It is found to be the very thing needed as a substitute for the "India Rubber Valve," which had been in general use since Melodeons have been manufactured, and which have caused so much trouble by the *dissolving* and *sticking* of the "India Rubber." All their instruments are furnished with improved valves, and can be recommended with confidence.

Also the "Divided Swell," secured by Letter's Patent, 22d May, 1855. By means of this Swell, solo passages may be played with the full power of the instrument, while the accompaniment is soft and subdued. All Melodeons now made by them are furnished with this attachment, *without extra charge.*

Prince is himself the inventor of most of the improvements in these instruments. As they are the pioneers and leading manufacturers of Melodeons in the world, they have, of course, the advantage of securing the services of the best mechanics in the business; and many of their workmen have been with them since they commenced the manufacture of Melodeons.

These Melodeons have the unqualified commendation of musical men everywhere, as of great excellence for schools, families and churches. The almost universal use of these favorite Musical Instruments abundantly attests their superiority, while the increasing demand proves that they are becoming still more popular. To keep pace with the demand they find it difficult, although their facilities for doing so are constantly increasing.

Messrs. Prince & Co. for many years have had a branch house in New York and one in Chicago, for the better accommodation of the great demand for these instruments.

Prince & Co.'s Melodeons have achieved a reputation throughout the civilized world as unique as our Photographers; and at the very head of the art of their manufacture stands Mr. George A. Prince. So perfect have these Melodeons at last been made by this firm, that they have offered to the world — on a fair forfeit, by any who accepts the challenge, — to give their best instrument to whoever will produce one to excel it. Their Branch Depot in Chicago, for supplying the trade, and also for retail, has been removed to 43 Lake Street, in Burch's Iron Block.

DSITILLATION OF PERFUMES AND COIFFEUR.

THE French have distinguished themselves above all other nations in the manufacture of perfumes and articles of utility and taste for the toilet. Lubin and other Parisian Perfumers have acquired a world-wide reputation in this elegant and important department of art. The impression has also gone through the world, that with the single exception perhaps, of the article of Cologne, all attempts to rival the Parisians would only prove hopeless. But as it has been left to the United States to demonstrate so many other things that have never proved true before, so it seems to have been left to us to show that there is no more difficulty in distilling the most exquisite and choice perfumes in this country. Hudson, under the Sherman House, on Clark Street, who is known as an ornamental Hair, Wig and Toupee manufacturer, and who has expended more time, talent and money upon his art than most Americans, after a series of most satisfactory experiments, determined to manufacture perfumes, having already ascertained that they could be produced here in the same perfection as in Paris. He procured from Paris, while a resident of St. Louis, some of the most accomplished and experienced of chemists, who are perfect masters of their business; and the result was attended with complete success. The successful establishment in the United States of the manufacture of the finest perfumes known in the world, is hailed with great satisfaction, and there are many reasons why it should be so. The exceedingly volatile and delicate character of fine distillations renders it next to impossible to transport them far, especially by sea, without some sacrifice of their original qualities. Owing, also, to the great popularity of foreign Perfumes, their labels are everywhere falsified, and it has become almost impossible to procure, in this country, a bottle of the best perfumes of Europe. Nearly all that are represented as European are put up in Philadelphia, and sold for foreign Perfumes.

Hudson stands pre-eminent among the Coiffeurs and Wig-makers in the West. No civilized nation bestows so little attention on the cultivation and arrangement of the hair as the Americans. With the one sex, it is generally thought to be enough to comb smoothly, and twist up behind with some expensive comb. With the other, to dash through with a brush, or dressing comb, leaving it to arrange itself for the rest of the day. Little care is taken in purifying the head; there is an indiscriminate use of dyes, and we every where see the consequences. Our hair turns gray, grows thin and falls earlier than any other people; the hair dye destroys the beauty and texture of the hair forever. Hudson remedies all this. *Les elegantes* of our fashionable world depends on his skill and taste, for not only the most delicious and *recherche* perfumes — but for Toupees, Wigs, Curls, Braids, and every texture, shade and arrangement of hair. *Combs, Brushes, Fancy Soaps, and Toilet articles*, form a part of his stock. There are several hair dressers and wig-makers in Chicago, but Hudson may be called the leader. His store is corner of Clark and Randolph Streets, in the basement, under the Sherman House.

LUXURIOUS BEDS.

THIS is an age of luxury, and well it may be, for a nation of working men are walking on a continent of gold. Mankind not only love good living and the refinements of civilized society, but also the luxury of repose. Nothing makes one in better humor with himself and "the rest of mankind," than a comfortable bed and refreshing sleep — to obtain which the bed is an indispensable requisite. The soldier may live through his campaigns, sleeping on the ground, or on a "soft plank," that offers its scanty accommodations for his acceptance; the prisoner in his cell feels thankful for his pallet of straw, and the rover is content with his blanket; yet it is not probable that either would select these modes in preference to the modes of more refined life. From the earliest period, men have bestowed much attention on the appliances of the couch and the bed chamber. In the year 1782, says Hoyne's Every-day Book, that extraordinary empiric of modern times, Dr. Graham, appeared in London. He was a graduate of Edinburgh. He opened a mansion in Pall Mall, called "The Temple of Health." The rooms were superbly furnished. Among other articles of furniture in this temple was a *celestial bed,* which he pretended wrought miraculous effects on those who reposed on it. He demanded for its use during one night *one hundred pounds;* and such was the folly of wealth, that several persons of high rank acceded to his terms. This brings us to speak of a *celestial bed* that the writer of this article reposes on in the year 1862; doubtless outrivaling, in point of luxury and health, the one spoken of, in Dr. Graham's Temple of Health, and at somewhat of a reduction in point of cost, for such an inestimable luxury. The miraculous effect it nightly produces upon our wearied body, is to our mind the best evidence of its great merit, for its *comfort, durability* and *cheapness.* The bed we refer to is of recent invention, and now, for the first time, being introduced to the Chicago public, by Mr. H. S. Huntington, at No. 172 Clark Street. It is known as B. F. S. Monroe's Improved Spiral Spring Bed Bottom and Mattress.

Few men have lived, who, by a single, simple invention, have acquired in so short a time, so handsome a fortune as the patentee of this Improved Spiral Spring Bed Bottom and Mattress. It is, wherever introduced, acknowledged to be the most perfect, and every way desirable bed in use. It has been subjected to the severest test and criticism. No one who has tried one feels satisfied without being the owner of one. The price comes within the reach of the man of moderate means. They are recommended by physicians and others for their combined advantages, which no other Spring Bed or Mattress offers — healthfulness, comfort, cleanliness, convenience, labor-saving, durability, economy and beauty. The springs are so arranged that they are not liable to get out of order; and the longer they are in use the more elastic they become. The springs are not in the Mattress, but underneath, and so arranged that each spring receives an equal pressure. The Bed Bottom, embracing the Springs, protected with a canvas covering, is sold with or without the Mattress, which may be made of the best curled hair, or of a substance known as rattan shavings, which is preferred by many persons for its airiness and lightness, being more healthy to sleep on than hair.

Mr. Huntington is offering them for sale, by the single one or to the trade — also, Territorial rights.

THE FASHIONABLE COSTUMER.

BEFORE the Atlantic was bridged by steam, and the telegraphs had annihilated distance, the devotees of fashion on this continent were obliged to wait with patience for the fickle winds to waft the old packets to our shores. From the time of Louis XIV., nobody had the audacity to question the right of Frenchmen to rule the fashions of the earth, until within the last few years. Formerly, American gentlemen who were particular in their dress, sent to Paris for coats, vests, pantaloons and cloaks; but we have now the best tailors in the world; and in Chicago, one of the best on this continent. Mr. EDWARD ELY, No. 9 Tremont Block, has been artistically educated in the school of fashion for gentlemen's wear, and has not only made it a business of life, but has been a student of art, in which he has cultivated the most refined taste for clothing "the human form divine." To him is accredited the "Leader of Fashion," in that department of trade for Chicago. Having always on hand the best selected and most fashionable stock of English and French goods — employing none but French or French-educated workmen — devoting his whole time and best energies for the highest development of the art, and benefit of his patrons; it is not a matter of surprise that he should control nearly all the best trade in this branch of industry in Chicago. Nearly all his work is made for regular customers, who are so well suited that they never go anywhere else. One unvarying price, the latest style, the best material, absolute precision, promptness and accuracy, have given to Mr. Ely a rank in his business which has been attained by few.

Beyond question, one of the most satisfactory things to a man of taste and refinement, is a garment that fits the person. The fabric may be coarse, or even threadbare, yet if fashionably made, and well fitted, it covers up a multitude of deformities.

Mr. Ely's stock of Cloths, Cassimeres and Vestings, is selected with great care from importers of French and English goods. He also has one of the most complete assortments of choice Furnishing Goods, where a gentleman may obtain any article required to supply his wardrobe in the most luxurious manner.

The manufacture of Shirts and Shirt Collars, although a distinct, organized and extensive branch of industry, yet Mr. Ely's arrangements are such that he stands among the best in this department of manufacture, giving constant employment to a large number of persons. These Shirts are well made, and range in price from $24 to $60 per dozen. The manufacture of Shirt Collars and Bosoms, is often a business disconnected from that of Shirts, and has attained a rapid development since the introduction of sewing and stitching machines. Hand-needle work would be totally incapable of meeting the demand. Besides, the machines perform with more uniformity and durability than is possible by hand, and relieves females of the most laborious, unhealthy, and least lucrative portion of the work.

About ten years ago, Mr. Ely came to this city with a small stock of goods, employing two persons, and occupied a store in the block of low wooden buildings which formerly stood on Dearborn street, opposite the Tremont House, where now rises in architectural beauty, the substantial block known as "Dickey's Building," from which place he removed to his present location, No. 9 Tremont Block, where for the last six years he has been making patrons, who rely upon his judgment, and are governed by his suggestions in the style of their dress. Steadily has he pursued his onward course, gathering strength, reputation, friends and fortune, until now he stands at the head of his profession, dictating the fashions of the North-West. His entire stock of rich and fashionable goods are selected with great care, from the best importations, and purchased entirely for *cash*, which enables him to sell *cheap*, and for *cash only*.

COMEDY IN CHICAGO.

McVICKER has domesticated Comedy among us. He alone has been successful in making it a constant, never-failing, permanent amusement. Others have made the attempt, but every such attempt witnessed a failure. McVICKER'S THEATRE is devoted to Tragedies, Comic Drama, Operas, and Grand Concerts. From the night it was opened, October, 1857, with the exception of about seven weeks, it has always been filled — always been kept open to the public, in successful operation; and although other theatres in the West, with the excitement and parade of actors of celebrity, and taking scenic effects, have sometimes witnessed successful runs for a season, yet no theatre, perhaps, in this country, has, for a series of years, been so uniformly well attended, nor by such intelligent audiences. Nothing has ever been badly done by McVICKER; the public never have been disappointed in any of the representations of his Theatre. He has not only had, in the long run, the best comic company of any Western theatre, but his own genius for representation is unrivaled. Take him all in all, he is the most effective, irresistible Comedian our stage has ever had. Aside from his native genius and blood-felt love of Comedy, he possesses unfailing resources in his intellectual acquirements. He commenced histrionic pursuits in New Orleans, at the St. Charles Theatre, in 1841. In May, 1847, he left St. Louis for New York, via Chicago, on a tour of pleasure and observation. While here he was favorably impressed with the city and the people, and settled here for life. He became stage manager of Mr. J. B. Rice's Chicago Theatre, which was first located on Randolph street. It was destroyed by fire, but subsequently rebuilt on Dearborn street.

Mr. McVicker learned the history of the Drama of America; he studied the causes of its failures and successes, in this great Valley of the West. When the present magnificent structure was erected, known as McVicker's Theatre, covering an area of eighty-two by one hundred and ninety feet, at an expense of eighty thousand dollars, besides the scenic and interior fittings, which cost some twenty thousand dollars more, he became its master, and started out with the resolute purpose of establishing the

Comic Drama as a permanent institution and amusement among our people. With him histrionic art was idolatry. Mr. McVicker has from the first, while giving to the public first-class "stars," so guided his representations, especially of the modern Comedies and farces, he has so put his pieces on the stage, and so perfectly adapted them to his characters, and the characters to them, that each part seemed almost equally attractive — for each one was completely filled.

Under such auspices his Theatre has flourished. The owner of his Theatre, and complete master of it and all its arrangements, Mr. McVicker has always developed the talents of every member of his company, with a generous disposition not only to give fair play to all, but to each one a fair opportunity to distinguish himself. The great scope of his efforts seems invariably to have been *the simple delineation of human nature.* His own acting is always characteristic; for it is like himself, and unlike anybody else. He not only carries the standard of impersonation further than most Comedians, but in the modern Comedies he adds appropriately to the familiar parts — without injustice or injury to the author — happy strokes, that bear upon the excitements and topics of the day; and honest country people have often gone away with the impression that he made up his part as he went along. And in fact, these simple country people are nearly right in this supposition; for McVicker so easily and unaffectedly blends his actions and feelings with the characters he impersonates, that the most constant *habitue* of the Theatre is left with nearly the same impression. That overflowing of human nature always witnessed on his stage, in all his plays, breathes an atmosphere through his theatre that is indescribably charming. "One touch of nature makes us all akin."

These qualities have made McVicker's Theatre what no other in this Western country has ever been — *a familiar home, drawing-room and family circle.* Here is the secret of its unparalleled success. There is no place, perhaps, in this city, where are witnessed such a constant succession of smiles and laughter — of intellectual and inspiring amusement, and often the unbidden gushings of genuine feeling.

ROOFING.

THE importance of a good Roof cannot well be over-estimated; and in a great city, the selection of a material that is *Fire Proof,* as well as Water Proof, seems to be a duty which a builder owes to the public. Shingles, of course, from their combustible nature, if for no other reason, cannot be recommended. Of Metallic Roofs there are a great variety, presenting claims to public attention and public confidence. In

Chicago, Slate is used to some considerable extent, and Tin still more extensively, as a material for Roofing. Zinc has not been found well adapted to the climate. Within a very few years, Composition Roofs have become very popular, and the manufacture of them has constituted an important business in this city. Of the thousands in use in Chicago, we have yet to find the first man who is fully satisfied with them. They are continually getting out of order, and few of them long continue water-proof. Architects give it as their opinion, that no better Roof can be put on a building than *Slate* or *Tin*. They are more durable — are Water-Proof — and the most important feature they present is, they are Fire-Proof. A Roof covered with Slate will resist the devouring flame, and endure perfect, Fire and Water Proof, for a century.

Mr. P. F. Shesken, whose office is at No. 143 Lake Street, is known throughout the North-West as a practical and reliable Slate and Tin Roofer. During the last ten years, he has covered many of the public and private edifices, not only in this city, but throughout the North-West. Having the agency for one of the most extensive Slate Companies in Vermont, and having always a large stock on hand, he is enabled to sell to the trade at Eastern prices. His facilities for conducting this business are such that no one can successfully compete with him.

The time is not far distant, when corporations and the public authorities in large cities will pass ordinances prohibiting the erection of wooden buildings, covered with combustible materials, fit for the devouring flame — the combustible that lights the meteor fires that flash from every city.

CIVILIZERS.

WHATEVER tends to divert the attention and interests of men from war, and attract them towards peace, by displaying or developing the greater nobleness and utility of peace pursuits, is a civilizer. Man is nobler this day, over half of Christendom, with scythe, or hammer, or axe, or plow in hand, doing honest, useful toil, than was ever lawless cavalier, or crusader, rioting around the holy sepulcher. The grain fields to-day rank before the battle field, the builder of steam engines before the forger of Toledo or Damascene blades, the manufacturer of labor-saving Agricultural Implements, before the manufacturer of implements of war. Each step taken to increase the home comforts, the individual independence, and the general prosperity through peaceful industry, strengthens the empire of peace. Ignorance and misapprehension have done much to retard the civilization and happiness of man, by clinging blindly to the present. The farmer struggled to save his ruder implements from the grasp of science and labor-saving machines. The noblest revolutionizers of society, instead of being generously accepted, have often been most bitterly opposed, either by selfishness of those whose inferior inventions they threatened, or by the prejudice of classes who think that whatever answers a purpose, in any way, is good enough and must be let alone. Whatever invention abridges labor, is naturally regarded in cities, or dense communities where labor is in surplus without machinery, as the enemy of labor. It was a long time after their invention before the old farmers would touch the iron plow—the side-hill and sub-soil plows—the horse rake, patent threshing machine, corn sheller, cultivator, and hundreds of other noble improvements in the farming implement line; and the great reason for their stubborn conservatism, was that *they could do all their work in the old way, and these new-fangled machines would deprive them of good hard toil and make them idlers.* If hard work with head and hands were the only object and pleasure of life, it would be cruel to disturb the race in slavish toil from ten to eighteen hours per day. But the machinery that helps the farmer to more leisure, abridges his labor, is a blessing, and the men who by invention and manufacture of Agricultural Impliments suited to the advance of the age, are doing more to advance civilization and develop the agricultural interests of a nation, than any other class of men in the community. In Chicago, the manufacture of Agricultural Implements has become a distinct and leading branch of trade of vast proportions. No men in Chicago, perhaps, are more favorably represented on the prairies of Illinois and adjoining States, than Messrs. FURST & BRADLEY, the only manufacturers of Agricultural Implements in Chicago. This firm produces a superior article of Old Land, Stubble and Sod, Michigan Double, Cast-iron, and Corn Plows, also Single and Double Shovel Plows, Corn and Grain Cultivators, for one and two horses, Harrows, Horse-hoes for cultivating corn, Sulky Hay Rakes with spring teeth, Hay Rakes of all kinds, Garden and Railroad Wheelbarrows, and almost every implement used upon the farm. They are introducing an improved Cultivator, claiming for it superior advantages over all others hitherto offered for sale—for putting in grain or tending corn. Its great merit consists in performing more work, and in a more acceptable way than any other similar implement, hitherto introduced to the public.

About nine years ago, this firm commenced business in this city, with a small capital, and by the enterprise and industry of its proprietors, it has attained a magnitude and importance which may well be called a representative business, illustrating one of the great manufacturing interests of Chicago. They give employment to from forty to fifty hands, employing a large capital; their trade extending over the North-Western States. They are extending their facilities in order to meet the rapidly increasing demand for their goods.

Within a comparative few years the demand for Wagons of a peculiar construction has elevated the business of Wagon making into the rank of manufactures. The wheelwright and the blacksmith are no longer able to supply the wants of Express and other similar purposes, and establishments are required that can purchase lumber and iron in large quantites, and which are provided with all the requisite machinery and appliances for turning out heavy vehicles with expedition and rapidity. This establishment have the facilities for making Buggies, Express, and heavy Lumber Wagons in the quickest possible time. If they say an article is good, the public have faith in its quality. Messrs. Furst & Bradley's manufactory is located at Nos. 56 and 58 Jefferson Street, and their salesroom at No. 90 West Lake Street.

PAPER WAREHOUSE.

THE art of Paper making in the United States has attained a high degree of success, and the manufacture is daily increasing.

In the year 1725 a Paper Mill was erected in the State of Delaware, a short distance from Philadelphia, by James Wilcox. The kind of Paper then made was what is termed, fuller's press-boards, such as are used at the present day for pressing cloth. An act of Parliament existed at that time, prohibiting the manufacture of any other kind of paper in the Colonies. The paper which was manufactured by Mr. Wilcox, at a later day than mentioned above, was used by Dr. Franklin, in publishing his paper in Philadelphia. From the Revolution until the year 1825, very little improvement occurred in Paper-making machinery. But few books being published, there was not a demand for paper, but as it slowly increased, more mills were erected. The art of Paper making in the United States has attained a high degree of success, and the manufacture is daily increasing. Machinery is used exclusively, and that of American invention, of which there are about one hundred and thirty different patents. It is stated that more Paper is manufactured yearly in this country, at the present time, than in any other country, and perhaps in all other countries together. This is well attested by the large number of papers printed and the millions of books yearly published, giving evidence of national industry and our proudest characteristic, national intelligence. The demand for paper in the United States has arrived at such a state that we begin to feel the want of paper material from which to draw an exhaustless supply. Says a recent writer, "We are emphatically not a nation of rags, while rags have been the principal source of material." But experiment has been busy, and our inventors have in a measure been rewarded with success. The time is not far distant when the American inventor will make the discovery for which thousands in both hemispheres have been so earnestly seeking — of producing Paper from some vegetable substance, that will not only cheapen the production but furnish an exhaustless supply.

Many patents were granted in the United States from the year 1790 to the year 1836, for the manufacture of Paper from plants, &c., but a description of the inventions was lost by the burning of the Patent Office in 1836. Among the different articles which they claimed to use for the manufacture, we may mention, curriers' shavings, corn husks, seaweeds, pelts, straw, leather, wood, rope. Up to the present time, none of these different materials have proved a success; but that sooner or later some American genius will discover this much-coveted secret of nature, is beyond a doubt.

To manufacture paper uniformly of superior quality, four things may be said to be essential — clear, pure water, superior machinery, good stock, and the requisite skill. All these are combined, perhaps, to a greater perfection in the production of the fine book papers manufactured in Connecticut, the reputation of which extends over this continent.

The Paper trade in Chicago by regular paper houses will probably exceed half a million dollars annually, beside the wrapping sold by grocers and other houses. Most of the Book and other fine Papers sold in Chicago are manufactured to order in the Eastern States.

Among the most substantial and extensive Paper dealers in the Northwest is the firm of G. H. & L. Laflin, established in 1854; their stock is, perhaps, the largest of any west of New York City. They have a resident partner in the East, which affords them facilities unequaled by any other Western house for purchasing stock at low rates, and having paper made to order at short notice, and qualities according to contract, not surpassed by any other house. The paper upon which this book is printed was in process of being manufactured, at a mill in Connecticut, the next day after the order was given for it by the publisher, in this city, and the paper was received here in about ten days thereafter. In 1856, Mr. J. G. Day became a member of the firm. They are now doing business at No. 42 and 44 State Street, in a building erected by them one year ago, especially adapted for their extensive trade.

STEAM TURNING AND SAWING MILLS, AND MANUFACTURING OF BUILDING MATERIALS.

THE establishment of WILLIAM B. PHILLIPS, successor to Goss & Phillips, located on the corner of Clark and Twelfth Streets, is one of the most remarkable and extensive of this kind in the North-West. It is remarkable both for the superior character of its machinery, and for the variety of its departments, and the quality of its productions.

It has been remarked, that in no branch of manufacture does the application of labor-saving machinery produce, by simple means, more important results than in the working of wood. Nowhere else have we seen this fact so fully demonstrated as in this establishment. They were among the first to introduce improved machinery into the business. In this manufactory may at all times be seen a greater variety of remarkable machines for this purpose than can probably be seen anywhere else in the West. Here we saw in operation, *Farrar & Lester's Planer*, adapted for all kinds of shop planing, and will plane from five thousand to six thousand feet per day. H. B. Smith, and Fay & Co.'s *Tenoning Machines*, for all kinds of Tenoning, Coping, etc., each one of which will do the work of a dozen men. Also *Sash* and *Moulding Machines*, of the same makers, which will turn out five thousand to six thousand feet of moulding per day; and *Power Mortising Machines*, for doors and sash, making two hundred cuts per minute; Scroll Saws, for brackets, and all kinds of scroll-work; and Circular Saws, for squaring and ripping.

This firm presents one of the fairest illustrations of enterprise in connection with improved machinery, that is to be found in this city. They commenced business here in 1850, in a comparatively small way. Now they give employment to about one hundred men, and do a business of one hundred and fifty thousand dollars per annum. Their facilities enable them to furnish every article necessary to erect a building, from the tasty modern cottage to the more substantial palace for the millionaire, or the most costly Church edifice — every piece of timber jointed and fitted — every moulding, door, window, and ornament, requisite to the most magnificent structure; also Painting, Glazing, and Hardware, all prepared and delivered on the site selected for the erection, in less time and at less cost than any carpenter or builder can perform the same. Their orders of this kind are not only from this city, but from every part of this Valley of the West — one order for a large Church edifice, they furnished in all its completeness of detail; also one for several residences, to be erected in the State of Tennessee.

The advantages conferred by a great manufacturing establishment of this character, upon the vast population occupying the prairie lands of our own and adjoining States, are inestimable. Chicago being the great lumber mart of this extensive region, it is of the utmost importance that here we should have an establishment of this magnitude, embracing all the combined and modern improvements in machinery, capable of supplying the rapidly increasing demand in Building Materials. Architects, carpenters, builders, and contractors would find it a very different matter to find a similar establishment in the West, where their wants and requirements could be so readily and promptly supplied. Every description of this kind of work which cabinet-makers and carpenters have not the facilities for doing to advantage, is got out with despatch, neatness and at less cost than can be procured without the aid of machinery, and this is one of the great elements of success, which has given this house its extensive trade, and won for them such a strong hold on public confidence.

We would recommend those who take an interest in the subject, to visit the establishment of W. B. Philips.

The manufacture, in this city, of building material has for several years been steadily on the increase. There are about ten establishments engaged in the business, having an aggregate capital of two hundred thousand dollars, producing manufactured articles amounting, probably, to five hundred thousand dollars, giving employment to about four hundred and fifty men.

For the greater convenience of architects, and their numerous customers, they have prepared, at great expense, a neat Catalogue and Price List, containing specimens of Mouldings, Doors, Windows, Sash, Frames, Pickets, etc., with their respective sizes and prices. With the aid of said Catalogue a person may select the style and size of every article wanted.

They also keep a full assortment of builders' Hardware, Window Glass, Paints and Oils. They also manufacture Refrigerators, Ice Chests, etc. Send for a Catalogue, free on application.

GOING TO HOUSEKEEPING.

WHEN the bride's honey-moon is over — and honey-moons cannot last forever—she must go to housekeeping. She may board, indeed, at a fashionable hotel, or a private house, or she may live with her old friends. But this will only do for a while. She will find the days grow longer, and at last she will tire of the same room, and the same table, be they the finest. She will tire of course of a private family, and there can be no remedy found for it but housekeeping. We know it is up hill work to keep house in America, where you have to wait on your servants, instead of being waited on yourself. But it is, after all, the smoothest road for the married woman to keep house; and rough as the path may be, all the flowers that never fade in wedded life, grow there.

If you would make a fair start, go to VAN SCHAACK's great store, No. 47 State Street, in the beginning, and take a deliberate look. He has upwards of thirty thousand different kinds of articles there, a great many of which you must have, before you can keep house half an hour. You have very little idea of what they are — you could not think of half of them in a week. But you need not think of any of them, Mr. Van Schaack will anticipate your wants, and save you that trouble. He set up that large establishment on purpose, and he has talked with a thousand housekeepers, and traveled in every American city or manufacturing town, and paid art a fortune — and you get the fruits of all this for nothing. To assist the young housekeeper, he has published a catalogue of the more prominent articles, which are required for housekeeping, from which a list can readily be made out, and old housekeepers gladly avail themselves of this list of housekeeping articles, kitchen utensils, etc., etc. At Van Schaack's your house can be more completely furnished, with all the modern housekeeping implements, and for half the money it would cost to hunt up the things here and there and everywhere for yourself. This establishment is in many respects a remarkable one;

remarkable in its character — for the enterprise of its proprietor, and for its rapid success. There is no similar one in this city to compare with its advantages and facilities. Those who have the pleasure of knowing its proprietor (and their names are legion) know of what we speak. Among some of the leading articles introduced by Mr. Van Shaack, we may be permitted to name a few.

First, that indispensable — a Cook Stove; of these there are a great variety, both for wood and coal, with prices within the reach of the most limited purse. In looking over this great variety, we were attracted particularly to one, whose ornamental design, was plain and bold — the moldings being round and smooth, so as to prevent the accumulation of dust, presenting a substantial and massive appearance, and finished in every respect, in the highest style of mechanical skill; its very name appealed to our admiration, "The Peace Maker," and we doubt not it would prove such, in the culinary department, even with the usual appendage in that department—"poor help." We were particularly attracted with the roasting and broiling chamber, where the roast is cooked on a spit before the open fire; and the broiling is performed without the escape of fumes and smoke in the kitchen, from which it escapes into other parts of the house. All this being accomplished without additions being made to the stove. Baking can be done at the same time in the regular oven, while its capacity for boiling is equal to any range. It has a movable reservoir for hot water, and is furnished with hot water pipes, for heating water for the bath room, etc. Of this one style of Stoves, Mr. Van Schaack has put up over one hundred during the past fourteen months. We also found an old friend here, in the "McGregor Cooking Stove," called the "Leader," which has proved *a leader* among cook stoves, gas burning and ventilating; also the "McGregor Heating Stoves," for churches, halls, offices, parlors, etc. The large number sold in this, and other cities, and the constant and increasing demand for them, is a sufficient guarantee of a superiority over all heating stoves. These celebrated stoves is expected to appear in a new dress the coming season, the design of which we have seen, and can promise no more ornamental Stove will be in the market, than the "McGregor." One fire will last the entire season without rekindling.

LITTLEFIELD'S BASE BURNING COAL STOVES.—The Secretary's office of the Board of Trade, several of our city banks, manufacturing establishments, offices, etc., are furnished with this stove, while many of our citizens have their whole houses heated by the Littlefield Base Burning Coal Stove, called "Railway Coal Burner," "Parlor Furnace," "Double Heater," or the "Morning Glory." In the last two seasons three hundred of the Littlefield Stoves have been sold by Van Schaack, and the sale could have been largely increased the past year, had they been manufactured early in the season.

Nearly every article required for househeeping will be found collected in one establishment, which is saying a good deal; still we hazard the assertion, that at Van Schaack's, no person need to seek further for any article ever made for household purposes — kitchen utensils in Enameled Ware, French Tinned Ware, Iron Ware, Wire Work, Tin Ware, Copper Ware, Wooden Ware, etc.— all may be found here, at this bureau of Household Articles. While in fine goods, his stock surpasses that of any other house in Chicago for elegant designs of Tea Trays, Toilet Ware of every description, Britannia Ware, planished and plain Tin Ware, Table Mats, Brackets for Statuettes, Ornaments, Flower Baskets, Book Racks, Folding Chairs and Tables, Camp Stools, Bathing Apparatus of every description. His Ice Boxes, Refrigerators, Water Coolers, and Patent Ice Cream Freezers are a simple apparatus, the very name of which in a warm day, "cooleth the brow, cooleth the brain, and maketh the faint one strong again." Also, Kedzie's River and Rain Water Filter.

One visit to this establishment, will convince the visitor that Van Schaack has something they want. In closing this article, we would mention the workshop connected therewith, where many articles of Tin Ware are manufactured, as well as all the sheet iron work connected with stoves. Van Schaack's is the place to send for men to put up stoves, repair bell wires, door locks, in fact, nearly every assistance a housekeeper may need. Send an order to Van Schaack's for aid. Sign of the Golden Tea Kettle, 47 State Street.

SCALES, BALANCES, ETC.

ONE of the great things of our Republic is, that it opens to every citizen all the paths that lead to wealth and honor. Here there is freedom for glory as well as struggle; wealth as well as toil. In tracing the progress of the mind of America, we are arrested at almost every step by some sign of the electric advancement of this country in whatever enriches or adorns civilized life. The genius of invention on this continent has achieved, during the present century, marvelous victories over seeming impossibilities, which have been the theme of philosophers, orators and poets. Heralded in rapid succession to the world, they have almost ceased to be regarded with astonishment. It seems to be the mission of the genius of modern invention, to give to the whole world what ancient art gave only to princes and kings. The strife of nations at the World's Fair in London, offered a spectacle more sublime and significant than history furnishes in all its battle-fields. It was the first time that nations had measured their progress with each other. America made a poor show in the beginning, and for the first few months our countrymen blushed over our exhibition, and hunted about for some plausible excuse for the shabbiness of our appearance at that grand bazaar of nations. But sometimes the moment of the greatest obscura-

SPRING PLATTFORM.

tion to the spectator shows him the broadest stretch of the heavens. The moment of awe is the one of deepest eclipse, and the darkest hour of the night is just before the breaking of the morning. McCormick's reaper passed over the fields of England —Hobbs had picked all the locks in the world — the Collins steamers had outstripped the Cunarders. All England hurried to the coast to see the yacht that beat the world, built by our young Neptune, George Steers. It was the second invasion of England, and this young American was our William Hastings. It was a nobler scene, too, for it was an invasion of the arts of peace. The English are the most prejudiced people in the world, and yet they will change their opinions if you give them a practical demonstration; and when they are divested of their prejudices, they become the most magnanimous nation on the earth. From that day to the present, that nation have been preparing ovations for American Inventors, as one by one some new and wonderful invention has been achieved by us.

The object of nearly all modern inventions has been to avert some portion of the curse pronounced upon our great progenitor, "in the sweat of thy brow thou shalt eat bread," — to increase human power, lessen human labor, and extend the dominion of man over the forces of nature. To this end, the brain of genius has, during this century, been wrestling almost with impossibilities. It has achieved a thousand already — so many indeed, that we have ceased to wonder. Our own city of Chicago has contributed her full share to this material progress of the race. Among one of the most important of these inventions, we may mention "Hitchcock's New Patent Scale," — constructed on an entire new principle. Mr. Hitchcock has devoted the best energies of his life in perfecting the manufacture of Scales and Balances. Like other men that have led the way to new fields of discovery, he has been the object of envy; but he has outlived all these feeble attempts to chill the ardor of his enthusiasm. He has triumphed over the strongest combinations; and now, from the step where he stands, he not only controls the fortunes of the men that opposed him, but the respect of all who know him, or his valuable inventions.

About the year 1830, Mr. Fairbanks, of Vermont, obtained the first patent issued in the United States, for scales. That patent expired some sixteen or eighteen years ago. Up to that time Mr. Fairbanks enjoyed the full benefit of his invention, proving superior to all others. But that patent was far from covering all the advantages in the science of scale making, and improvements of later years. It was left for another to perfect. An American genius, whose brain has been wrestling for years to solve the problem, has at last discovered the working of a principle, entirely new, by which he has produced the most perfect scale extant. S. S. Hitchcock's manufactures will become the standard scales of this continent. This new principle in scale making is destined to revolutionize the present system in many important points. First in adjusting the beam, so that it turns with the least possible weight — simplicity of construction, quickness and accuracy of weight, durability, non liability to get out of order, and for Track and Hay Scales, the slight depth of excavation or vault necessary for erection, with no checks and little or no wear on the fulcrum, so adjusted that it leaves the scales free to act, without a possibility of its becoming disarranged.

The Scale swings on a hollow cylinder, therefore does not require any braces underneath to strengthen it. The leverage is so constructed that there are no levers passing through the centre of the scale, having only two, one at each end at right angles to the beam. The fulcrum which the foot of the platform usually rests on, in this scale is covered for protection, by an artificial plate, acting like a hinge; on the top of the plate, is a wear fulcrum, so adjusted that it produces little or no wear on the fulcrum itself. On the top of said wear pin, is a clevice, with concave steel sections, which hangs about eight inches below, to receive the foot of the platform in such a manner that it requires no checks to keep the platform steady weight, which will always hang plumb and easy. The platform always swings free, and settles instantly. By moving back and forth, it always adjusts and frees itself from the edges without the aid of the tender. For simplicity, cheapness, durability, correctness, and ease of management, they are superior to any scales manufactured. Most scales require an excavation or vault, of from three to five feet, while this scale requires from top of platform to bottom of pit only fifteen inches for Hay and Coal Scales, and twenty-four for Track Scales.

For many years Mr. Hitchcock has devoted his time and talents to the manufacture of scales, and for the last twelve years has been sealer of weights and measures in Rochester, New York, and in Chicago, during which time he has had most of the standard weights and measures, of all the principal manufactures, from different towns and cities, from this section, brought to him to regulate and adjust, which has afforded him greater facilities, perhaps, than any other man engaged in the manufacture of Scales.

Hitchcock's Scales, manufactured with his improvements, on the principle of Fairbanks, have been awarded one hundred and thirty-four first premiums, over all other Scales, by County, State, and United States Fairs, held in New York, Ohio, Illinois, Wisconsin, Michigan, Indiana, also in the British Provinces, in direct competition with Fairbanks. Mr. Hitchcock is a practical manufacturer, possessing a rare combination of genius and constructive skill in the mechanic arts.

Mr. Hitchcock has recently admitted as a partner Mr. H. NUTTING. They are extending their facilities for manufacturing, to enable them the better to supply the increasing demand for the New Patent Scales.

They also keep on hand and make to order, Letter Copying Presses, Improved Sugar Mills, Store and Warehouse Trucks, Wheat and Hopper, Coal Cattle, Depot, Dormant and Warehouse, and Portable Platform Scales. Hitchcock & Co. are located at No. 39 South Canal Street.

THE INHERITANCE OF LETTERS — A CENTRALIZATION OF LEARNING.

ONE of the highest tests applied to the civilization of nations, has always been considered to be the prevalence among the greatest number of persons, of Books and universities of learning. One of the most significant and encouraging signs of the progress of learning on this continent — in this great centralization focus of the Valley of the Mississippi, where are culminating the arts, commerce, and political power of this nation — where the eye of the scholar, or the man of science, whose sympathies are with the progress of light and learning, turns with the most interest and encouragement, is the Publishing House of S. C. GRIGGS & Co., on Lake Street. The establishment is a massive edifice, with an ornate iron front elevation, to protect it from the devouring flame and the wreck of time, known as "Burch's Iron Block," majestic in its appearance, as becomes a pursuit whose prerogative it is to move the arms that move the world. There is little pomp or parade to attract the eye of one who passes by, for all the goods of this vast concern are received and shipped from the rear entrance; but compared with any other place in this Western world, it is to the scholar what the Parthenon was to the Athenian which stood on the summit of the Acropolis, and was dedicated to the Goddess of Wisdom. The intellectual life of this continent is just dawning. We have been building a Republic, and we have had less than a century to do it in. It took Rome seven centuries to consolidate hers; and the Ptolomies a longer period to give perfection to the Alexandrian Library.

We no longer erect temples, except to the true God, whom Paul preached from Mars Hill. But if there were another temple to be erected, we should build it to Minerva; for as the foundations of this great government were laid by the wisest and best of men, so will it be perpetuated only by the same spirit. We have read of Cadmus bringing letters to Greece, and we trace with unutterable curiosity and delight, their progress from nation to nation, as like the sun in his circuit, they go to illume the globe. But we are witnessing here in this latest-found Hesperian home of the struggling races of men, a spectacle which enkindles a deeper enthusiasm, and awakens more illimitable hopes than all the records of Alfred or Cadmus. Being the latest among the nations of the earth, and destined, perhaps, to hold the fortunes of civilization itself in our hands for coming ages, Heaven has made us the heirs of all the learning of all the centuries that have swept by, and we have now pouring in upon us streams of learning, broader, deeper, richer, than have ever rolled in upon any preceding nation. There never has been a great nation, until this, with a universal language without dialects. The Yorkshireman cannot now talk with a man from Cornwall. The peasant of the Ligurian Appenines drives his goats home at evening over hills that look down upon six provinces, none of whose dialects he can speak. Here, five thousand miles change not the sound of a word. Around every fireside, from every tribune, in every field of labor and in every factory of toil, is heard the same tongue. This we owe to Webster, whose genius has presided over every scene in the Nation. His principles of language have tinged every sentence that is now, or will ever be uttered by an American tongue. It is universal, omnipotent, omnipresent. No man can breathe the air of the continent and escape it. This great work of the Lexicographer is one of the standard works always found on sale at this great representative house of Messrs. Griggs & Co. No person should be without a copy.

There is but one larger Book House on this continent than this; and there is no Book-store outside of New York city that can hold any comparison with it. It occupies one of the largest and most eligible stores in Chicago, in "Burch's Iron Block," the salesroom being forty-seven and one half by one hundred and sixty-five feet, filled with almost countless thousands of volumes, embracing every department of knowledge. Not less than three hundred thousand volumes are always in store, and sometimes the number will exceed half a million. The name of S. C. Griggs & Co. is borne upon the title page of over one million volumes annually. Its annual trade in School Books nearly equaled the *entire* sale of School Books in all the Southern States, previous to the Rebellion, while its sale of Miscellaneous works is far greater than any other house in the West.

Of Photographic Albums, that recent beautiful and useful invention, Messrs. G. & Co. keep a very extensive assortment, embracing every size, style and price, from seventy-five cents to twenty-five dollars a. Their sales in this one item for the six months ending May 1st, exceed $10,000.

In Subscription Works this house deals largely. In 1856 its subscription list for Benton's Abridgement of the Debates in Congress, (a work costing forty-eight dollars in the cheapest form,) was five hundred sets; and the same number was taken of Ticknor & Fields' household edition of the Waverly Novels in fifty, volumes.

Of Kane's Arctic Expedition, over six thousand copies were sold; and more of the Encyclopedia Britannica were sold by this house than by any other outside of Boston, New York and Philadelphia, costing about one hundred and twenty dollars per set, complete in twenty-two volumes.

The present subscription list of Appleton's New American Cyclopedia, exceeds five hundred sets, or nearly thirty thousand dollars' worth.

They are *Special* Agents for Messrs. Ivison, Phinney & Co., D. Appleton & Co., Harper & Brothers, Ticknor & Fields, Gould & Lincoln, J. B. Lippincott & Co., and SHELDON & Co., having such terms as enable them to furnish the publications of these houses to merchants at the same rates as charged by them.

We noticed, among other valuable works, two copies of Roberts' Views in Palestine — a large English quarto, costing four hundred and fifty dollars per set. It is one of the most magnificently illustrated publications extant, of which there are very few copies in the country.

Also a celebrated illustrated French work — "Musee Francais," in four volumes, royal quarto, costing three hundred and fifty dollars; a rare and beautiful book, of which we believe there is but one other copy for sale in any book-store in the United States.

They publish, in connection with Messrs. Ivison & Phinney, that popular list of School Books, known under the name of the "American Educational Series," of which upwards of half a million copies have been sold by the Chicago house within twelve months.

As a great distributing depot for Eastern publishers, it stands confessedly above all others. Prince Napoleon, who visited it while here a few months ago, expressed his wonder and admiration at the extent, the richness and the variety of the stock, and remarked to Mr. Griggs, that he "had visited all the leading Book-stores of the Continent, and that Europe could produce no stores to equal this." "The young City of Chicago," he remarked, "may well be proud of such a house." What a commentary this, upon the social and moral grandeur of the great North-West. What a commentary upon the integrity, perseverance and business character of the man who stands at the head of this great house, contending manfully on the great road of literary enterprise, halting at no obstacle, disheartened by no discouragement, pursuing his daily occupation of furnishing thought to others, and scattering light through the world, and giving to the whole American people the best editions of the best books in the world. Every civilized man, woman and child in the North-West is personally interested in this great Book house of S. C. Griggs & Co.; for the books they sell embrace the genius and learning of the most gifted men and women who have illuminated the world, and left their own example and intellect to illustrate heroism and virtue, and to embellish life. These are the books, which they sell, that we need for the education of the young millions that are bursting into life on this continent. This is the spirit in which this house are sending forth their works, and millions greet them as fast as issued.

How important, then, the mission they are fulfilling; and under such circumstances, how favorable are the prospects of American publishers! A new world is continually opening to their enterprise. Where the waste wilderness stood forth in primeval solitude and majesty ten or twenty years ago, or where the prairie then extended in ocean-like vastness, without the intruding foot of civilization to trample down its wild flowers, or disturb the repose of the wild turkey or pheasant, there are now hundreds of populous cities and towns, prospering in art, commerce and manufacture. And where, less, perhaps, than five years since, the smoke of European and American progress had never circled above the pine and elm tops of our ancient forests, there are now churches and academies innumerable; village schoolmasters, village politicians, and village editors. But the stream of civilization is ever onward. Every individual, and every village, town and city in the land, are slowly contributing their various mites to the development of an American universal literature. Our population grows with unparalleled rapidity, but certainly not faster than our enlightenment.

Opulence, which many of our citizens have long since attained, will give leisure for study, and enable the cultivator of the beautiful to enrich himself with specimens of art, or books. Every emigrant, almost, who sets foot upon our shores; every fresh school established in the land; every church erected; every appeal made in behalf of mental culture, is to the publisher an encouraging prognostic.

A brief review of the origin of this House, and changes of firms, may not be uninteresting. In 1845, the house of W. W. Barlow & Co. was established here by the New York firm of Mark H. Newman & Co., on Lake street, between Clark and La-Salle streets. The store was afterwards removed to the Tremont House, and again to 121 Lake street. In March, 1849, Wm. Bross succeeded Barlow. In October of the same year, S. C. Griggs, for six years a Bookseller in Hamilton, N. Y., came to this city, and in company with Mr. Bross, purchased two-thirds of the stock of the firm of Wm. Bross & Co., which at that time belonged to the house of Newman & Co., the style being changed to S. C. Griggs & Co. In May, 1851, they removed to 111 Lake Street, Mr. Griggs, having during the month previous purchased Mr. Bross' interest in the business. In the spring of 1854, Egbert L. Jansen, who had been with the house five years, was taken into partnership, the style of the firm remaining unchanged. In April, 1857, this enterprising firm removed to Nos. 39 and 41 Lake Street, in Burch's Block, their present eligible situation. In 1858, Messrs. Griggs and Jansen purchased the interest of the New York firm.

One cannot pass through this store without being impressed with the thought that the genius of all ages presides there, from Moses to Hallam, each one having made contributions. Greece with all its classics; Rome and the historians of her eternal annals; modern Europe from the revival of learning to the startling revelations of Layard — the lights of a thousand guiding, shaping intellects of the world. This house is prepared to furnish almost every book that can be named; it has become head quarters for furnishing information upon every subject appertaining to books. There is an uninterupted stream of intellectual wealth flowing from the ancient fountains of learning in the old world, to the new. One by one, in those old seats of misgovernment, the foundations of civil order are giving away, and successively are being transmitted to us the lights of ancient learning. What Europe parts with, we inherit; and this vast legacy is growing richer every hour. Sooner or later, the accumulated literary wealth of all ages will come to us. Heaven has decreed it, and his providence will bring it about.

In this aspect then, as the medium through which we derive this ceaseless and exhaustless stream of light, we see in the firm we are speaking of, who are the gleaners of this intellectual wealth, something more than merchants and salesmen. They are doing for us, in this first florid period of the cultivation of letters, what the Medici did for the Florentine Republic, after the fall of Constantinople. It is time for our eagle, that has spread his pinions over such vast territories of the earth's surface, to begin to wing his flight into the Empyrium, where he will achieve conquests in the empire of learning, more lasting than the sceptre of the Cæsars. Crowns, thrones, presidencies vanish, and are lost in the midst of the ages as they sweep on, but science is eternal.

ARCHITECTURE.

GENIUS, history proves, is not hereditary. The children of a king are not necessarily kings, nor the heirs of an architect, artists. Nor has art any preference for particular times or countries, being a universal fact of human development. But the aspect and forms of art are as different as the spirit of different ages and climates. It need be no discredit to us in America, that we have not originated a style of Architecture; for art is strictly related to the circumstances of life that surround it. That art, therefore, will have its proper place in our national development, is not a matter of speculation, but of science. It is not proved by the erection of Greek temples for banking-houses, or of ameliorated Gothic Cathedrals for Protestant Churches; but it is to be found in the thousand new aspects that belong to our new life.

Architecture, in its artistic sense, meaning the ornamental structure of buildings, receives attention and progresses with the advance of civilization. It regards not only the exterior of the house, but the details of the interior. It is encouraging to mark the great progress made in the United States during the last few years, in the general appreciation and patronage of Architecture. The public mind is becoming fully impressed with the importance of these subjects, and it is moving in the right direction. It needs, however, constant watchfulness to guard against the errors growing out of a tendency to admire what is overwrought or extravagant, and to substitute costliness of material for beauty of form and elegance of design. No building of public character, or of any considerable cost, either public or private, should be undertaken without the aid of full specifications and complete working drawings, made by those whose study and professed business it is to do this very thing in a tasteful and proper manner. The

Wm W. BOYINGTON

Architect.

Office, Cor. State and Randolph Sts.,

CHICAGO, ILL.

Having removed my office from No. 82 Dearborn Street to more conveniently arranged rooms, I would call the attention of my patrons and friends to the accommodations offered them, which I trust will be of mutual benefit, and facilitate the transaction of business.

Having met with such a degree of success during a residence of eight years in Chicago, I take pleasure in referring my patrons, as well as others, who may be about to build, to some of the more important structures that have been erected from my designs, and under my immediate supervision, viz:

Sherman House, corner Clark and Randolph Streets,	cost,	$200,000
Newhall House, Milwaukee, Wis.,	"	150,000
Metropolitan Hotel, corner Randolph and Wells Sts.,	"	60,000
Massasoit House, cor. South Water and Central Av.,	"	30,000
Orient House, corner Van Buren and State Streets,	"	25,000
Garrett Block, corner State and Randolph Streets,	"	60,000
Wadsworth and Keep's Marble Block, corner Wabash Avenue and Lake Street,	"	50,000
Mills', and others, Marble Block of seven stores, cor. Wabash Avenue and Lake Street,	"	140,000
Laflin's, and others, block of nine stores, cor. Wabash Avenue and South Water Street,	"	150,000
Walter, Rogers and Norton's block of three stores, River Street,	"	60,000
Reynolds, Ely & Newhall's Block, four stores, corner Michigan Avenue and South Water Street.	"	60,000
Loomis' Marble Block, cor. S. Water and Clark Streets,	"	20,000
St Paul's Church, (Universalist,) Wabash Avenue,	"	65,000
First Presbyterian Church, Wabash Avenue,	"	80,000
M. E. Church, Wabash Avenue,	"	55,000
North Presbyterian Church, cor. Indiana and Cass Sts.,	"	25,000
Second Baptist Church, Quincy, Illinois,	"	25,000
First Baptist Church, Dayton, Ohio,	"	25,000
Lombard University, Galesburg, Ill.,	"	30,000
University of Chicago, (partly built,)	"	150,000
Young Ladies' Seminary, at Hyde Park,	"	8,000
Illinois State Penitentiary at Joliet, by Boyington & Wheelock, now in process of erection. Present cost,		600,000
Marble Terrace, Michigan Avenue, containg eleven dwellings—average cost $20,000,	"	220,000

And some thirty separate first class marble front dwellings, on Michigan and Wabash Avenues and cross streets, between said Avenues, costing from five to forty thousand dollars each—averaging $15,000, - - - - - - - - - - $450,000

Together with some two hundred buildings in different parts of the City, State, and adjoining States, such as churches, school-houses, and blocks of stores, public halls, and private dwellings, at various grades of cost.

Having successfully accomplished the various undertakings before mentioned, to the general satisfaction of some four hundred different proprietors, to any of whom reference may be had, which I am persuaded should be a sufficient guarantee that works entrusted to my charge will be executed with integrity and ability.

As I have on hand a large collection of the designs and plans above referred to, I shall take pleasure to show them to persons about to build, from which they may gain valuable information.

Please give me a call at the new office.

W. W. BOYINGTON.

difference between a building made up of patch-work features, stolen piecemeal from one and another existing structure, and one whose every feature has been determined by a competent and comprehensive knowledge of Architectural principles, though it may not be apparent at once to every eye, will sooner or later reveal itself; and that difference is as wide, almost, as the poles. And if Architecture should either be satisfactory to good taste, or be the means of cultivating it, then surely attention to its quality in this respect is not out of place or unimportant.

There is the same reason for employing the professed and competent Architect, as there is for employing the rightly educated and skillful lawyer or physician; and we would as soon entrust an important legal cause to the merest pettifogger, as leave it to one who only knows how to joint boards and mortise timber to build a house for us. There are, indeed, in many of our towns and villages, those of the plane and saw who also have an eye for Architecture as an art, and such men often build very unexceptionable structures. But the majority of carpenters have hardly more sense of what is really involved in Architecture, than is needful to the building of a barn. The fine lines and just and graceful proportions, the lights and shades, the proper effects of shape and material, in impressing the mind, satisfying or cultivating taste, and touching the heart, while answering at the same time, the grosser and primary purposes of any structure; these capabilities and adaptations of Architecture, the ordinary builder commonly knows little or nothing of. He is a mere hewer of timber, or, at best, a copyist of what others have done, and too often without the judgment necessary even to copy appropriately. And so we see such builders putting Gothic windows, perhaps, under a Grecian pediment; or mixing all sorts of mouldings and characteristic architectural features, in one and the same building. The consequence is, that as those who use the building grow in taste, while the building remains the same from year to year, the latter becomes more and more unsatisfactory, and instead of being cherished the more the longer it stands, is soon despised, and ere long deserted, or pulled down to make room for a better. It deserves to be considered, too, in this connection, that the principles of Architecture apply to one structure as well as another; to the humblest and simplest, as well as to the most imposing and elaborate. They have place as truly in the building of the plainest cottage as in the erection of a palace; in the shaping of the garden fence or the kitchen chimney, as truly as in the arrangement of a portico or the hanging of a dome. They are principles altogether independent of cost in their application. The question of fitness and propriety, as well as that of size and adequate strength, comes in wherever a board is to be sawn or a timber hewn.

This young city of forty years' growth — of giant proportions, which has sprung into existence with its unparalleled activity, can claim a degree of architectural beauty and taste in many of its public and private edifices, which can be said of few cities of its age and proportions. For this diffusion of architectural beauty and refinement, we are indebted to our architects, among the foremost and leading of whom is Mr. W. W.

BOYINGTON. We take pleasure in referring to some of the more important structures that have been erected from his designs, and under his immediate supervision; among which may be mentioned, the Sherman House, Garrett Block, Loomis Marble Block, St. Paul's Church, First Presbyterian Church, University of Chicago, Young Ladies' Seminary, at Hyde Park; also, Lombard University, Galesburg; Illinois State Penitentiary, at Joliet, besides very many others of equal merit, which will long continue as monuments of his architectural skill and taste. Mr. Boyington has been a resident of Chicago for the last eight years, and by the interest he has manifested, not only in Architecture, but in every good work whereby civilization could be advanced, and suffering humanity relieved, has secured for him a wide circle of friends. He has recently removed to "Garret Block," corner of State and Randolph Streets, where he has fitted up a suite of commodious rooms, for the better accommodation of his increased business.

MEDICATED BATHS.

BATHING is a practice of great antiquity. It prevailed among the Greeks as early as the heroic age; and we even find mention made by Homer of hot baths in the Trojan times, although these seem to be rare. Although bathing among the ancients, made, as it were a part of diet, and was used as familiarly as eating or sleep, yet, as we learn from Pliny, Hippocrates, and Oribascus, it was in high esteem among their physicians as a cure for certain diseases, and hence their frequent exhortations to washing in the sea, and plunging into cold water. The first instance of cold bathing for medicinal purposes is that of Melampus, who bathed the daughters of the king ot Argos, and the first instance of warm bathing is that of Media, who was said to boil people alive, probably with some reason, since Pelias, king of Thessaly died in a hot bath under her hands.

The modern baths consist of hot, warm, tepid, and cold baths, in which the water and vapor used, are either pure or variously medicated. The Turks and Persians have regarded the bath with more interest than any other people. The Russians are such lovers of vapor baths, that St. Petersburgh contains an immense number of these establishments; whole families, men, women, and children, from the noble to the serf, make it a religious observance.

The baths used by the modern European and Americans differ essentially from the Turkish and Russian baths, in that the vapor of water, or steam, is rarely made use of during the process of bathing; the operation being limited to washing or immersing the body in water of varied temperature, according as the person wishes a tepid or hot bath. The vapor bath is infinitely superior to the warm bath for all purposes for which a warm bath can be given; and as a medical agent in the removal and alleviation of certain chronic diseases, can scarcely be over-praised.

Within a few years past more attention has been given to the bath not only as a luxury, but as a medicinal agency. The experience of other nations has been handed down to us, and we are beginning to profit thereby. In cities, and large towns, baths are established under the management of medical and skillful men. In the autumn of 1856, Mr. R. C. GREER opened a bathing establishment at No. 178 Madison Street. The rapidly increasing patronage of this place has rendered it necessary, for increased facilities and greater convenience for his patrons, to secure a more commodious building, located at No. 185 Madison Street, where he is fitting up the entire building for permanent occupancy. The basement will be fitted up for a swimming bath nineteen by thirty feet, and five feet deep, supplied by a continuous running stream. On the floor above will be eight or ten vapor baths, the medicinal properties of which are admitted by the highest medical authority. These baths possess the power of producing profuse perspiration in any state of the body; therefore its effect must be salutary, efficacious and powerful. Its immediate effects are agreeable and pleasant, cleansing the whole system, causing an equal stimulation of the functions of the skin, producing animation, liveliness and a desire for food. It is also said to be a reliable remedy for fevers of every kind. Sulphur vapor, and Mercury baths, are most beneficial, and in many instances a certain cure for Rheumatism in all its most aggravated forms, also for Salt Rheum, Scrofula, Throat Diseases, Dyspepsia, Costiveness, Nervous Irritability, and all Cutaneous Diseases. Mr. Greer proposes to furnish the Oriental bath, the same in principle as the celebrated Turkish bath, but with substantial improvements. This establishment is patronized by physicians, clergymen, and the highest class of our citizens. In all respects it is a first class institution, receiving, and meriting the full confidence of the community. Its management could not be in safer or in better hands. Mr. Greer is a competent, genial, accommodating gentleman, devoting his whole time and talent to this institution. It is patronized by ladies of the best class. All improper persons are strictly excluded.

Location No. 185 Madison Street.

WOOD ENGRAVING.

AMONG the miracles of the present time is the taste for the Fine Arts, which forms a prominent characteristic of the American mind. Instead of the tasteless, coarse, vulgar pictures which within living memory, embellished illustrated books, we now have the beautiful engravings on wood, executed in the finest style of art. In no branch of art has progress been so palpable and satisfactory as in wood engraving. It is now the associate of the studio—it is the beloved of poets, the best friend of the publishers, and the real servant and benefactor of the people. The first illustrations in our popular works are done on wood. The art of wood engraving is a law into itself, and each worker at the shrine becomes responsible for his labor to the great public whose taste is to be gratified, and whose sense of propriety is not to be outraged. As each engraver is the carver of his own reputation, we instance the case of the Messrs. CHILDS, whose meritorious works of wood engraving have made for them a fame which will be enduring.

Mr. S. D. Childs, was the pioneer engraver of this western country. As early as 1837 he commenced Wood Engraving in Chicago, when it was comparatively a village; but being the only engraver here at that time, he was sought for to do all other kinds of work in the engraving line, such as seal-cutting, stencil cutting, marking jewelry, cutting steel stamps, copper engraving, printing, etc., and often to keep employed he busied himself in carving and sign painting. Since then Mr. Childs has raised a family of sons, who also have become Engravers, keeping pace with the progress of the age in Engraving, and to-day this establishment represents one of the leading firms in this business in the North-West.

Steadily have they progressed in their art career, winning an enviable reputation, and the patronage of an appreciative public. Only a few years ago, publishers of the North-West thought it necessary to send to Philadelphia for their wood engravings. At the present day, the best productions of Chicago will compare favorably with anything produced in Philadelphia.

The highest and most difficult range of wood engraving consists in landscape scenery, and historical pieces. Wood is capable of developing any effect which can be brought out by steel or copper, with the single exception, perhaps, of the mezzotint, which is neither prized nor appreciated, except by a practical artistic eye. Wood engraving is superior to a lithograph, or a work on copper or steel. First, in the greater rapidity and economy with which they can be transferred, and stereotyped, and put in various forms, by which they can be multiplied *ad infinitum*, preserving the original work of the artist, which is never destroyed. Besides, Wood Engravings admit of producing deeper colors, and consequently broader effects of light and shade. There are certain elements of nature that can be wrought upon by wood by the engraver, as they never have been, and can never be, on copper and steel. Water can be made more translucent; the fish can be seen deep as he is in the stream; the light is caught and trembles, and held glancingly, dancingly, ripplingly, sheen-like, as it can never rest on the paper which comes from its impression on copper and steel; wherever scenery can be thrown in, in deeper, richer, lighter masses; there is more freedom in it; you can see further into the forest engraved on wood, there is more transparency of atmosphere, there is more vigor, vitality, life, power, than can be infused into any other style of art.

It is no longer a question — will it add to the interest and value of a book to illustrate well; that it will be is regarded as a matter of fact; and it therefore, is the study of publishers and authors how to do it within the limits of a reasonable expense. There is no doubt but that *nine-tenths* of the books and magazines published would be beautifully illustrated if the expense could be afforded by the publisher — so clearly is the taste of the people in favor of these miniature and easily attainable works of art — for such works they are, though of all degrees of excellence, of course. That this taste is a promising one, needs little argument to show; for, as in the case of the more ambitious efforts of the studio and the pallet, the more love and encouragement of the reader, and early attempts of the artists, it will be sure to culminate in a more familiar knowledge of art, and a taste for the best forms of expression.

It is surprising to what usefulness the wood cut can be adapted. Is there a design or mechanical drawing required — is a house to be daguerreotyped — is a landscape to be reproduced — is a history or fiction to have its scenes and characters depicted — the infallible Wood Engraving is called into requisition, and the service is performed admirably and cheaply. By aid of the electrotyping process, *fac similes* of the engraving can be produced to any number; and it is doubtful if half the actual usefulness of the wood process has yet been understood, since it is now chiefly employed in book and newspaper illustrations, while it is adapted to many uses in ordinary business.

In England, illustrated books have long held a supremacy in market, and the American publisher, with a few exceptions, prefers to have his work done abroad, for he says, "what smells of London ink sells best to American tastes." We do not believe this is true. If a work is handsomely printed, appropriately illustrated, and artistically bound, we do not think any purchaser would stop to inquire the nationality of the hands which produced the volume. It is true, as specimens of beauty and artistic excellence in typography and illustration, those exquisite editions of Longfellow, Bryant, Poe, etc.— the "Court of Beauty," "Shakspeare's Heroines," were produced abroad. It only requires that our publishers and authors should recognize the ability of our best engravers to have as exquisite work from their hands, if we may judge from the various specimens of Messrs. Childs, which have come under our notice.

By the foregoing remarks, we would not have our readers infer that the art of Wood Engraving is chiefly adapted for book and paper illustration. It is particularly fitted to more practical uses, such as envelope illumination, (now become so popular with business houses,) bill-heads, circulars, stamps, labels, etc., etc. It is now becoming a matter almost of necessity to every good business house, to use this beautiful and economical system of advertising. A tint block is engraved the size of the envelope — the name of the person or firm, and business and address, being sunk so as to appear in semi-relief; and thus we have the business card covering the whole face of the envelope, yet in such faint lines as to mar it in no way for the superscription with the pen. This "tinting" process can be applied to various things, such as bills, letter-heads, etc., and, ere long, will be very generally used. We may advise all who commission Messrs. Childs — who are doing a large amount of this serviceable work, and have facilities for doing it at moderate prices — that they will give entire satisfaction.

Parties at a distance, who wish any kind of Wood Cuts, can have them executed at this establishment with promptness and perfectness, simply by giving correct drawings. With a good photograph, or ambrotype, or daguerreotype, the engraver will provide a correct portrait on wood in a short time. Thus it is easy for persons at a distance to obtain any required engraving they may order, on the shortest notice.

Messrs. Childs are located at No. 117½ Randolph Street, next-door to Kingsbury Hall.

SEED AND IMPLEMENT WAREHOUSE.

THE Seed trade of Chicago, though in comparison with many other branches, one of very limited extent, is nevertheless entitled to consideration, when discussing the industrial pursuits of our citizens. We cannot claim for its extent and management hitherto all which it should have been, for a great commercial centre like Chicago. The objections which have hitherto existed, it is to be hoped, will in a great degree be removed, and here we shall have all the facilities extended for procuring Seeds of the most accredited quality and description that can be desired. Many of the Seeds formerly sold in this market were obtained in Europe, where the effect of cheap labor upon prices, coupled with freedom from imports at home, enables the importer to purchase many articles for sale here at a cost far below the actual expense of production in this country. The humid climate of Great Britain, from which country the major portions of all are obtained, is not favorable to ripening seeds, and many kinds suffer by a sea-voyage — so greatly do they swell that the twine on papered parcels is not unfrequently embedded or burst by the expansion; and in either case, there is reason to believe Seeds already impaired by age are shipped to this "Western wilderness." Still, so low priced are many, in comparison with the American, that the mere dealer, whose study is to buy cheap, imports his stock — perhaps not recklessly, but trusting for the best, and anxious to quote low prices to the country merchant — a fatal policy — affording pleasure or profit to none in the end. The merchant who retails them, enticed by low quotations, is beset by indignant planters; and the market-gardener who has unfortunately staked his crop upon the issue, finds his land and labor for the season have been cast away — far better for him had he paid the full price for American or imported seeds of reliable character. Loud and bitter have been the denunciations by our agricultural community against these dealers—and, perhaps, justly and deservedly so.

There never has been a period in the history of our country when so much interest has been manifested as at the present time in procuring rare, valuable and reliable Seeds, not only from every section of our own country, but from every part of the civilized world. This indicates a higher civilization and the advance of science in the domain of agriculture. As the wants of a people increase, facilities adequate to the demand are usually to be found. The opening of another Seed and Agricultural Warehouse in this city, on a scale commensurate with the wants of the people, by Mr. A. H. Hovey, late of Boston, Mass., gives very general satisfaction to all who are interested in agricultural pursuits. That he is "the right man in the right place," we need only advise the public that Mr. Hovey is of the Boston stock of the same name, and by them was educated in this most important branch of trade.

Mr. Hovey, having acceded to the proposition of Western men, to locate in Chicago, has taken the spacious store, No. 73 Lake Street, and opened a Seed and Implement Warehouse, for the sale of the best seeds grown in this country, raised by old and experienced raisers at the East; and such as cannot be procured in this country are imported from some of the most reliable Seedsmen in Europe. Here may be found not only the best seeds, but the best assortment the country affords. His facilities for supplying any seeds he may not have on hand are such as to enable him to execute orders for large or small quantities with dispatch. The Flower Seed department is becoming a leading feature in this branch of trade. Mr. Hovey will keep not only all the old and most favorite varieties, but any new and rare kinds which may be introduced at the East. He will promptly execute all orders for Trees, Plants, Shrubbery, Bulbs, etc.

Many new and ingenious articles of Garden and Farming Implements; also Books on Horticulture, etc., etc., will be found at this store. We have seen no other place in the West, which, in all its management, arrangement and completeness, reminds us so much of "Thorburn's," of John street, New York, as this Seed and Implement Warehouse of Mr. Hovey's. The rapid increase of the farm garden and orchard interest of the North-West—the great influx of emigration throughout the rural districts—the unparalleled development of our agricultural resources, give an importance to the location of a house of this character in this city, which will be beneficially felt throughout the vast region from whence Chicago derives her extensive trade.

MERCANTILE UNIVERSITY, OR ILLINOIS SCHOOL OF TRADE.

AMONG European nations, mercantile education in the theory and practice, is regarded quite as essential as those ordinary studies, which among us are considered indispensable in every system. We rejoice that in this respect at least, the European standard of education is being gradually introduced into this country; and the success which Prof. DYHRENFURTH'S ILLINOIS SCHOOL OF TRADE has met with is one of the encouraging signs visible, from which we borrow the hope that the period is not far distant when our children will be favored with as high facilities for this branch of education, which are universal among the better classes of other nations, as they are now favored with in the ordinary departments of intellectual culture.

The cultivation of trade, which is now deemed a most important branch in the administration of paternal governments, has always stood foremost among the claims which the American people exact from its governing power. Our best historians have too clearly defined the advantages a country derives materially from a well directed commerce, to dwell with any doubt on the subject, and we, as a people, have, and do bend all our energies in that direction to become, if we are not so already, the first commercial nation of the globe, or what amounts to the same, to establish our country as the centre of trade.

Trade is a science to be acquired by study only, the practical application of which is to teach us to avoid the many errors which are daily occurring in a mercantile community from a want of knowledge of the true principles of trade. The first nation to appreciate the advantages of a thorough systematic business education were the Germans. The government granted liberal endowments for establishing institutions for commercial education, the first of which was located at Hamburg, in 1867, the *Ecole speciale de Commerce et de l' Industrie.* The most important one was established in Paris in 1820, and it was followed in 1831 by the school of Trade at Leipsic which rose to great fame. Since then schools of a similar kind have become general on the European continent; and it has in some respects become necessary for all aspirants to mercantile employment, to pass a regular course of instruction in one of these schools of Trade.

Within the last few years Commercial Colleges have been established in this country, and are receiving gratifying encouragement — for the people have felt their necessity, and are nobly responding to their patronage. Under competent instructors much theoretical business knowledge is imparted to the student, and he is thoroughly made acquainted with practical book-keeping in all its minute details — thoroughly fitted on leaving the school to take charge of the books of the counting house. There is in this respect an assimilation, in a degree, to foreign schools. But this does not satisfy the demands of our practical business men. While we give much credit to the Germans as great theorists, we pride ourselves upon giving life to their theories, by carrying them into practice, and thus it is necessary for our business students to learn in these schools how to carry the theories of business into practical life. This subject has been fully appreciated and carried out by Mr. Dyhrenfurth, one of our most talented and practical teachers, whose early education at the Leipsic School of Trade, and for more than twenty-five years had the advantages of a practical business experience in our own and foreign countries, as merchant and banker, has peculiarly fitted him to manage a mercantile institution of this kind. Few men have enjoyed the same facilities, of acquiring a thorough practical knowledge of this peculiar branch of education, and possess the genius and tact in imparting it to others, as Prof. Dylirenfurth. At the request of some of the most influential business men of Chicago, who had been advised of the successful operations of Prof. Dylirenfurth's School of Trade, established at Waukegan, in 1858, he was prevailed upon to establish a similar school in this city for the better education of our young men, who are preparing for mercantile persuits. As a citizen of Chicago we are proud to welcome Prof. Dyhrenfurth as an educator of our young men in the practical science of commercial pursuits. That this institution is becoming fully appreciated, is fully attested, by the great number who seek admission as students. One such institution as this, located in our midst, will effect an influence for good, which will be felt in all coming time. It is not the moderate price of twenty-five dollars for a life scholarship, which ensures the success of the college; but the thoroughness with which students are there prepared to became intelligent and practical business men will always be appreciated. It is regarded as one of the noblest and most useful institutions in the West. Here are culminating, and centralizing all the elements of commercial influence and power, and doubtless, will yet become, and at no distant period, the most extensive inland commercial city on this continent. Chicago of to-day presents one of the most remarkable instances of sudden rise to commercial importance to be found in our age. Then here we should have established and *supported liberally*, the best schools for educating our young men in the science of trade and commerce.

A preparatory class for boys has lately been added to the School of Trade.

Prof. Dyhrenfurth's College of Trade in located in Burch's Bank Building, corner of Lake and LaSalle Streets.

AUCTION AND COMMISSION.

ONE of the most important branches of trade and commerce, in every city and town of note, and one of great convenience and advantage to those who wish to make quick sales and sure returns, and those who wish to purchase and get their money's worth for the money, is the Auction and Commission House. The Auctioneer, who is the presiding genius, or the middle man between the purchaser and buyer, of tact and commercial talent, is presumed to know the wants of all the customers who visit his establishment; therefore exposes to sale the right goods at the right time, to the customers. An Auction room is also a place where wit and mirth often hold "high carnival," and an hour spent with the jovial Auctioneer is of more benefit to the dyspeptic and hypochondriac, than the most exhilarating elixir or the physician's best prescription. "Laugh and grow fat," is an old axiom, and if coupled with the fact that you can get what you want, and that at a "great bargain," then, indeed, was the philosopher quite right in saying that "at the Auction Room one gets *his money's worth for his money.*"

There is no legitimate branch of trade, where so great a number and variety of articles are so readily disposed of as at auction, because a great number of persons attend the sales, and they all go with the determination of buying if the articles they want are offered, and provided some one else does not bid more than they are inclined to pay. This is the only branch of trade through which the purchaser gets articles at his own price.

There seems to exist a prevalent idea, that only a second rate class of goods are sold at auction, and that Auctioneers are all disposed to overrate and misrepresent the articles offered by them for sale. The fact is that this is as honest and legitimate a branch of business as any other class of merchandising, when conducted on high toned and honorable principles. That we have in our community, men of this latter class, who are engaged in this business, has never been disputed. Among the number, as an illustration, we would instance the popular Auction and Commission House of JOHN PARKER, at 115 and 117 Dearborn Street. Having been engaged in the business in this city for the past twelve years, he is a thorough master of it, in all its detail, and his integrity and capacity as a business man and as a salesman, receive the unqualified confidence of the consignee, and all who enjoy the pleasure of his acquaintance. His aim is to do a straight-forward legitimate business, regardless of the course pursued by others.

The new fire-proof brick building of Mr. Parker, designed and executed especially for the business, is the best, largest and most convenient building for that purpose in this or any other western city, or perhaps in the United States. It is centrally located on the east side of Dearborn Street, that great thoroughfare for pedestrians, where one can step in without going out of one's way.

The Auction Room is forty by one hundred feet, well lighted and admirably arranged for convenience. The second floor is also a salesroom of the same size. He sells wholly on commission, at public or private sale, and his consignments embrace almost every article that can be imagined, principally Dry Goods, Clothing, Groceries, Boots and Shoes, Yankee Notions, Furniture, Musical Instruments, etc., etc. We look upon his as a model Auction House, and Mr. Parker as a model Auctioneer.

WHOLESALE DRUGGISTS.

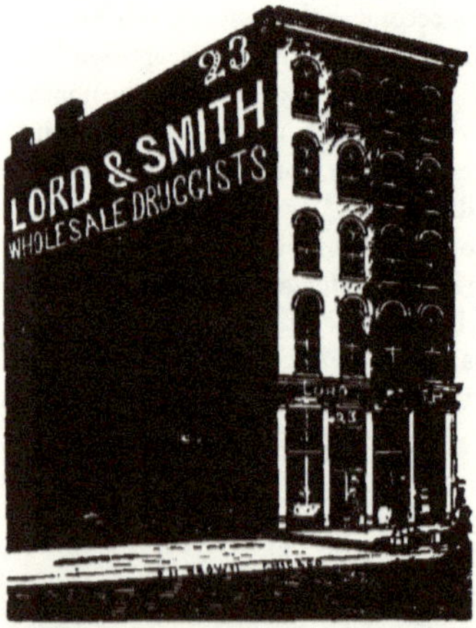

WHEN Prince Napoleon visited Chicago last summer, in nothing was he more surprised than in the extent of our commerce — the magnificence of our stores — the extent and richness of our merchandise — and the intelligence, and business education of our merchants, several of the leading representative houses of which he visited, and expressed his surprise at our combined commercial advantages, and at all the elements of wealth and prosperity culminating here, to be developed to a still greater extent. We first heard of the Prince at the great book and publishing house of S. C. Griggs & Co. — then at other representative houses in various branches of commerce. On visiting the wholesale Drug House of LORD & SMITH, which occupied the next door to Griggs', he remarked, after looking through their extensive establishment, "If this does not represent the right arm of power, and the true dignity of American merchandising, then I have not seen it on this continent." And Prince

Napoleon was right! In Chicago we have many such merchants of true mercantile dignity—mercantile integrity—and mercantile education, in the fullest acceptation of the term. These are the men who are not only laying broad and deep the foundation, upon which is to be reared one of the largest and most prosperous cities on this continent; but are shedding luster and prosperity upon the present, and diffusing intelligence and virtue, thereby advancing civilization in this great valley, and throughout the regions of the North-West, which are rapidly being settled by refugees and emigrants fleeing from the crumbling thrones and despotisms of the old world.

The Drug House of which we have spoken above, is one of our oldest, most respectable, and strongest firms in Chicago—moving on quietly, yet boldly and successfully, because justly and perseveringly; rising superior to all obstacles, and becoming more widely and favorably known throughout the North-West,

Among some of the leading articles represented by this firm, we will mention only a few, for want of space — Drugs, Paints and Oils, Brushes, Window and Druggists' Glass, Kerosene, Acids, Chemicals, Varnishes, Patent Medicines, Alcohol, Surgical Instruments, Extracts, Perfumery, Concentrated Preparations, etc., etc.

Messrs. Lord & Smith are the chief dealers in Patent Medicines for the North-West, of which they send forth large quantities, the healing balm to alleviate the distresses of the wounded, bruised and sick. These remedies are very often successful where the regular practitioner pronounces the case hopeless. Patent Medicines have their opponents, not less than advocates. There are other men besides those who belong to the established school of medical science, who have changed human affairs, and affected the destiny of their fellow men all over the earth. The manufacture of chemicals in the United States may be said to date from the war of 1812. The commercial restrictions which preceded that war, caused such a scarcity and dearness of chemicals, that the preparation of the more prominent articles offered an attractive field for the enterprise. The chemicals kept by this house have an enviable reputation for purity, exactness and beauty. They sell no others but those they can safely recommend. Of Oils, they deal largely in Lard, Coal, Kerosene, Linseed, and others. Druggists' Glass-ware has become a leading business, represented in this city by only a few firms. Lord & Smith have always on hand a full supply, such as Druggists' Vials, Jars, Demijohns, Carboys, etc. This kind of glass is made of ordinary materials — generally sand with lime, and sometimes clay and alkaline ashes of any kind; but great care and experience are required, particularly in making bottles that are to contain effervescing fluids. The materials must be carefully and thoroughly fused, and the thickness uniform throughout, to resist the pressure of the contained carbonic acid. Reliable houses, only, should be dealt with in this line. Of Acids, their list includes Soda-ash, Alum, Copperas, Aquafortis, Nitric and Muriatic Acids; all the various preparations of Tin for the use of dyers. Of Surgical Instruments, here a full assortment may be selected, of the most approved manufactures.

There is, perhaps, no establishment in the North-West that keeps so large a stock or better assortment of pure Medicinal Preparations; as Solids, Extracts, Concentrated Preparations, Fluids, Fluid Extracts; also, Pharmaceutic Sugar-Coated Pills and Granules, with all new preperations, as this house of Lord & Smith. These last named articles are mostly the preparations of Tilden & Co., so well and favorably known to the medical faculty, wherever the healing art is practiced.

A large supply of pure Native Wines and Brandies for medicinal and sacramental uses, may be found at this establishment.

Mr. Lord, the senior partner, has been engaged in the Drug business, without interruption, for twenty-four years, and for the last five years in Chicago. He succeeded the firm of Bay & Baldwin. Dr. L. H. Smith became a partner in 1859, since when the firm has been Lord & Smith. They removed from No. 43 Lake Street, about the first of April of the present season, to their present elegant location, No. 23 Lake Street. Their store is six stories high, including a fine basement, main building twenty-six by one hundred. This is probably the most extensive drug establishment in Chicago. They do a cash business, and short time to cash purchasers. The whole amount of the drug trade in Chicago will probably exceed $3,000,000 per annum.

SHERMAN HOUSE

CHICAGO, ILLINOIS.

THE SHERMAN HOUSE.

OPPOSITE, we present a fine view of the latest and one of the grandest Palatial Hotels in the metropolis of the West. It is a bijou of architecture and taste, and occupies one of the best sites of any hotel in Chicago. It stands on the north side of the Court House Square; its southern aspect overlooking the park with its fountains and foliage. Chicago has long been celebrated for the extent and science of her hotel keeping. But this vast and superb structure, that lifts its marble front on the corner of Clark and Randolph Streets, in the Italian order of architecture, seven stories in height — counting its basement — with a front on Clark and Randolph Streets of three hundred and thirty feet, and a height of ninety-six feet from the lower floor, excels all others hitherto erected in the great West. It was built by the man whose name it bears, who is one of our oldest and most esteemed citizens. Standing on the corner of two great thoroughfares, it is accessible from every quarter; and when at last it was adjudged entirely complete, with the exception of a Master, whose experience, urbanity, hospitality and taste would ensure for its guests a warm and genial welcome, Mr. P. B. Roberts consented to conduct the new Hotel. A vast sum was expended upon the house itself. It was furnished with all the conveniences and luxuries of the most princely palace. The furniture is rosewood, the curtains are silk and damask, the carpets are velvet. No improvement has ever been introduced into an American hotel, which is not found here. Those who explore it, and examine all its machinery, will find that it embraces a combination of everything that the spirit of invention, taste, hospitality or elegance could suggest. Its perfect arrangements in the halls, parlors, and suits of rooms, its attendants, its exuberant larder, and its exquisite *cuisine*, are the admiration of every guest. As to the manner in which the hotel is kept, there is but one opinion, and although so much has been written about it, and a capricious and exacting public had been led to expect everything, yet its opening so far exceeded the expectations, that it carried the public captive.

No private establishment, however expensive, can hope to equal in these particulars the accommodations, luxury and style of this Hotel; while the table, with its unrestricted field for good breeding, and good manners of every style, is a great high-school of refinement, in which the greatest boor from the country, and the most hopeless case of *mauvaise honte*, gets his asperities rounded off, his awkwardness smoothed away, and the wrinkles ironed out of his character and carriage. A man or woman will learn more of the world, and of that *je ne sais quoi* which distinguishes the cosmopolite from the countryman, by a brief residence at such a hotel, than by making the grand tour of Europe. It is in effect a very considerable approximation towards all the advantages, improvements and economics possible in the household of a rich and refined gentleman. One can live at the SHERMAN HOUSE in a style of the most *recherche* luxury, excelling anything found in any private house on any terms, and at a rate not greater than it requires to subsist in the meagerest and most commonplace manner in a solitary and out-of-the-way private dwelling.

There was a degree of elegance and refinement, of harmony and taste, and yet withal of chasteness and unostentation, that the guests seemed to feel, and certainly they acted, less as though they were in a public hotel than a private palace. While this will be a grand Mecca of hospitality, it is supposed that its Master will make it the great rallying place in the North-West for the travelers from every part of our country, and from the old world, to many thousands of whom the proprietor has many years been known, for his kind, genial and generous hospitalities. Among the *attaches*, and intimately associated with the management of this house, is Mr. S. Hawk, formerly "mine host of the Richmond House," the man to whom all the West has paid its tribute, as its most distinguished hotel-keeper, and from whom he has won golden opinions. This Hotel has all the charms of home, for it has all its elements of comfort, quiet, independence and luxury.

METROPOLITAN HOTEL.

CHICAGO for many years has been famous for its Hotels. On the south-west corner of Randolph and Wells Streets, in former years stood the old "Planter's House." In the years 1855 and 1856, it was taken down, and on its eligible site was erected the present commodious building, known all over the North-West as the Metropolitan; kept by that social, genial and kind-hearted man, Mr. B. H. SKINNER, formerly of Boston, who takes pride in being the keeper of one of the best Hotels in Chicago. He has a fondness for seeing everything go right; and it has long since ceased to be a burden to him to administer the affairs of a vast House. His equanimity is never disturbed; he is always happy to see his old friends, and every new guest feels, before they have been in his house twenty-four hours, that they may number him among their acquaintances.

In September, 1861, the Hotel May, adjoining on Wells Street, containing sixty rooms, was added to the Metropolitan, which now contains two hundred and twenty sleeping rooms, neatly furnished throughout, well ventilated, lighted with gas, and furnished with luxurious spring beds. Its *table d' hote* is not only enriched by every luxury, but served as noiselessly and unostentatiously as a private table. Its head cook (Mr. John Murray,) for fourteen years occupied the same position at the Warriner House, Springfield, Mass., formerly so widely and favorably known to the traveling public. It is free from the rush or confusion of many other places; and while it maintains the celebrity it has so justly won, it will continue to be resorted to by those who think more of luxury and taste than of noise and parade — of perfect cleanliness in everything, than of mere show.

This Hotel has long been known to the lovers of clean, neat and airy apartments, and "good cheer," with a *table d' hote* surpassed by no other — and prices uniform and low. The names of those guests who have enjoyed the home-bred hospitalities of the Metropolitan, as recorded in the register by their own hands, amount to many thousands; of this great number, not one ever went away dissatisfied, unless he demanded what personal attention and ungrudging generosity could not give.

This House has all the charms of home, for it has all its comforts. It is resorted to by the Western people as a favorite and familiar spot, where all their taste for neatness and domestic economy is gratified. It is the resort of traders generally, being central and convenient, and the charges moderate for one of the best Hotels in Chicago. One dollar and fifty cents per day is the regular charge of the Metropolitan.

Rooms are always reserved for passengers arriving by the various trains during the night. The management of the Metropolitan could not be in better hands. May B. H. Skinner long continue to be its worthy Master.

RAILROADS OF THE WEST.

A FEW years have witnessed a mighty revolution in the Western States in facilities of communication, increase of population, wealth, and commerce, chiefly through the agency of Railways. Before their construction, these States were dependent upon the navigation of the Ohio and Mississippi, and their tributaries, for outlets to the markets of the world. From four to six months in the year, the navigation of these rivers was always interrupted, and often rendered impassible by low water or ice. But Railways have opened to the vast commerce of the West artificial channels of communication which defy the inclemencies of the seasons, and triumph over the obstructions of nature. Railroads are talismanic wands. They have a charming power. They do wonders—they work miracles. They are better than laws; they are essentially, politically and religiously — the pioneer, and van-guard of civilization. They announce to the world as the angel announced on the plains of Judea, "On earth peace and good will toward men." Let then every man, village, town, city, county, state and territory in the land co-operate with Congress in creating these new channels of internal improvement, and uniting their efforts to sustain them, that "swords may be turned into plow shares and spears into pruning hooks," that mountains and valleys may be leveled and crooked places made straight, that produce and persons, as well as thoughts and feelings, may enjoy the speediest inter-communication between the heart and the extremities of the country, that the internal improvement of the land may keep pace with the internal improvement of the spirit in man. The gigantic system of public works that has been constructed during the last few years, by the Western States, has no parallel in history. The Corsican soldier never opened such avenues of communication between territories of such vast magnitude; nor, indeed, do we find in all the records of history any system of public works at all comparable in grandeur of conception, or results, to these Western Railways, except when we go back to Rome.

The boldness of the projection, the vigor of prosecution, the startling rapidity with which these herculean labors have been preformed, have successively amazed and electrified the world. Nothing could have justified so daring a system of expenditure but the anticipated results upon the value of all real estate in this mighty valley.

As if by the wand of enchantment, the dwellers on our wide extended prairies have in a day seen distance annihilated, so that the farmer of these Western States, whose home a few years ago was in the wilderness, now feels like the farmer on the banks of the Hudson, the Ohio, or the Mississippi.

Here are concentrated a hardy race of industrious people, by whose united effort these wonderful resources of nature are being developed, thereby adding millions annually to our national wealth. They come from every nation and every clime; the hardy sons of toil from New England's sterile soil — the newly arrived fugitives from the crumbling despotisms of the old world—brave, industrious men from every quarter of the globe. Here let them come and settle upon the virgin lands in the vicinage of these Railways. In this way hundreds of thousands will become independent land owners and cultivators of the soil; and we shall witness their rapid progress on the road to more civilized life, which gradually brings the embellishments of refinement, and builds up great and prosperous communities, with free schools everywhere distributed among them, and books and newspapers carried to every door. Snobs from despotic Europe have charged us, in this country, with lack of refinement, which is the boast of European courts and capitals. We can afford to put up with all this. We can point to a million of happy homes in the free West, owned by fathers and families — a great people starved out of Europe — escaped from the house of bondage, like God's chosen people from Egypt, who say, "Here are the achievements of a Republic," (which now, since the "Slaveholders' Rebellion," will become a hundred fold stronger, and more glorious in the eyes of the civilized world.) "If we do not make courtiers here, we make men — something which despotism never did — at best it only made gilded slaves."

NORTH-WESTERN RAILWAY.

One of the most important of these Railways, which centre in Chicago, is the CHICAGO AND NORTH-WESTERN RAILWAY. This very popular Railway is now in complete order, having added largely to its equipments and motive power, as well as a thorough repair of its entire track, which renders it in every respect a first-class road.

This is one of the most important roads entering into Chicago, and when it shall have completed all its projected connections, especially that with the Lake Superior mineral region, it will do more to enrich this Capital of the West than any other iron-belted avenue which centres here. Its connections with so many different roads, steamboat and stage routes in the North-West, must eventually make it one of the most remunerative corporations in the West.

By a glance at the map on the last page of this volume, our readers can form some idea of the many points in the North and North-West that can be reached by this road.

This Road, without doubt, is one of the most important to the interest and trade of Chicago, among the many that terminate in this city. Located, and running as it does, through the very garden of the agricultural country of the North-West, its many railroad connections in Wisconsin, give it an opportunity to compete successfully with the trade of Milwaukee, the capital of Wisconsin. It crosses every railroad in the State tributary to Milwaukee, and at every crossing arrangements have been made to transfer cars to its track; consequently it commands a large share of the products of the North-West, which, without this road, would be obliged to seek Milwaukee as its only market. Having a direct connection with Northern Illinois, Northern Iowa, Wisconsin, Minnesota, etc., the increase of business as the country fully develops itself, must be immense.

The main line of this Road extends from Chicago to Appleton, Wis., a distance of two hundred and thirteen miles, and is now being extended from Appleton to Green Bay, a distance of thirty miles, which extension will be completed and running by the middle of September, 1862, making the total distance of the main line two hundred and forty-three miles. The completion to Green Bay will be of great importance both to the road and to this city, as it will open a trade to Chicago that heretofore has had no outlet, except by lake to Buffalo, and during the close of navigation has had no outlet whatever.

The importance of the Chicago and North-Western Railway, we are pleased to learn, is fully appreciated by our business men. It has also a direct connection with the Mississippi River from Dunleith, Prairie du Chien and La Crosse, and most naturally commands a large share of the resources of Minnesota, Iowa, etc., both in passengers and freight, from its northern terminus. It now receives an immense trade from the great lumbering country in Northern Wisconsin; and before long, in accordance with the design of its projectors, it will penetrate into the great mining and mineral districts of Northern Michigan. Probably no road in the North-West has such peculiar advantages in its location as this. Almost every point is tributary to it, and it must eventually prove, as the country develops itself, one of the best paying roads in the country. The capital of the road is as follows:

Capital Stock	$2,955,236.17
Preferred 1st Mortgage Bonds	1,250,000.00
General 1st do do	3,000,000.00
do 2nd do do	2,000,000.00

The following are the officers of the Road:

Wm. B. Ogden, President; P. H. Smith, Vice President; Geo. L. Dunlap, General Superintendent; E. DeWitt Robinson, General Passenger Agent; Geo. P. Lee, Treasurer; Chas. S. Tappin, General Freight Agent.

Company's Office, corner of Lake and Clark Streets.

PITTSBURGH, FORT WAYNE AND CHICAGO.

THIS great Railroad, which is doing so much to develop the commercial position of Chicago, was completed to this city in 1858. It is over four hundred and sixty miles in length, extending from Chicago to Pittsburgh, completing, in connection with the Pennsylvania Central Railroad, the great Western line from Philadelphia to Chicago. The fact of its being the *shortest* route to the sea-board, one of the safest, best conducted and most pleasant, the fare as low as by any other route; and in connection with the Pennsylvania Central, extending from the shores of Lake Michigan to the placid waters of the Delaware, a distance of eight hundred and fourteen miles, passing through four different States, embracing some of the most beautiful landscape scenery, which may be termed the Switzerland of America, with all the sublimity of Alpine grandeur, to the more quiet charms of lovely and romantic valleys, and the wide-spread prairies, at once renders it one of the most popular and interesting routes in this country.

The herculean labors performed by these two companies, the boldness of the projection and the final result, electrifies the men of the other hemisphere, who dare not grapple with such undertakings. And yet these two roads, so substantially constructed, so thoroughly equipped, so well officered by men possessing the best railroad talent of the age, and now becoming so profitably managed, are but the opening of a great Appian way, now linking the great chain of lakes with the tide waters of the Delaware, and destined at some future day to connect with that other road of iron, *to be* built by a great and free people, which will link the two earth-encircled oceans by iron, electricity and steam. Who can foresee the future of these two roads, as they directly contribute to the commercial supremacy — the unprecedented growth and prosperity of this Metropolis? The citizens of Chicago ought always to award a generous support to the Pittsburgh and Fort Wayne Road; it is their true interest so to do, for it is one of the great arteries that nourish the vitals of our commercial greatness.

This Road has caused a mighty revolution in the sections of country through which it passes, in facilities of communication, increase of population, wealth and commerce. It has opened a channel of communication which defies the inclemencies of seasons. Every acre of land in the region through which it passes has more than quadrupled in value, and wealth is rushing in to enrich their owners. It connects at Crestline with the Cleveland, Columbus and Cincinnati Road; at Lima, with the Dayton and Michigan; at Fort Wayne, with the Toledo, Wabash and Western; at Mansfield, with the Sandusky and Newark; at Alliance, with the Cleveland and Pittsburgh; at Rochester, with the Steubenville and Indiana. At Fort Wayne, the company have recently erected a first-class Dining Station, that oasis so grateful to the sight of the hungry traveler; its table is all that the most fastidious epicurean could desire. Improvements of a similar kind are continually being multiplied, which will add to the comfort and convenience of the traveler. At Chicago, there is in process of erection a magnificent structure, to be known as the "Union Depot." It is worthy the spirited and popular companies who, conjointly with the Pittsburgh, Fort Wayne and Chicago projected it.

Two through trains daily leave each terminus of this road. The speed is the highest attainable with safety; the cars are spacious and well ventilated, constructed with all the modern improvements, including the Sleeping Cars, which are the finest on any western road.

The principal officers, under whose immediate supervision it is managed, are men of accredited Railroad ability and give universal satisfaction. Mr. William P. Shinn is the General Passenger Agent at Pittsburgh.

PENNSYLVANIA CENTRAL RAILROAD.

ONE of the great facts of the age, which has been fully demonstrated by this unholy Rebellion, is the advantages and value of Railroads to the Government in the hour of its peril.

No Railroad, perhaps, in this country, has contributed so much strength and assistance to the Government, as the Pennsylvania Central — one of the best constructed, best equipped, and best officered roads on this continent; managed by men possessing superior railroad ability — the highest integrity; forming the great Appian iron-belted way across the mountains, from the tide-waters of the Delaware to the Valley of the Great West. It has accomplished more in the protection of our Capitol from the threatened assaults of the Rebel Crusader, whose hosts had encamped on the banks of the Potomac, with the lighted torch in one hand and the sword of the destroyer in the other, than any road in this country.

It has been so well and ably managed, not only in a financial point of view, but always consulting the best interest of the public, whose servant it has ever been; that it has become a popular, wealthy and powerful corporation — reaching out its giant arms on every side, extending its influence and aid through new channels, to intersect with other roads, thereby enriching the great national domain, by extending the boundaries of civilization, and aiding the material greatness of the age.

The present managers of this road have accomplished three very important things: first, they have reduced the expenses; second, they have increased receipts; third, they have multiplied the accommodations for the public — and it may safely be laid down as a rule, that no railroad in the world can fail of success when it contains these three great elements of power. This road is earning more money, affording greater accommodations, and carrying passengers literally by the million, with less loss of life and limb, than any other road of the same extent and amount of business. We only wish that this example could be imitated by the other Railroads of the United States, into which so many millions of money have been thrown by confiding stockholders; for then we might show a clearer record of our railroad operations that we boast so much of in this country.

As the great highway for travel, from every section of the great Mississippi Valley South-West, and more especially from the North-West, which is so rapidly becoming the seat of a dense population, and centralization of inland commerce and trade; its advantages, in connection with the Pittsburgh, Ft. Wayne & Chicago Road, can hardly be estimated, in developing our commercial greatness.

As a through route for travel or freight from this point, there is none, perhaps, that offer greater or more combined advantages, than the Pittsburgh, Ft. Wayne & Chicago, in conjunction with the Pennsylvania Central. Baggage can be checked through to Philadelphia or New York; the cars are commodious, and the sleeping-cars contain all the modern improvements — the fare always as low as by any other route. The principal officers may always be found at their post of duty, guarding the interests of the road with untiring vigilance.

The Pennsylvania Central runs three through daily passenger trains between Pittsburgh and Philadelphia, connecting direct, in the Union Depot at Pittsburgh, with through trains from all Western cities, for Philadelphia, New York, Boston, Baltimore, and Washington City; thus furnishing facilities for the transportation of passengers, perhaps, unsurpassed, for speed and comfort, by any other route. Freights of all descriptions can be forwarded from Philadelphia, Boston, New York or Baltimore, to any point on the railroads of Ohio, Kentucky, Indiana, Illinois, Wisconsin, Iowa or Missouri, by Railroad direct. It also connects at Pittsburgh with boats which float upon all the navigable waters of the West. The efficient and active officers of this road are, H. H. Houston, General Freight Agent at Philadelphia; L. L. Houpt, General Ticket Agent; Thos. A. Scott, General Superintendent, Altoona, Pa., and W. H. Holmes, General Western Agent, Indianapolis.

THE IMPERIAL CITY.

NEW YORK has fully vindicated her claim to the title of the Empire State; for she has concentrated or developed on her soil the highest elements of supremacy. Standing as her chief city does, on the verge of an European ocean, with the gigantic arms of the sea thrown around her, and washed on the west by the lordly Hudson, which came down from her distant hills, she still cast a glance of exploration towards the chain of great inland lakes, and determined to bring the tribute of their waters to her feet. It was a startling conception; but under the guidance of Clinton this work was done. It was the boldest and the best work that had been achieved by mankind since the days of the Cæsars.

The Erie Canal had, however, been opened but a few years before the indomitable genius of New York enterprise began to think of opening an iron road direct to the shores of lake Erie, a distance of four hundred and seventy miles, bringing the chief sea ports of the Atlantic within forty-two hours of the Mississippi valley. But the immediate execution of this more than imperial work was beyond even New York daring. It was arrested by the terrible revulsion of 1837, which struck down the nation. In 1841, less than fifty miles had been built. But the recovered energies of the Metropolis were once more directed to the work, and from that period it went on. Through forests and mountains, across rivers and gorges, this Roman Road forced its irresistible way till at last, in the summer of 1851, the inspiring announcement was made that a train of cars, bearing the President of the United States and his Cabinet, would leave the Metropolis for the great lakes of the West. Once more the firing of cannon proclaimed the opening of a new avenue through the Empire State, and within an hour from the first note on the Hudson, the reverberations had penetrated every valley and crossed every mountain and river, and gone rolling along the blue waters of lake Erie. This immense road, after many financial embarrassments, is now in full and successful operation.

The management of this Railway with the expenditure of upwards of twenty million dollars, has called into requisition talent enough to have administered a government, and genius enough to have conducted a great campaign.

Its present management, under the new corporation, which change occurred at the commencement of the present year, are cheerful indications of a highly prosperous future. No better or more competent set of officers ever presided over the interests of any Railway company. Mr. Charles Minot, who occupies a very responsible post — that of Superintendent — is equal to its duties, and by his assiduous habits of industry, clear head, and indomitable will, has earned a proud station among prominent business men for his Railroad management. Mr. E. S. Spencer, the Western Agent, at Chicago, is every way fitted for this important post of duty, socially, not less than in a business point of view. The interests of the Erie Railway, in Chicago, have fallen into the keeping of a representative man.

Arrangements have recently been made by this company, which will enable persons desiring to go to Europe, to procure through tickets at the lowest rates of fare, at their office 64 Clark Street, for all the principal European cities, thereby avoiding delay in New York and the risk of being swindled by ticket agents. The time by this road is as quick and the fare as low as by any other route. This broad gauge road affords ample room for wide night berths, in cars with all modern improvements, in which the weary traveler can enjoy a night's rest without interruption.

ST. LOUIS, ALTON AND CHICAGO RAILROAD.

THIS Road runs from Chicago to St. Louis, making a distance of two hundred and eighty-one miles, of which thirty-six miles of the Joliet and Chicago Railroad, and twenty-four miles of the Terre Haute and Alton Railroad are leased and employed. In December, 1859, owing to embarrasments, the road passed into the hands of James Robb, Esq., as Receiver, and has since been under his exclusive management. Its outstanding liabilities are as follows:

1st Mortgage Bonds	$2,000,000.
2nd do do	1,585,000.
3rd do do	1,000,000.
Receives Liens about	600,000.
	$6,185,000.

Its receipts for 1860 and 1861 were as follows:

1860	$ 938,041.
1861	1,098,464.

A charter has been obtained from the Legislature of the State of Illinois for a new organization, to be styled the Chicago and Alton Railroad Company. The line of this road is the most direct between the cities of Chicago and St. Louis, and twenty-four miles shorter than any other existing route, it penetrates a region of country of great advantages and fertility, and is one of the most important Railroads in Illinois.

GALENA AND CHICAGO UNION.

THIS is the parent of the railroad system of Illinois. The first forty miles of the road was opened in 1849, and completed to Freeport, its terminus, in 1853 Here it merges into the Illinois Central. From 1849 until 1856 its prosperity had scarcely a parallel, and since the latter date its business had been encouraging, considering the circumstances governing nearly all railroads in the Western States. From the first opening the company have earned and paid an average dividend of twelve and one half per cent. per annum upon the capital. It has numerous important connections, and as a general thing it does a profitable business. The stocks of the company are regarded as among the best of our western roads. The season of its largest traffic is yet to come, when it will again pay a dividend approximating its more prosperous days. Its present officers are WALTER L. NEWBERY, President; WM. H. BROWN, Vice President; EDWARD B. TALCOTT, Superintendent; WM. LARRABIE, Secretary; GEO. M. WHEELER, Geneal Ticket Agent. Trains leave on this road from North Wells Street, corner of North Water Street. Freight Depot, South Canal, below West Twelfth, and North Dearborn, corner of Water.

CINCINNATI & CHICAGO AIR-LINE RAILROAD.

THIS last constructed iron-belted way—this new candidate for public patronage—this new right-arm of power to accelerate commercial prosperity, by linking in an indissoluble band the two most prosperous and powerful inland commercial cities on this continent, was finally consummated in May, 1861, at which time this great event was fully announced by deputations of hundreds strong, from either city, interchanging visits and congratulations, making and comparing notes of the advantages and facilities most to be derived from this new acquisition of power. The result has been, from the first opening of the Cincinnati & Chicago Air-Line Road to the present time of writing, just a year ago, that the capacity of this road has been taxed to the utmost power of its rolling stock, to enable them to forward the immense amount of freight. In anticipation of the increase of business, the Company have added largely to their rolling stock, freight and passenger cars; the latter possessing all the modern improvements—the night cars with commodious sleeping accommodations, not surpassed by any other road.

This road secures another link in our great railway connections, of vast importance upon the commercial future of Chicago. It opens up a great trade between our Lake coast—the rich prairies of the North-west—and the waters of the Ohio; it forms another bond of alliance to Chicago, the great heart of the North-West. The business from this city, already very large, is daily increasing. The financial position of this road is most gratifying; not a dollar's worth of stock is hawked upon the market; the price rules so high that men who are the fortunate possessors are quite willing to hold it as a good investment.

The entire length of road is 280 miles. The distance by this route is 42 miles less than any other between Chicago and Cincinnati, and 33 miles shorter between Chicago and Louisville. Two express trains leave daily, through to Cincinnati and Indianapolis without change of cars. Through freight cars leave daily, without breaking bulk. Connections at Cincinnati, for Hamden, Marietta, Parkersburg, and points on the Ohio River. Running time over this road, only 11 hours.

Officers, W. D. Judson, President, New York city; J. Brandt, Jr., Superintendent, Richmond, Ind; Chas. E. Follett, General Ticket Agent, Cincinnati; S. W Chapman, General Freight Agent, Cincinnati; N. A. Moore, General Agent, Chicago.

DISTILLING AND RECTIFYING.

DISTILLATION is the separation of two bodies which may be mixed or combined, by converting the more volatile one into vapor, with the aid of heat, and condensing this product. On heating sea water, the vapor which passes off leaves behind the impurities mechanically mixed, and the salts that were held in chemical solution; the steam condenses upon cold surfaces and forms drops of pure distilled water. Such is the rain, and such are the dew drops, which in nature's laboratory are distilled from all fluid surfaces exposed to evaporation, even the most impure. By this process a more volatile liquid may be separated from others less so, as ether, alcohol, or ammonia, etc., from the water with which they may be mixed. The preparation of a highly intoxicating liquor, by separating the more volatile portion of the fermented juices of sweet fruits and infusions of grain, does not appear to have been understood by the ancients. There are but few nations at the present time who are not in the habit of preparing some form of intoxicating liquors by distillation.

Great improvements have been introduced into the modern stills. Continued scientific investigation has resulted in producing an apparatus for the production of fine spirits and whisky, superior to anything hitherto made. Mr. A. F. Croskey, one of the most enterprising Distillers, has, after long experience and great expense, succeeded in constructing a still which is the most efficient in its results of any in the United States. It is too complicated for any intelligent description to be given of it without drawings. It collects the condensed fluid of all degrees of strength, and of the utmost purity. By this new apparatus he is producing a superior quality of Alcohol Cologne Spirits, for the use of Druggists, Perfumers and wholesale Liquor Dealers. It is the highest proof ever produced in this country, and not excelled, perhaps, by any manufacture in the world. It more than accomplishes the highest expectations of its enterprising owner, to whom it will give the control of this market, for fine Cologne and high proof Spirits.

The consumption of Spirituous Liquors, both as a luxury and in the arts, is so vast that their manufacture necessarily involves considerations of great commercial importance. This is comparatively a new branch of business in Chicago; the demand for Alcohol and Spirits having been, until within the last few years, supplied from Cincinnati, St. Louis and Buffalo. The home demand has become so great as to induce men of capital to invest large amounts in perfecting machinery with all the modern improvements, for producing not only a superior quality, but an abundant supply; having all the raw materials ready at hand, in greater abundance and at less cost than any other point or great commercial centre in the great valley of the West. Therefore this city is becoming the centre of manufacture for Whisky and High Wines. In 1862, there were distilled in this city and vicinity, about one hundred thousand gallons of Proof Whisky, consuming, if we allow one bushel of corn to every three gallons of spirits, 33,000 bushels of corn. There are but eight concerns engaged in distilling Whisky from rye, corn, etc.

The leading business connected with the manufacture of Spirituous Liquors in Chicago is *Rectifying* Whisky. There are at least eight or ten firms engaged in this pursuit. The leading and most extensive one is that of A. S. Croskey. This house, which was formerly W. S. Shufeldt & Co., was among the first to open this business in this city, having commenced here in 1856. Mr. Croskey has a large capital employed in this business, and in the manufacture of his well-known Fine Rye and Monongahela Whiskies, which is said to be equal in flavor and quality to the celebrated Whiskies of Ohio and Pennsylvania, and which, on account of its purity and freedom from any disagreeable smell, is preferred and much used by perfumers and druggists. Mr. Croskey, controlling a large capital, can keep his liquors in store until time imparts that flavor which it is said age alone can give. In addition to articles manufactured by this house, their stock consists in Camphene, Burning Fluid, Scotch Whiskies, Cherry Brandy, also the finest Imported Liquors, Wines and Segars; the imported articles always kept in the United States Bonded Warehouse in this city, which he offers to the trade at the lowest rates and most favorable terms.

Alcohol, it is generally known, is distilled from Whisky — nine gallons of the latter making five gallons of the former. Alcohol for Burning Fluid is ninety-five per cent., while Druggists' Alcohol is but eighty-four per cent., being reduced to that standard after distillation. Burning Fluid, which this firm deals in quite extensively, is made by the admixture of one gallon of Pine Oil to four gallons of Alcohol.

DENTAL SURGERY.

THIS includes the surgical treatment of the teeth — their extraction, the remedying of their serious defects, and the mechanical operation of making and fitting artificial teeth to supply the place of those lost. Although it is less than a century since this art has taken the rank of a distinct profession, attention was directed from the earliest periods to the means of preserving and improving the beauty of the teeth. The ancient Hebrew writers evidently appreciated their importance in giving expression to the countenance, as when Jacob blessing Judah says, "His teeth shall be white with milk," and Solomon compared a fine set of teeth to a flock of sheep even shorn. In the time of Herodotus the art of Dentistry appears to have been practised in Egypt, as a distinct branch of surgery. Little, however, is known of the attainments of these early practitioners. In the ancient tombs of these people, artificial teeth of ivory or wood were found by Belzoni and others, some of which were fastened upon gold plates. It is also stated that the teeth of the mummies have been found filled with gold. Thus it would seem that the Egyptians understood processes of the art which are commonly regarded as only inventions of the refined nations of modern times. In the year 1836, the eminently practical work, "Principles of Dental Surgery," of Leonard Koecker, M. D., who had practised dentistry from 1807 to 1822, in Baltimore and Philadelphia, appeared in London, and fully established the claims of the art to take rank as a distinct branch of science. It appears that in 1776, Duchateau, a chemist of St. Germain en Laye, succeeded with the aid of Dubois, a Dentist of note in Paris, in producing artificial teeth. They imitated the color of the natural teeth and gums by the use of mineral oxides, and obtained royal letters patent from Louis XIV for the invention. The practice of Dentistry was introduced into the United States by Le Mair, of the French force which joined our army during the revolutionary war. About 1788, Mr. John Greenwood established himself in New York, the first American of this profession. In 1795, he carved in ivory an entire set of teeth for Gen. Washington.

The process of Dentistry as a science has been necessarily consequent upon that of anatomy.

The Dental science involves an acquaintance with the anatomical relations of the organs of the mouth with all parts of the system.

In all these processes various kinds of professional talent and mechanical skill are called into requisition, and the operator, in order to give the natural expression of the mouth, imitating the true colors, and proportions of the teeth and gums, must even possess a certain degree of that genius and taste which guide the pencil of the artist, or the chisel of the sculptor.

At the commencement of the present century those who were unfortunate with their teeth, either by injuring them through some severe accident, or by the improper use of pernicious medicines, or who were deformed by having them grow improperly in their places, suffered through long years of misery, totally unconscious that science would ever, to any practical extent, relieve the defects. Now, however, things have changed, deformed grouping of teeth is corrected into charming regularity, decaying teeth are arrested in their progress to ruin, and by the use of incorruptible gold, restored to almost pristine soundness; as those entirely gone are replaced by such wonderful imitations of nature that the most critical eye is deceived, and the wearer scarcely conscious of his premature loss. And by these improvements how much has been added to the sum total of human happiness of mankind — how much suffering has been alleviated, how many sensitive minds have been relieved from the agony of a disagreeable, and perhaps, a repulsive appearance — but, aside from physical comfort, so long as beauty calls forth a response from the human heart, so long will the pearly row of teeth form a battery from which are flashed the sharpest arrows of Cupid's bow. The forehead may lack a marble whiteness, the cheek may be even sallow, and the eye dull, but let the parting lips display a set of pearly teeth, and cold indifference at once turns to admiration, and warms into love — but the ruddy cheek glowing with health, the wavy ringlet, or the eye soft with sensibility and flashing with intellect, when associated with decayed and neglected teeth, only serve to render the unfortunate possessor more positively repulsive than if cast in a plainer mould.

In Chicago there are some twenty-five Dentists. Among the number there are a few men of science and skill in the dental art; men who are thoroughly educated in the science, who have made it a life study, and acquired a reputation for eminence by their high artistic skill and long practice. Among those who have in a remarkable degree secured high consideration as practical Dentists, is Dr. Lorenzo Bush, whose office is at 136 Clark Street. Dr. Bush has had many years practical experience in the most complete as well as simple operations of his profession. He is now prepared in every department to bring a more than usual degree of skill to the relief of his patients.

Dr. Bush adds to the most intense study of his profession, a genius which appreciates the highest triumphs of art. It is to him a source of refined pleasure, to restore to almost primeval beauty the decay of nature and the ravages of disease. With a mind highly cultivated in matters of taste, and a mechanical skill that has become almost creative power, he adds to the charms of youth and contributes to the comforts of age — and knowing what is necessary to make every department of his profession as perfect as possible, he has surrounded himself with every appliance of utility and luxury demanded in an enlightened age.

WHIPS.

THE manufacture of Whips is a business entirely distinct from that of saddles and harness; but the relations existing between them are so intimate that they may properly be considered in the same list of manufactures. In this city, however, the Whip manufacturing is principally in the hands of Mr. G. W. King, who has devoted his life to this branch of productive industry, and is therefore complete master of it in all its details. The Factory of Mr. King is located on Randolph Street, under the Metropolitan Hotel. Here are manufactured all kinds of Whips, from those that sell for one dollar and twenty-five cents per dozen to those which sell at fifty dollars per dozen. The materials used for the stock are Whalebone, Rattan, Fancy Woods, Leather, Gut, Gum, Pitch and Glue; for the lashes, Leather, Gut and Thread; for the handles, Wood, Ivory and Bone; and for the mountings, Gold, Silver, Ivory and Pearl. Machines are used for plaiting or weaving the gut covering. The machine is a circular frame, around which is a series of bevel cogs, driven by a crank-handle in the hands of the operator. The Whip stands in the centre, and receives its gut from numerous spools which surround it; the machine at the same time plaiting the gut over the stock. They are of different capacities, one plaiting sixteen threads, and the other twenty-four.

The great difference in the cost of Whips — some selling as high as fifty dollars per dozen, and even more than that — is mainly in the character of the mountings. Mr. King uses in all his Whips the very best material; and the reputation of his manufactures is unsurpassed by any in the United States. He furnishes the trade to a large extent, both in Chicago and through the North-West. He is able to produce a better article for less money than many of the Whips brought to this market from the East. His business has gradually increased from small beginnings to quite an extensive trade.

The Whip manufacture has suffered severely from the enormous expansion of ladies' skirts, and the consequent demand for whalebone hoops. Again the fashion has changed in skirts, and this time it favors the whip-maker, as the ladies found whalebone to be an imperious master, not yielding readily to their wishes.

The great demand for whalebone for ladies' skirts caused an advance four to five hundred per cent. Now, since the price has receded to its old standard, Whips are sold at less prices by Mr. King than at any previous period.

AGRICULTURAL IMPLEMENT WAREHOUSE.

THAT the cultivation of the soil may be carried on to the best advantage, it is necessary that the farmer be provided with a sufficient stock of machines and implements of the best construction. Very great improvements have of late years taken place in this department of mechanics. The great agricultural societies of the country have devoted much of their attention to it; and under their auspices, and stimulated by their prizes and exhibitions, manufacturers of skill and capital have embarked largely in the business. In many instances the quality of the article has improved and its cost been reduced. The lower price and extended use of iron in the construction of Agricultural Implements has materially added to their durability, and generally to their efficiency, and is thus a source of great saving. While great improvement has taken place in this department, it too commonly happens that the village mechanics, by whom a large portion of this class of implements are made and repaired, are exceedingly unskillful, and lamentably ignorant of the principles of their art. They usually furnish good materials and substantial workmanship, but by their unconscious violation of mechanical laws, enormous waste of motive power is continually incurred and poor results attained. This is being remedied by the construction of the more costly and complex machines being carried on in extensive factories, where, under the combined operation of scientific superintendence, ample capital, and skilled labor, aided by steam power, the work is so performed as to combine the maximum of excellence, with the minimum of cost.

That all these various articles of Agricultural Implements may be better placed in position for sale, where the agriculturist and the merchant who deals direct with the farmer can obatin their supplies, Agricultural Implement Depots have been established, under the management of men who are either agents or extensive purchasers from the manufacturer of every Implement of accredited utility, and every new invention of skill, which will lighten toil and multiply the agencies to greater ease and comfort to the gardener and the farmer.

The House of W. H. KRETSINGER, at No. 91 Water Street, established upon this principle, has added greatly to the facilities of the whole agricultural class of the North-West, and many of these Implements of great utility and simplicity, introduced by him, have inspired new hopes and stimulated to greater activity the cultivator of the soil. We can hardly over-estimate the beneficial results of an establishment of this kind in Chicago, upon our entire agricultural community. Much credit is due to Mr. Kretsinger for the industry, perseverance and skill he has manifested in accumulating into one establishment so many valuable Agricultural Implements. But they are here to be scattered again, for like the wandering Jew, they have a restless immortality. As the Agricultural Goods trade proper embraces a very wide range of Implements and tools, many of which are cumbrous, such as Reapers, Mowers, Threshers, Plows, etc., it becomes necessary for a division of trade; the heavy goods being placed on sale through the country, of easy access to the farmer, while the others are gathered in such an establishment as this of Mr. Kretsinger. Among the leading articles are Scythes, Forks, Snaths, Hoes, Horse and Hand Rakes, Grain Cradles, Scoops, Shovels, Spades, Scythe Stones, etc., etc.; the amount of sales of these articles is immense.

Since the establishment of Mr. Kretsinger's House in Chicago, in 1857, he has been steadily adding to his facilities for extending his trade. He represents one of the oldest and most extensive manufacturing firms in Ohio, whose implements are everywhere accredited as superior in finish, pattern and make. Mr. Kretsinger stands at the head of this business in Chicago, and is worthy of the liberal patronage bestowed on him by merchants who make their purchases in this market. The Agricultural Implement Warehouse of Kretsinger ought to be known by every dealer in the North-West. No purchaser of these goods should visit Chicago without looking through his stock.

In addition to Agricultural Goods, he also deals extensively in Wagon Makers' Wood Stock.

Remember, Kretsinger's Agricultural Implement Warehouse, No. 91 South Water Street.

PUTNAM'S GREAT EASTERN CLOTHING EMPORIUM.

BUT few are aware of the vast extent to which the sale of *Ready Made Clothing* is carried on at the present day. Probably no branch of business has so rapidly increased in its manufacture and sale as this. But a few years ago, it was confined to goods of very inferior quality, style and make, worn mostly by seamen and laborers. But now the most fashionable, exquisite or fastidious taste, can be suited in a short time, with goods which for price and finish would rival the most celebrated tailors of London and Paris. In the cities of New York, Boston and Philadelphia alone, the yearly sale of Ready Made Clothing is estimated to exceed $70,000,000.

If the ancients, who first donned the skins of wild beasts, or covered up their nakedness with the leaves of the forests; or even the matrons of more modern times, who occupied their leisure hours in weaving home-spun, while the juveniles were lulled to sleep by the music of the spinning wheel, could once more visit the earth, their astonishment could be no greater than that of the recluse purchaser, who for the first time enters PUTNAM's Great Eastern Emporium or Ready Made Clothing Establishment, where combined art, industry, perseverance and capital have instituted a new era in the Ready Made Clothing business, producing a *better article* for *less money*, and more *accurate fits* and fashionable styles than formerly was accorded only to the more wealthy.

The enterprise and ingenuity of the Yankee has perfected, by the aid of machinery, all this — and that most wonderful little piece of mechanism, the sewing machine, which has so recently been added to the list of inventions, has brought about a new era in the Clothing trade, whereby the man of most humble means is enabled to support garments of as *recherche* style as the man who can boast of his thousands. We would call attention to the fact, that but few cities can boast of a more magnificent store for the sale of Ready Made Clothing than our enterprising friend, PUTNAM, proprietor of the Mammoth Eastern Emporium. Mr. PUTNAM is yet a young man, and has been with us but a few years. Still, by an indomitable energy, he now outrivals all competitors, and leads all others in the sale of FASHIONABLE READY MADE CLOTHING. At his store may be found piles and piles of goods, of every quality, make and finish; and the crowd of customers who daily throng the establishment, is a sufficient guarantee that he has accomplished the great aim he had in view — making his fortune by selling an enormous quantity of goods at the lowest living profit — depending upon his increasing sales for his profit. Mr. PUTNAM is not slow in using printer's ink; and he informs us that his success depends, in a measure, upon advertising. He has fully demonstrated the value of a liberal and judicious system of advertising. From small beginnings, a few years since, he has realized a fortune, and built up an extensive and successful trade. He believes that if a bad article can be sold by a vigorous system of pushing and advertising, much more so a good one; and herein lies the secret of his great success. During the last ten years he has paid twenty-five thousand dollars for advertising — some weeks, even as high as from three hundred to five hundred dollars. We are proud to record the names of such men, to be handed down to posterity, who, by industry, perseverance and liberality, have carved out an honorable fortune.

Such enterprise certainly deserves success; and we would most cheerfully say, that by a visit to his establishment, you will find his clerks polite and attentive; and his goods and prices cannot but induce you to make your purchases at the Emporium, when in need of any articles in the way of Clothing. Go and be convinced of the fact, at PUTNAM's MAMMOTH EASTERN CLOTHING EMPORIUM, 116 and 118 Randolph Street, Chicago.

MECHANICAL BAKERY.

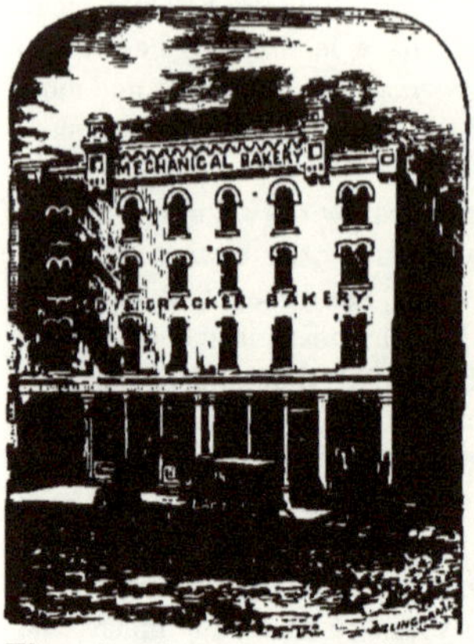

BREAD is the staff of life among all civilized nations, and on the European continent it is nearly the only solid food of the peasantry of large provinces. For this reason many inventions have been made in every country to improve and cheapen the manufacture of this great staple of existence, only two of which have, thus far, been successful. They are those of Hiram Berdan of New York, and J. F. Rolland of France.

Berdan's Machinery was established in Brooklyn in December, 1856, and was destroyed by fire in May following. A large establishment, on the same plan, has since been erected in Chicago, capable of converting two hundred and fifty barrels of flour into bread daily; the building is four stories high. There is one oven twenty-seven feet high, twenty-six feet long, and ten feet wide, passing from the basement into the third story. It is heated by an ordinary coal furnace underneath, through brick arches which form the bottom of the oven to fire brick flues, which run up the sides and carry off the smoke to the chimney. The heat is thus radiated into a close chamber. The temperature is regulated by dampers moved by iron rods, which close and open by hand. Within the oven are three endless vertical chains supporting the cars containing the bread. These cars are twenty-six in number, continually in motion one above the other, passing and repassing. The chains move slowly around, so that the cars move upward on one side of the oven and downward on the other. The oven has four doors, two on the first and two on the second story. On the sides where the chains move upward the cars containing the bread enter the oven through the upper door and are delivered at the lower door, the reverse is done on the other side. These bread cars are made of wrought iron frames on which the unbaked loaves are placed. The car being charged with loaves by hand, the door of the oven opens mechanically, an iron arm comes out, pulls in the car on railroad tracks and the door closes. When the car arrives opposite the other door the bread is baked; this door is opened, the car is pushed out by an iron arm, the loaves are dumped from it into baskets, and the car moves on a track to the front of the other door, where the attendant stands ready to load it with new loaves.

Machinery is used for kneading, by which ten barrels are kneaded in ten to fifteen minutes. The dough is made into loaves by another machine. They are all equal weight according to adjustment. The fuel used is coal. It is claimed that there is an economy of fifty per cent. on this combustible, and thirty per cent. on labor, with a gain in the quality and weight of the bread, so that with one Bakery of this kind nearly as much work can be done, as with twenty built on the common plan. And herein consists the unparalleled success of the Mechanical Bakery Company, with a man at the head of its interests of untiring energy, indomitable courage, capable of surmounting every obstacle. This great representative establishment is conducted under a corporate company, composed of gentlemen of high respectability and business talent, one of their number, Mr. H. C. Childs, who acts as general superintendent, devoting his time and interests to the conducting and developing its great interests. Its officers are E. C. Larned, President, J. T. Ryerson, Secretary, B. W. Raymond, and George F. Rumsey, are Directors.

When this establishment first went into operation, with its present efficient board of officers, it became evident it would prove a successful venture, as has subsequently been demonstrated in the highest degree. And to-day the "Chicago Mechanical Bakery" is regarded in the light of a well founded, successful, commercial enterprise, the result of bold energy, persevering efforts, and skilled business management — one of the institutions of interest to our commercial prosperity, and the development of science, in multiplying the necessities of life, cheapening the production, and lessening toil. These advances are encouraging signs of a higher civilization and national prosperity.

The cost of erecting the building was $14,000 and the lot upon which it stands cost $30,000. The capital invested for transacting the business amounts to $82,000. The Bakery went into operation in June 1858, since when it has been continually increasing in its capacity and the perfection of its arrangement. During the last year in addition to its already extensive operations, they have supplied the army in Kentucky, Tennessee, and Western Virginia with six million pounds of bread. Their trade in Crackers, such as Soda, Butter, Boston, Graham, Wine, Water, Pic-nic, etc., go to supply the best dealers in twelve different States. The business amounts to nearly a million of dollars annually.

They give employment to one hundred men. There are four distinct departments, comprising Soft Bread, Hard Bread, Crackers, Pastry and Cakes, consuming about seventy-thousand barrels of flour annually. The motive power of this great establishment is driven by a fifteen horse power steam engine. It is located on North Clinton between Lake and Randolph streets.

FURNITURE, CHAIRS AND UPHOLSTERY.

THIS branch of industry has very much progressed, both in point of taste and extent of production, within the last few years. In 1845 there were but few furniture stores in this city, and they were mostly small ones, keeping samples of the styles of goods, but relying mainly on orders from their customers to supply work for their employees. A spring seat Sofa or Chair was then a luxury — almost a novelty. The art of veneering was just beginning to be understood. Previous to this period a crotch of mahogany wood was cut into veneers by a narrow blade saw, drawn laterally by two men. They could not get more than four veneers out of an inch thickness, and it could only be applied to flat work or very slight curves. About this time circular saws, some of which were seven or eight feet in diameter, were introduced, and gradual improvements were made so that at the present time it is not uncommon to produce sixteen veneers to the inch. Mahogany, rosewood and walnut, and all the finer woods are now used in veneering, with such skill that elliptic ogees and oval surfaces of common wood are covered with a thin coating of fine wood, thus reducing the consumption, comparatively, of finer woods. In course of time mahogany became scarce, and growing in mountain fastnesses it was procured only at great expense. Rosewood has always been equally difficult to obtain. American Walnut was examined and on trial it was found equally suitable for finer Furniture. Walnut is now used more than all other woods combined. The supply on the rich bottom lands of the Western States, generally, is almost unlimited, and the quality of it so superior that large quantities are shipped to Europe. The result is that an immense Furniture manufacturing business has sprung up in this city, which has given Chicago a well merited reputation for the production of fine Furniture; the carved work is really superb, and the less elaborate known as Cottage Furniture is distinguished for excellent workmanship, high polish, tasteful painting and moderate price.

In Messrs. HALE & BROTHER's establishment on Canal, between Lake and Randolph Streets, our attention was attracted to an ingenious method which this firm practice, of staining all their Walnut to a perfect imitation of the finest Rosewood. The stain passes into the grain of the wood, making it durable and susceptible of retaining its Rosewood appearance as long as the wood will endure. Messrs. Hale & Brother have been engaged in business in this city about seven years. They give employment to about fifty hands, and have supplied Furniture for some of the finest mansions in this city. Their principal business consists in supplying the trade, to which they sell large quantities, supplying dealers in most of the towns of the North-West. They have been very successful in the selection of their customers, consequently now occupy a worthy position at the head of the Furniture business of Chicago. We have been unable to arrive at the statistics of the Furniture manufacture in Chicago, but from all the facts collected, the Furniture and Upholstery business will reach five million dollars.

This house connect Upholstering and Mattress manufacturing with the Furniture business. It embraces the manufacture of Curtains, Pew and other Cushions, and the making of Hair, Moss, and other kinds of Mattresses, etc. They are also engaged in the manufacture of Chairs of every description. They devote a good deal of attention to the manufacture of Church, Library, and Counting-house Furniture.

It has become a well-conceded fact, that every article of Furniture required to supply this market can be produced in Chicago and sold to the dealer at less cost than the same article can be brought from an Eastern market. This extensive establishment of Hale & Brother demonstrates what capital, energy and business tact will accomplish, in manufactnring all these articles in Chicago. Their facilities enable them to offer inducements to the trade, which has built up for them an extensive business with the North-West.

PATENT LAW AND SOLICITING OFFICE.

THE impetus and productiveness which our Patent Laws have given to the inventive genius of this country, are truly wonderful. It is only by wandering through the various departments of the Patent Office at Washington, that one can form any adequate idea of the immense number and variety of inventions pertaining to every branch of industry and usefulness, that the wise policy of our Patent system calls out.

Under its protection, the march of invention has been so rapid, and the number of inventors has become so great, as to give rise to and demand a distinct profession, devoted exclusively to their interests. Patent Soliciting has become a necessity to Inventors, and Patent Lawyers are a disideratum to all who have anything to do with Patent Rights.

In the growth of the West, in wealth and substantial prosperity, the inventive spirit of its inhabitants has not been left behind; and it is of great importance to Western Inventors, and something they will be glad to know, that a reliable Patent Law and Soliciting Office has been established in the Metropolis of the West.

Inventors who have hitherto been compelled, at an extra risk and expense, to send their inventions East to be patented, can now get their Patents secured, and everything done that an Inventor needs to have done to secure his rights, nearer home and in the most careful and and reliable manner.

R Messrs. COBURN & MARKS, Attorneys and Counselors at Law, established their office in 1860, and making Patent Law a specialty, are thoroughly prepared to do any kind of Patent business, either as Solicitors of Patents for Inventors, or as Attorneys and Counselors in cases of Patent Right litigation.

Inventors having inventions on which they desire to obtain Patents, will find it for their interest to send for one of their circulars; and any information they may want in regard to Patents will be promptly given.

Their office is in Larmon's Block, corner of Clark and Washington Streets. Chicago.

THE EPICURE'S HOME.

THE last Steamer from Europe brought to our shores a time-honored citizen of Chicago, whom everybody knows that knows what good living is, and are epicurians enough to enjoy the cherished luxury where it is attainable. The arrival home of Mr. JOHN WRIGHT, the gentlemanly proprietor of "Anderson's," is an event of no little interest to many of our best citizens, who have so often regaled their taste with rare delicacies at his tables, and remembered him with gratitude a thousand times, around the festive board, at the bridal party, the evening sociable, or the sumptuous banquet, given by some gentleman of fortune to some honored guest. If Mr. Wright has heretofore been considered the prince of caterers, what may we not expect from his increased knowledge and ripe experience, after visiting the *Cafe de Paris*, and all the Hotels and *Restaurants of note* in Europe, with an eye keen to the acquisition of knowledge in the epicurean art, and the power of dispensing luxuries and dainties with elegance and greater refinement?

"Anderson's" has become an institution of as great importance to the families of fortune and favor, as well as to *all* whose palate craves a dainty or a luxury, either from *his* tables or at *their own*, around their own fireside in the retirement of their homes.

Every conceivable thing that is pleasant to the eye or grateful to the taste can be ordered at Anderson's, and when "weighed in the balances not found wanting," in all those requisites so essential to the highest attainable luxury.

During the coming summer many a grateful remembrance will be had of John Wright, by the thousands who will regale their tastes with his celebrated Ice Cream made by steam. The rich fruits in their season — the delicate pastry and confectionery — the luscious shell-fish expressed daily from their watery element — all are to be had at Anderson's in their greatest perfection. For the benefit of strangers, we will state that "Anderson's" is No. 83 South Clark Street, opposite the Court House.

BOOKBINDING AND RULING.

BOOKBINDING is the art of fastening together the sheets of paper composing a book, and enclosing them in pasteboard, covered with leather of various kinds, also cloth, paper and wood; the object of which is the preservation of the book, and its protection from injuries while in use. It involves, in addition to skill in securing the sheets, no little knowledge of decorative art; for from its commencement it has gone beyond the mere necessities of utility, often to heights of noble extravagance. In respect to expense, the limits have never been defined, ostentation of display having at times superseded the binder proper by the goldsmith and the lapidary. At times when books were rarities — either manuscripts, produced by patient, secluded labor, or the productions of the printing press, during the infancy of typography — they were naturally very highly prized; and as much labor, skill, care and expense were bestowed upon the protection and embellishment of a cherished folio, as would suffice at the present day for the building of a house. The wooden cover of a book, with its metal hinges, bosses, guards and clasps, seems, in all but dimensions, fit for a church door; but since the great improvement in the mechanical arts connected with the production of books, together with the extension of education to all classes, and the consequent diffusion of knowledge, literature has become almost as necessary as clothing and shelter to the comforts of civilized man; hence the multiplication of books, and the gradual but radical changes witnessed during the present century in the art of Bookbinding.

This great art still lacks its historian; it is much to be regretted, that on a subject so well deserving attention of the curious and learned, no researches have been made into the origin, progress and decline of the art. Beyond a few incidental and fragmentary passages in the writings of bibliographers and travelers, merely description, we may seek in vain for reliable information.

It would be exceedingly difficult to determine what the art of Bookbinding, or that which occupied its place, was during the middle ages, as no evidence remains, and the light of discovery has not been thrown upon it. All that we can at present learn is, that in the ninth and tenth centuries, owing probably to the impulse given to letters and to everything connected with literature by Charlemagne and the princes of his line, the external decoration of manuscript was carried to a high state of perfection. The parchment in leaves was inclosed between two tables of wood or ivory, inlaid and incrusted with jewels and precious stones, bosses of gold and silver, sometimes with hinges and clasps of these metals.

The library of the Louvre contains the the celebrated *Book of Hours*, written with letters of gold upon purple parchment; it is covered with red velvet. This book was given to the city of Toulouse by Charlemagne.

It was only in the eighteenth century that binding assumed an importance as an art. The present tendency of the art is toward neatness in general effect, and where ornament is at all conspicuous, to emblematic truth. The introduction of Cloth binding has had the effect of combining considerable durability with economy; and a large portion of books now made are in that style. Leather, Morocco, Velvet, occasionally Ivory and Mother-of-pearl, and sometimes highly polished Wood, are used for the more expensive bindings; while with books intended for presentation, much latitude is allowed in respect to intrinsic adornment.

At the Crystal Palace exhibition, held in New York in 1853, the first premium for Bookbinding was awarded to William Mathews, for a copy of Owen Jones' "Alhambra," on which the Bookbinder's work was estimated to be worth six hundred dollars. The material and decoration of the binding were solely such as properly belong to the art, including no jewels or precious metals, and its value consisted entirely in the manual labor consumed in its production.

Among the Bookbinders in Chicago, we have those who produce binding equal to any made in the United States. For artistic finish, excellence of workmanship, neatness in general effect and emblematic truth, there is no one who ranks higher than Mr. WILLIAM J. WILSON, whose Bindery is located in the building known as Rounds' Type Foundry, on State, near Lake Street. Mr. Wilson has devoted thirty years of unremitting toil and perseverance in perfecting himself in this growing art. His early education in Bookbinding commenced in England, where his early advantages have not been lost in his subsequent experience in this country during the last twenty years. Some of the best volumes that ever left a bindery from this city have come from Mr. Wilson's.

A very important branch of his business consists in Ruling and Blank Books, which in Chicago has become a very extensive business. His ruling machines combine all the modern improvements, which is a great gain on those of former years. No nation or people equal this for Blank Book Binding. Mr. Wilson stands pre-eminent in this branch of the trade, his facilities are such as to enable him to execute orders with despatch and in the best possible manner.

MUSIC PUBLISHERS.

THE musical composers who furnish our songs and whose productions have the widest popularity among the masses of our people, and are educating them for a higher civilization, are known to very few even by reputation. The new melodies and songs, sacred and secular, that greet the public ear week after week, and are sung, whistled and hummed by the thousands all through the valley of the West, in the sacred temple as anthems to the great Jehovah, in the concert room, in the *Salon* of fashion, around the fire-side of the cabin and the hovel, in the camp and on the tented field, and wherever human voices are heard; thumped on piano fortes, thrummed on banjoes, breathed on flutes, tortured into variations; all indicate our growing love for music. Every nation has had its native music, and records of national songs have come down to us from the remotest antiquity. We too have have a native music, such as Yankee Doodle, Hail Columbia, and some other national songs; but as artistic compositions, they are so inferior that they indicate a national spirit for independence, rather than a taste for music.

In America we are inaugurating a new reign for music, which has long been an exotic. We are beginning to study it in common schools, like the Germans — we are beginning to enthrone Apollo in our homes — and will yet enshrine his glorious image in our hearts. Since the shrill clarion of war's alarm has summoned the nation to arms, most of our music composers are weaving into songs and melodies historic and national souvenirs, which are becoming everywhere popular, and will have no unimportant agency in preserving many incidents and embellishments of history.

One of the most important agencies in diffusing these songs and melodies throughout this entire valley is the great Music Publishing House of Messrs. Root & Cady, No. 95 Clark Street. This firm represents one of the fairest and most extensive music publishing houses in the West.

The firm is composed of George F. Root, E. T. Root, and C. M. Cady. All of them are musical men, the first named is the celebrated musical composer — they devote their whole time to the interests of the business — these three make our Trinity of musical fame in this valley of the West. Messrs. Root & Cady are the sole agents for this city for the celebrated Steinway & Sons' Patent overstrung grand and square Pianos, which are considered the best manufactured, and warranted for five years. They have received medals over all others made. Thalberg, Benedict, Strakosch, and other illustrious composers of Europe, have given homage and written their unqualified commendations, and one by one composers, preformers, and lovers of music throughout the world have greeted them with delight wherever they have been known. In sweetness, power of tone, solidity of construction and elasticity of touch they are probably superior to any other Piano manufactured.

Messrs. Root & Cady have recently extended their facilities for publishing, by adding to their already extensive business a music Composition House, enabling them to prepare their own illuminated title pages and sheet music, with great care and correctness, and produce any piece of sheet music or bound volume at the shortest notice. They are the originators of music publishing in the West, and the *only* house having their facilities.

These elegant music rooms on the first and second floors of No. 95 Clark Street are a constant resort for sociable, musical, loving spirits.

THE PRESENT METALLIC AGE.

THIS might with propriety be called *the blended metallic age;* for although silver has been very scarce, yet gold and iron are in abundance. Iron is doing more for mankind than gold. It is revolutionizing the world. England digs little or no gold from her soil, but iron has made her the richest nation on the earth. Iron is stronger than armies; it is mightier than kings — the most powerful of all metals, and the most bountifully provided in variety and general distribution of its ores. It is applied to the greatest number of purposes, and consumed in larger quantities than all other metals combined. The most massive metallic works are made of it, and also the most delicate instruments, as the hair springs of watches, in which the metal attains a far higher value, weight for weight, than that of gold itself. No material is so enhanced in price by the valuable qualities imparted to it by labor. A bar of iron worth five dollars is worth ten and one-half dollars when made into horse-shoes; fifty-five dollars in the form of needles; three thousand two hundred and eighty-five dollars in pen-knife blades; twenty-nine thousand four hundred and eighty dollars, in buttons; and two hundred and fifty thousand dollars, in balance springs of watches.

The art of working metals is a very ancient one. The Scriptures tell us that Tubal Cain was an instructor of every artifice in brass and iron.

The multiform uses of iron are beginning to be understood by the American nation as by no other. One small vessel, built of iron, planned and perfected by our own countryman, "ERICSSON," has by one single trial of her skill and power, electrified all the naval powers of the world, and is destined to revolutionize the whole system of naval architecture. Iron is beginning to be used in building our cities. The establishment of our empire in the gold-land, fringed the Pacific with meteor cities, that flashed in flame and were rebuilt only to become heaps of ashes. There men have begun now to build what the fire cannot consume; and the weary gold hunter deposits his treasure where he defies the flames.

Iron is doing more for Chicago than gold and silver in the hands of our artizans, founders and machinists. Men of enterprise, genius and business talent, are furnishing rails for our great Appian ways, which open up to us communication with towns and cities whose commerce is enriching us and making us a great people. To few of our citizens is society more deeply indebted than to P. W. GATES, President of the "Eagle Works Manufacturing Company." His efforts in establishing this gigantic manufacturing interest in Chicago cannot be too highly appreciated. The Herculean efforts which this man has made to convince the world that iron was intended by the Creator for great and noble purposes, developing its power and influence in moulding the destinies of nations, have been astounding.

More than twenty years ago, Mr. Gates laid the foundation of this great representative establishment in an obscure blacksmith shop, with a capital amounting to just twelve and one-half dollars, which comprised his stock in trade. He was burdened with a debt of seven hundred and fifty dollars, caused by the failure of the State to pay contractors on the canal; and in consequence of the general embarrassment of the country, by failure of crops, etc., he made slow progress for several years. He possessed the energy that knew no discouragement; his heroism was equal to all exigencies. He has passed through trying times; for he has been a bold man, daring to do good where it was hazardous business, venturing to trust neighbors when they did not confide in each other—but there never was an hour when those who knew him did not trust him with the greatest confidence. His name became known not only through this valley of the West, but in almost every place where gold is dug on this continent; for Gates' Steam Engines and Boilers, *high and low pressure*, Sugar Mills and Evaporators, for making sugar and syrup from the Sorghum, or Chinese sugar cane; Quartz Mills and machinery for the gold regions and Lake Superior copper mines; Flouring

Mills, Saw Mills, and in fact nearly every article of machinery required in the North-West. In 1857, the sales of this establishment amounted to six hundred and twenty-five thousand dollars, giving employment to some four or five hundred hands. The buildings and grounds occupy most of three blocks. Since the crash of 1857, the Eagle Works have been obliged to reduce their force; employing at the present time from seventy-five to one hundred and fifty men, with facilities and every prospect, when the country shall be restored to peace, that this establishment will equal if not exceed its former prosperity.

Under a new organization of the Company, which went into effect January 1st, 1862, the name was changed, and will hereafter be known as the "Eagle Works Manufacturing Company," operated under a most liberal and special charter. Its officers are, P. W. Gates, President; Geo. W. Gage, Vice President; James W. Scoville, Secretary and Treasurer; Thomas Chalmers, Superintendent; D. R. Fraser, Draftsman.

The Board of Directors is composed of Geo. W. Gage, Geo. Steel, Wm. B. Ogden, Matthew Laflin, Samuel Hall, and Charles B. Brown.

HIDES.

THE extent of the Hide trade is becoming of so much importance in a commercial point of view that a brief review in regard to the rise, progress, and present position of the trade, as also its extent and progress in Chicago, and the party who most fairly represents it in its largest interest, may not be uninteresting to our readers.

Hides, in commerce, are known as the skins of some of the larger animals which are especially adapted for the manufacture of leather. The term is applied chiefly to those of cattle, the horse, the hippopotamus, and of the buffalo, when intended for tanning. The skins of young cattle are distinguished as kips, those of the deer, sheep, goat, seal, etc., even though intended for leather are called skins. Ox hides, which may be considered as including all the skins of the bovine kind designed for leather, and horse hides also, are articles of large export from South American countries. California also, has furnished great quantities of them. The animals from which they are principally obtained roam in vast herds over the pampas, the property of the estates upon which they may be found. They are lassoed and slaughtered only for the hides, and are immediately dried in the sun for exportation. Those obtained in the tropics does not make so good leather as the hides of temperate latitudes. The East Indies also supply a large portion of the hides of commerce, especially to the

English market. They are also obtained from the West Indies, the cape of Good Hope, from Holland, and the countries up the Mediterranean. The skins of domestic animals add to the supplies, and under the name of green hides, are rated as of a better quality than the dry or salted foreign hides. The heaviest hides and those which make the best sole leather are the skins of steers. Those of the bull are thickest about the neck and parts of the belly, but in the back they are inferior in thickness and in fineness of grain to the hides of oxen, or even of cows and heifers. But hides differ much in quality when obtained from animals resembling each other in size and in other respects, and their relative excellence cannot always be determined on examination. The best are made into the heavy leather used for the best trunks, soles of shoes, belts for machinery, harness, and other purposes. The lighter qualities serve for the uppers of common boots and shoes, and some are employed in European countries without tanning for covering trunks. Kips and the skins of calves make the best leather for the uppers of fine boots and shoes.

Hides were an important article of trade with the ancient Egyptians, being largely imported from foreign countries and received as tribute from the conquered tribes. In the paintings on the walls of the tombs at Thebes, skins of the leopard, fox and other animals are seen laid before the throne of a Pharaoh, together with gold, silver, ivory, rare woods, and various productions of vanquished countries.

The hide trade of Chicago has become one of vast commercial interest and rapidly increasing. The first shipment to the sea-board from this city commenced in 1845. They arrived in this city from the interior of Illinois, from the States of Missouri, Kansas, Nebraska, Minnesota, and the Lake Superior region. The hides shipped from Chicago annually, to Pennsylvania, New York, the New England States and Canada, amount in value to about $3,000,000. The meat from which these various hides are taken form another large article of commerce, most of it prepared for shipment, amounting to nearly or quite $10,000,000. In the early part of the business green hides were abundant in this market at one dollar each, or two cents per pound for green, and four cents per pound for dry, and many hides in the interior of the country were left to decay, the price ranging so low that it would not pay transportation, In 1857, green hides ranged in price as high ten and one-half, and dry from nineteen to twenty-one cents. These were extreme prices, such as had never occurred previously nor since that time. The present prices will average about six and three-fourths for green and fourteen cents for dry hides.

The principal hide trade of Chicago is entrusted to the hands of a man of large experience, having been thoroughly educated as a practical Tanner, and for several years conducting an extensive tanning business. For the past eighteen years he has had an intimate and practical knowledge of the hide trade in all its detail. Mr. Isaac S. Bush has, during the last ten years, given more encouragement and accomplished more in developing the hide trade than any other man in Chicago. Mr. Bush commenced with it when it was in its infancy, watched all its progress and development, and now stands at the head of it. He is the master and controller of the hide trade in Chicago and the North-West. His business with the packers of this city amounts to nearly three hundred thousand dollars per annum; and his trade through the country reaches a much larger amount. Mr. Bush acts for Eastern parties, who commission him to purchase; his long experience, thorough knowledge, unlimited facilities, and reputation for high commercial integrity, make him sought for in all transactions of any importance in this branch of trade.

The general dealers in the business purchase hides promiscuously—green, half green and salted, of all weights and sizes, and prepare them in a condition for shipment. Mr. Bush buys of the dealer, in such quantities, sizes and weights as will best serve the tanners in the Eastern market, by whom he is commissioned. He gives his personal attention to the purchase of every hide.

Having spent many years in the tanning business, and devoting his whole time to the hide business, he is necessarily a most competent judge of leather of every description, in which he also deals largely for the benefit of merchants throughout the country. To such men as Mr. Bush, Chicago owes much of her present greatness and unprecedented continued prosperity.

Mr. Bush's place of business is 163 Kinzie Street.

HATS AND CAPS.

IN some form man appears to have made use of a hat to protect the head from the cold of winter, the burning rays of the sun, or against blows in battle, from the most remote periods. It was constructed in various shapes, and of the greatest variety of materials according to the purpose for which it was designed. As a part of defensive armor the hat was the helmet, which still retains its primitive shape; as a protection from the weather it was the cap such as we see in ancient figures representing the goddess of liberty. The ancient Greeks appear to have employed several other kinds of head dress, the names and appearance of which have been faithfully presented in their writings as well as engraved upon antique gems.

The hat being the most conspicuous article of dress and surmounting all the rest, it was natural to give it special care and attention, to place in it showy plumes and jewels and surround it with bands of gold and silver. Its form and sometimes color were also made to designate the rank and character of the wearer; the monarch being known by his crown, the cardinal by his red hat, betokening his readiness to spill his blood for the sake of Jesus Christ, and the court fool by a cap with a bell. In one form it served to distinguish the military officer and in another the peaceful quaker. Among the great variety of hats used by the English, the forms of which are preserved in old pictures, none combine the elegance, grace and comfort to the wearer, of the soft hat of the Spaniards, which the latter have retained in use, while the English have been continually changing. The broad folding brims of past generations turned up to form the cocked hat, and various other styles, have almost entirely disappeared, the felt hat being the only representative of them in general use. The fashion for many years has been the stiff cylindrical hat with narrow brims, but fashion is again seeking an alliance with comfort and practical common sense, and the soft felt hats of wool and fur are largely manufactured again for common wear, and these of the most ordinary kind, differ but little from the ancient *petasus*.

The manufacture of hats has been carried to the highest perfection in the United States; no people have ever approached us in the elegance, ease and style of head dress, and in London and Paris the American is now frequently known as such by the excellence of his head dress. The American hats are superseding the Turban in Turkey. The fashions of hats, as a general rule, are not imported, but originate with the leading houses. In New York we have Leary, Beebe's and others; in Philadelphia that of Herst & Co., and in Chicago that of Loomis. This house may be said to represent the leading fashions in Hats in Chicago. Mr. Loomis has been engaged in this business for twenty years, eleven years of that time in this city, untiringly, perseveringly devoting his energies and talent in devising and moulding forms of beauty and grace, adapting them to the situation and times and the enlightenment and advancing of civilization. During this time he has passed through all the changes of this eventful city, has studied and knows the wants of the people more fully than any other man engaged in this business in Chicago. One may go to Loomis' and be suited to anything for head gear that can be found in any market, as also, Canes, Unbrellas, Gloves, and many other articles usually kept by Hatters.

Loomis is located in Larmon's Block, opposite the Court House, No. 97 South Clark Street.

IRON AND HEAVY HARDWARE.

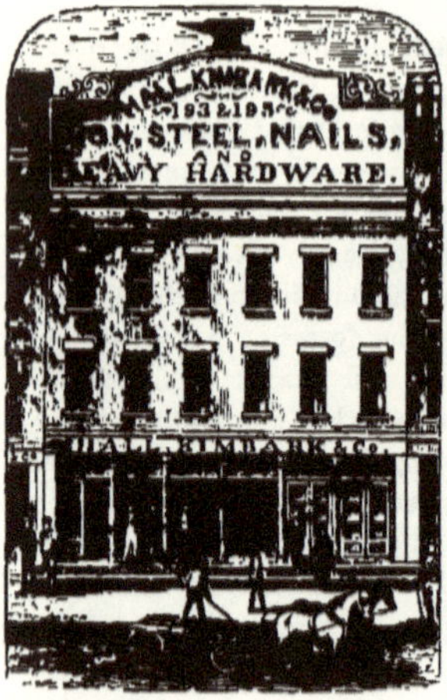

IT is probable that in no branch of the general commerce of Chicago is her interest becoming more rapidly developed than in Iron and the products of its manufacture. . The rapid increase of population in the North-West, the great demand for articles of Heavy Hardware, has induced men of capital and business capacity, men who have been educated in the hardware trade, to add Heavy Hardware to that of their former business.

The most noteworthy of these houses, perhaps, is that of HALL, KIMBARK & Co., who commenced business in Chicago in the spring of 1853, since which time they have continued to extend their business and increase their facilities, promptly meeting every engagement, and passing unharmed through the financial storms which have swept over our city, until at the present time they stand at the head of this branch of trade in this city, and represent one of the fairest and most reliable mercantile firms in Chicago. In order to secure a more central position and other business facilities, they fitted up the two stores, Nos. 193 and 195 Water Street, forty by one hundred and fifty feet, three stories high with a basement, opposite the Board of Trade Rooms, which they now occupy, and where may be found the largest and best stock of Heavy Hardware in the North-West. Their trade amounts to about one million five hundred thousand dollars per annum. In order to meet the increased demand for many articles in their line of trade, they employ all the working force, most of the time, of one of the largest foundries in the North-west. Among the many things they have manufactured, we may mention a few leading ones, viz: Improved Thimble Skeins and Boxes for wagons; Tire Benders; Blacksmith or Fire Drills; Road Scrapers; Fence Keys; Colter Hubs; Swedge Blocks; and a variety of Cast Iron goods; also extra quality of Plow Bolts, from best Charcoal Iron.

Thimble Skeins they make a speciality; having almost unlimited facilities, they could turn out one hundred set per day of finished Skeins, of as good a quality as has ever been offered in this market, having spared neither effort nor expense in bringing their patterns to perfection. They are prepared to offer the trade in this line the best article made in the United States. All the Skeins now manufactured by this house are chill-hardened, which will increase their durability at least one hundred per cent. Parties wishing to purchase Thimble Skeins should by all means buy chill-hardened Skeins, such as manufactured by Hall, Kimbark & Co., without extra cost. They are bestowing unusual attention upon this branch of manufacture; their object being to introduce the best article, without aiming to compete in price with brands of those inferior in quality and weight. Their sales of Skeins last year amounted to ten thousand sets, principally to wagon-makers and dealers who are fully competent to judge of their merits.

Their stock is at all times the largest, perhaps, of any similar business in the North-West. The efforts of this firm to supply the North-West with the best articles in their line at the lowest prices, entitle them to the confidence and patronage of dealers generally. It has been their purpose to stand between the manufacturer and the dealer and consumer. How well they have succeeded, an appreciative public have fully demonstrated by their very liberal patronage.

I. B. SEELEY'S TRUSS, ARTIFICIAL LEG, AND SHOULDER BRACE ESTABLISHMENT.

THE manufacture of Trusses and Artificial Legs demand, on the part of manufacturers who would rise to eminence, other elements of success than mere mechanical skill. His art is to aid the curative powers of nature — to manufacture appliances for surgical injuries and deformities, with their required modifications for special cases, or to compensate for lost members by artificial contrivances. The judgment, tact, inventive power and manual dexterity of the manufacturer, are important aids in carrying out his ideas.

The Truss, so necessary and indispensable to the afflicted, has of late years, in the hands of skillful and scientific men, undergone every conceivable modification and improvement, until an incredible number of different varieties have been produced. Science and experience have demonstrated the fact, that there are but two distinct varieties, viz., the *Convex* and the *Concave* Truss.

In view, then, of the qualifications required, it is no small compliment to say, as we can with truth, that the best Truss yet produced is that of Goodyear & Riggs' Patent

Hard Rubber Truss, manufactured by I. B. Seeley, who is the sole proprietor. They take pre-eminent rank over all others. They have received the unqualified commendation of physicians, surgeons, and men of all classes and positions in society — of the Surgeon General of the Army, where it is now used by members of his bureau in preference to all others; Chief Justice Taney, who by the advice of his family surgeon ordered one for his own use — and in fact wherever suffering humanity has been afflicted with Hernia, there have these Trusses gone, as angels of mercy, relieving the distressed, healing surgical injuries, and carrying the balm of consolation to the afflicted. Wherever they have been on exhibition, at State, County, Mechanical and Agricultural Fairs, they have been awarded the highest premiums.

Dr. Riggs after devoting years to the investigation and treatment of this disease, and becoming familiar with the practical working and effects of the various kinds of Trusses in use, at last devised this, with the view of combining all the good qualities of other Trusses without their faults, and the result is the production of the only successful Truss, which has everywhere met the requirements of the varied forms of Hernia.

Some of the advantages claimed in this Truss, are the construction of the pad — the material of which they are manufactured being hard rubber, which retains the hernia at the internal ring, with no pressure on the spermatic vessels—free from corroding — will not blister, because it is subject to no friction — it cannot chafe or gall — will not slip from the position it is placed — can be made stiff or limber, by which means it is more easily adjusted and adapted to the most intricate surgical injury. The spring being made of steel coated with rubber, it is always kept clean and good as new, which are combined advantages over all other Trusses ever presented to afflicted humanity.

Mr. Seeley has recently removed his rooms to 126 South Clark Street, where he has fitted up a handsome suite of rooms for the better accommodation of his rapidly increasing business.. Here may be found a general assortment of Trusses of every description, ranging in price from fifty cents up to twenty dollars; also Shoulder Braces, Abdominal Supporters, Silk Elastic Stockings, Suspensory Bandages, Surgical Splints, also a new and improved instrument for the treatment of Piles, a long looked for and most useful invention. Connected with this establishment is the manufacture of Dr. Wilcox's Improved Patent Artificial Leg, manufactured by Mr. C. Stafford, whose artistic skill, genius and experience of years has won for him a reputation second to no man on this continent; his testimonials come from the highest and best authority — those who are using Stafford's Artificial Limbs, of Wilcox's Patent.

Modern science and inginuity has been directed and devoted to the improvement of Artificial Limbs, until now the unlucky loser of an arm or leg, can be fitted with an artificial one of this patent that enables him to perform almost all that could be effected with the natural limbs.

This is the only regular establishment in Chicago where Trusses are fitted, and Artificial Limbs are made. Every article sold is warranted to be as represented.

WOOLEN GOODS.

THE trade in Cloths, Cassimeres, Vestings and Woolens, considered as a branch of commerce, is one of the most important of any now existing in this country. It controls a greater amount of capital, employs a larger number of persons, and distributes a greater value of commodities than any other branch of mercantile pursuit.

There are certainly "merchant princes" among those engaged in mercantile pursuits; but in capacity, energy and aggregate wealth, the dealers in Woolens, as a class, are emphatically THE MERCHANTS of our day and country. The immense capital and practical experience required to engage successfully in this business places it above the reach of transient speculators, and ensures to the fortunate possessor of the requisite knowledge and means, a successful and remunerative business.

A great deal has been said recently about cotton being king of trade and commerce. If so, it is a usurper, for as long ago as when the first little sail was hoisted over the briny waters, Wool was an extensive article of trade, and has continued so ever since. Wool being extensively produced all over the world, it does not make so much *noise* as cotton, but is vastly more comfortable to dwellers in this climate, where we have nearly or quite six months of winter weather. If those who minister to our comfort are public benefactors, then Field, Benedict & Co., of this city, should take high rank, having for the past thirteen years supplied a large part of the North-West with material wherewith to keep warm. Fine Broadcloths, Doeskins, Cassimeres and Vestings are a speciality with this house. They import their Cloths direct from the best makers in Europe, such as Hilger Brothers, Simoni, Bauendahl & Co., Jansens, etc. While they are head quarters for fine goods adopted to men's wear, they always keep on hand a full assortment of the best makes of American Woolen Goods, such as fancy and coating Cassimeres, made by Harris, Eddy, Salisbury Co., Milville Co., Seagraves, Farnum, Utica Mills, etc. In Satinets they keep a great variety, of different colors and qualities; as also Sheep's Gray, Tweeds, Ky. Jeans, F. & M. Cassimeres, Coatings, Pant Linens, and in short all kinds of Piece Goods adapted to men's wear, with the necessary trimmings to make them up with.

Field, Benedict & Co. commenced business in Chicago in the spring of 1849, and their long experience enables them to know exactly the kind of goods adapted to the Western trade.

On another page is a cut of the building now occupied by this house, located at 81 and 83 South Water Street. Their store is forty feet wide by one hundred and sixty-five feet deep, and being lighted on three sides, Dealers can see exactly what they are buying. With their facilities for importing fine goods, and with a resident buyer at the East, for the purchase of American Woolens, Field, Benedict & Co. are prepared to compete successfully with any jobbers in this country.

COFFEE, SPICES AND TEAS.

WITHIN the last few years, the demand for ground Coffee and prepared Spices has become so great that large amounts of capital have been invested in this branch of productive industry, and several firms in this city are engaged in their preparation.

Among the most note worthy, popular and reliable manufacturers in this city we may mention Messrs. Thompson & Billings, whose sales room and manufactory are located on Monroe near the corner of State Street. They have probably the best arranged mills in this city; and their facilities for grinding Spices and Coffee, and the preperation of Chocolate, and Mustards are probably unequaled by any other establishment in Chicago. From small beginnings their business has increased to an establishment possessing all the modern improvements — their machinery is driven by steam power. The business integrity of the proprietors are made evident in the celebrity of their establishment, by the purity and extent of their production, and the rapidly increasing demand for Thompson & Billing's manufactures of Coffee, Spices, Chocolate, etc.

.With a spirit of commendable liberality this firm have introduced a new mode of putting up their Coffee in air tight tin cans, containing from one to ten pounds each, for family use; thereby retaining for a great length of time all the rich aroma, which imparts to this exhilarating beverage, that delicate flavor so grateful to the lover of this delicious luxury. These cans are enameled in colors, presenting a neat and tasty appearance, which form an important appendage to every well regulated kitchen closet, or store-room.

The jobbing trade of this house has increased to such an extent that in order to supply the demand they are compelled to run their mill, much of the time, night and day. The improved mode of preparing and putting up Coffee has made it a leading business in every large city. Few persons at the present day purchase green Coffee for domestic preparation, for the fact has become fully demonstrated that Coffee prepared by a celebrated manufacturer is better and cheaper to the consumer, and put up in these air tight cans will keep for any desired length of time, retaining all its freshness and flavor.

Messrs. Thompson & Billings have added the sale of choice Teas to their stock of Coffee and Spices, and will always keep on hand a full supply of fresh Teas for the better accommodation of their rapidly increasing retail customers.

Dr. Thompson, one of the members of the firm, is a practical chemist of large experience. Having made chemistry a life study he has endeavored to utilize his experience for the advancement of commerce. For several years past he has been engaged in preparing for market Flavoring Extracts, which have found ready and extensive sale with Druggists and family Grocers, and gone into every state in the Union. This article of commerce now forms an important item in the jobbing department of this house, for "Thompson's Flavoring Extracts" are widely and favorably known to house keepers as well as to the mercantile community.

The mercantile reputation of this house is so favorably known throughout the North-West, that merchants ordering goods have only to name the quality and quantity to have their orders satisfactorily executed.

PROGRESSION OF INVENTION.

THERE is always progression, but it is a progression of invention; the destined works are too vast, too infinite to allow a long delay in the advancement of any one accomplishment. The rival and growing necessities of the human family, and the corresponding pressure which they impose upon the toiling hands and active intellects of the age, necessarily impart a corresponding importance to the element of time and the value of labor. This is true of every civilized country on the globe; it is especially so of the United States, as at once an industrious and progressive nation. Whether in multiplying the production of the soil or elaborating the luxuries of the wardrobe, the genius of invention, no less than the hand of toil, finds a still widening "scope and verge" for action. And new mechanical auxilliaries and appliances are in demand upon the farm and in the work-room. What the steam plow promises to be, and what the prize mower already is to the one, the Sewing Machine is to the other. The Sewing Machine comes as a boon to the delicate and overtaxed slave of the needle. In a comparative sense, it diminishes her toil to a fraction; it also insures her the compensation of *a day* for less than the fatigue and application of *an hour!*

But if in these latter lights the Sewing Machine may be regarded as a household treasure, it only becomes really so in proportion to the judgment exercised in its selection. Sewing Machines of innumerable styles, patterns and claims to patronage, constitute one of the most curious and prominent features among the present business rivalries of Chicago. Among those now before the public claiming prominence, we propose to speak of SIGWALT & WHITMAN'S PATENT DOUBLE LOCK TIGHT FAST STITCH SEWING MACAINES. It is what few machines are, just what it professes to be. Among some of its advantages, it claims, first, to be particularly adapted to family and manufacturing purposes, is made of the best materials, is substantial and durable, simple in its construction and working, easily managed, and pronounced by competent judges to be the best Machine yet presented to the public.

This Machine uses a straight needle, which is much preferable in many respects — it makes the Double Lock Tight Fast Stitch, and makes an elastic seam which will not rip, though every third stitch be cut. The combination of the movements is such that it is impossible for the machine to get out of order, as all parts must act in unison with each other. Its seam is known to be the strongest, smoothest and most elastic of any seam extant. No person in pursuit of a Sewing Machine should make a selection without seeing these, which may be found at Mr. B. F. WIGGINS', the gentlemanly proprietor of Wiggins' Merchant Tailor and Wholesale Manufacturing Establishment. These industrious little automaton co-workers, which neither require wages nor food, are silently, perseveringly enabling Mr. Wiggins to manufacture clothing at such prices that he can supply the dealer at reduced rates. This is the mission these truly simple and effective machines are destined to accomplish for any who will purchase and do likewise.

Mr. Wiggins employs these machines for making custom work and work for the jobbing department of his establishment.

He has also on hand some forty or fifty of the Sloat Sewing Machines, both for family use and manufacturing purposes, which he offers cheap for cash.

Mr. Wiggins' establishment is at 75 Lake Street.

OPTICS—MATHEMATICAL AND PHILOSOPHICAL APPARATUS.

OPTICS is the science which treats of the nature of and the laws of the phenomena of light and vision. The Optician, to be successful in his trade, must be a man of scientific attainment — must possess artistic skill and genius; all of which qualifications we can most truly claim for the well known and long established firm of Messrs. JAMES FOSTER, JR., & Co., of Cincinnati, who have recently established a branch of their house in Chicago, under the management of Mr. LOUIS BOERLIN, the junior member of the firm. We are proud to welcome to our city the representative of so scientific and important a branch of business from one of the oldest and best commercial houses of Cincinnati.

In order to fit the human eye with artificial aid of a proper kind, the Optician must needs be a scientific man, and of wide experience; such we can claim for Mr. Boerlin, who received his early education in Europe, at the schools of Switzerland; which with several years of practical experience in this country, well fits him for the responsible position he will occupy here in his new field of operation.

Among the leading articles comprising their well selected stock, we may mention Marine Glasses, Opera Glasses, Telescopes, Microscopes, Spectacles, Drawing and Surveying Instruments, including Burt's Solar Compass, every description of Field Instruments for Civil Engineers, such as Levels, Transits, Theodolites, etc.; also some of the best Philosophical Apparatus, perhaps, that has ever been brought to this city.

In 1836, Mr. James Foster, Jr., the senior partner, commenced in Cincinnati the manufacture of Mathematical and Philosophical Instruments, since which time he has steadily increased his operations, until now he takes rank with the first house of this kind in the United States. Mr. F. is a practical scientific workman, having spent a life time in its study. This firm are prepared to furnish every description of apparatus for school or higher scientific institutions, from the plain Electric Machine to the best Astronomical Clock, and the most complicated Galvanic Apparatus.

Mr. Henry Twitchell, one of the partners of this firm, was for twelve years the assistant of Prof. Mitchell at the Cincinnati Observatory. His early acquirements, and many advantages have enabled him to acquire a thorough practical knowledge of all the requirements of any piece of scientific apparatus. The Cincinnati house give employment to a large number of skillful and scientific workmen, excelled by no other establishment of a similar kind on this continent.

Any articles in their line can be ordered of their branch house in this city, located at No. 60 Dearborn Street, under the Matteson House.

UNIVERSITY OF CHICAGO.

THE fact that we have too many Colleges in this country is one which has long been admitted and deplored by all who have at heart the interest of education and sound learning. It is no exaggeration to say that if the hundreds of thousands of dollars that have been comparatively wasted in ill designed schemes for establishing collegiate institutions had been concentrated upon a few great seminaries, the standard of scholarship would have been far higher in America, the expense of education lessened, and the humiliating comparisons so often instituted between our own Seminaries of learning and those of England and Germany would never have been drawn. As it now is, every State has its Colleges, from one to half a dozen in number, the majority of which are constantly struggling "to keep the wolf from the door," equipped with libraries, cabinets, and philosophical apparatus, half paying their over-worked professors — accepting, from necessity, students half prepared at the Academy — and the results are seen in the low grade of culture of our professional men, in the sciolism and empirism that run riot in the community, and in many other evils which we lack space to particularize. That each State, or large section of a State, should feel an anxiety to have its own College is natural enough; but it is a theory of ours which will be borne out, we think, by facts, that the true seat of a University is at a great geographical and commercial centre. Such a centre is Chicago. Situated at the head of the great chain of lakes which connects the East with the West — grasping with one hand the commerce of the former, and with the other the exhaustless agricultural products of the latter — the focus of a perfect spider's web of railroads, whose net-work stretches to the very confines of civilization, and which pour into her lap the "*lactea ubertas*" of six great States—Chicago, which a few years ago was a mere trading post, has become a mighty city, whose influence radiates throughout the entire North-West; and hence the importance of making it a great educational centre, to which the youth of Illinois, Wisconsin, Michigan, Iowa, and Minnesota may resort, is obvious at the first glance. Appreciating this fact, the friends of learning have labored with much self-sacrifice to establish here a University—a University in fact as well as in name—distinguished alike for its endowment and its breadth of comprehensiveness of plan—Christian but not sectarian—answerable in short to a want long and deeply felt, and the result is to be seen in the UNIVERSITY OF CHICAGO. Though lacking the associations which cluster around the older institutions of the East, it is in the full tide of successful experiment, and is enjoying a prosperity which probably not one of them in its infancy could boast. Like Pallas from the head of Jove, it has sprung forth in full panoply, with its Law Department, its Literary and Theological Societies, its Clubs, Class Organizations, and Gymnasiums—and has a number of students of which any but the oldest institutions might be proud. Four years ago a dozen only were in attendance, and now they are counted by hundreds, and what is unprecidented, we believe, in the history of American Colleges—already the receipts for tuition exceed those of the oldest eastern Colleges. This fact speaks trumpet-tongued for the energy and ability of the management, the qualifications of the faculty of instruction, and the intellectual and moral advantages of the institution; a fact whose significance is intensified by the unparalleled embarrasment of the times in which this enterprise has gone forward. The University unites to its other advantages that of a charming location, in the grove on the bank of lake Michigan, sufficiently near to the city to render available all its advantages of libraries, lectures, refined and intellectual society, etc., yet far enough from the *fumum strepitumque Romæ* to ensure health and quiet. It will continue, we trust, to be thronged by hundreds of the youth of the West, till all its majestic proportions are complete, and it shall challenge comparison with the moss-grown institutions of Cambridge and New Haven.

HISTORICAL OUTLINE.—The University of Chicago, as before intimated, had its origin in the conviction of its founders, of the necessity of such an Institution, both to the city of Chicago and the great country to which the city is so intimately linked.

By many, aware from past examples how disastrous to any society is the too rapid and exclusive development of the spirit of gain, the unprecedented material prosperity of. both city and country had long been viewed with deep concern. The necessity of some corresponding development of educational and religious interests, was apparent, and it was foreseen that an Institution of learning, of high order, incorporated into the life of this community, while yet young and formative, sharing its growth, and standing as an exponent of its culture, would occupy a position of influence rarely equaled.

In the spirit of these views, the Hon. S. A. Douglas, in the year 1854, expressed his willingness to donate ten acres of beautiful grove, adjacent to the southern limits of the city, for the purpose of a University, so soon as responsible parties should be found ready to accept it.

On the 2d day of April, 1856, Mr. Douglas conveyed to Rev. J. C. Burroughs, in the city of Washington, the proposed site, on certain conditions. On the 6th of July following, at a meeting of citizens of Chicago, called for the purpose, a preliminary organization was effected, to which the grant, as originally stipulated, was transferred. On the 31st of the same month, the books were opened for subscriptions, and within two months, $100,000 were subscribed. This amount has been subsequently increased to about $225,000.

On the 2d day of April, 1857, an act of incorporation was obtained from the Legislature of Illinois. The Board of Trustees, held its first meeting on the 24th of May following, and elected officers. The Board of Regents provided by the charter with powers of visitation and supervision, especially of the internal affairs of the University, its courses of instruction, discipline, etc., was also organized. The Executive Committee were instructed to proceed immediately to make the necessary arrangements for the erection of buildings.

The plans prepared by W. W. Boyington, Esq., contemplates an imposing stone structure in Norman architecture. The part completed, about ninety feet front, has been universally admired for its beauty, convenient arrangement, excellent ventilation, etc.

On the 4th of July following, the corner stone was laid with public ceremonies. Immediately after, however, the financial embarrassments in which the country has subsequently been involved, were so clearly foreshadowed that the Trustees deemed it wise to suspend all further work on the building, and accordingly no progress was made for the next two years. In July, 1858, work was resumed, and the south wing of the building was pushed rapidly on to completion.

In the history of the University, the name of William Jones, Esq., one of the old and well known residents of Chicago, will ever occupy a prominent place, as one to whose energy and liberality the resuscitation of the enterprise, when it seemed almost hopelessly paralyzed, is in a great measure due.

At a meeting of the Trustees in September, 1858, it was resolved to begin the work of instruction. The President and two Professors were chosen, and on the 29th of the same month, small classes were organized in temporary rooms.

The building was dedicated on the 22d of July, 1859, when addresses were delivered by Hon. J. R. Doolittle, of the United States Senate, and Dr. A. C. Kendrick, of Rochester University.

In 1858 the Trustees resolved upon the important measure of organizing the Law Department, towards the endowment of which the Hon. Thomas Hayne had secured to the Board the payment of five thousand dollars. On the 21st of September following, the department went into operation, under the present Faculty, with an opening address by Hon. David Dudley Fields, of New York.

www.ingramcontent.com/pod-product-compliance
Lightning Source LLC
Chambersburg PA
CBHW032009060726
47497CB00017B/2420
* 9 7 8 3 7 4 4 7 2 4 7 7 7 *